Contents

5th Edition

The English Legal System

Jacqueline Martin

Hodder Arnold

A MEMBER OF THE HODDER HEADLINE GROUP

Orders: please contact Bookpoint Ltd, 130 Milton Park,
Abingdon, Oxon OX14 4SB. Telephone: (44) 01235 827720.
Fax: (44) 01235 400454. Lines are open from 9.00 – 5.00,
Monday to Saturday, with a 24 hour message answering
service. You can also order through our website
www.hoddereducation.co.uk

If you have any comments to make about this, or
any of our other titles, please send them to
educationenquiries@hodder.co.uk

British Library Cataloguing in Publication Data
A catalogue record for this title is available from the British
Library

ISBN: 978 0 340 94156 0

First Edition Published 1997
Second Edition Published 2000
Third Edition Published 2002
Fourth Edition Published 2005
This Edition Published 2007

Impression number 10 9 8 7 6 5 4 3 2
Year 2011 2010 2009 2008 2007

Cover photo © Royalty Free/Corbis
Typeset by Dorchester Typesetting Group Ltd
Printed in Italy for Hodder Arnold, an imprint of
Hodder Education, a member of the Hodder Headline
Group, An Hachette Livre UK Company, 338 Euston Road,
London NW1 3BH.

Preface

The book is intended for any first-time student of the English Legal System. In particular, the coverage of topics is suitable for the AS specifications in Law for OCR and WJEC but the book is also suitable for those starting degree or similar courses. The book does not assume any prior knowledge and starts with an introduction to types of law, in particular the critical distinction between civil and criminal law. The first chapter also introduces jurisprudential concepts and discusses law and morality and law and justice using recent cases. This section has been deliberately kept fairly brief as I have always felt that an 'in depth' study of jurisprudence at an early stage of a legal course is not desirable.

The order of topics is then fairly traditional, starting with the sources of law and going on to look at the criminal justice system, the civil justice system and legal personnel. The chapters on criminal justice take the student through the entire process starting with the commission of crimes and police powers, covering prosecution, both pre-trial and the process in the courts and finishing with sentencing. The civil justice chapters also endeavour to give comprehensive coverage including pre-litigation matters, the courts, tribunals, arbitration and ADR, remedies and enforcement of judgments. The chapters on legal personnel cover both the professionals and lay participation and the problem of financing litigation. The final chapter is a brief one on human rights.

I have tried to keep to the principles of explaining legal points simply and clearly, but at the same time providing sufficient depth for the more able students. Articles, cases and other 'live' material are used to illustrate points and to provide examples of the legal system at work today. Many of these items have also been used to give students the opportunity to do activities and exercises to help their understanding of topics. Key fact charts on many topics are included.

This fifth edition takes into account the changes made to the OCR specification. The examination questions at the end of chapters are, therefore, taken from the sample questions published by OCR or examinations between 2002 and 2004 when the style of question was similar to those in the new specification.

The law is stated as I believe it to be on 1 March 2007.

Jacqueline Martin

Acknowledgements

The author and publishers would like to thank the following for permission to reproduce copyright material:

Welsh Joint Education Committee for WJEC examination questions; OCR for the use of OCR examination questions; *The Independent* for the articles on pages 4 and 147 © *The Independent*; *The Times* for the articles on pages 4, 7, 87, 105, 178, 251 and 291 © NI Syndication, London (1990, 1994, 1995, 1996, 2001, 2006); Metro Newspapers for the article on page 5; Telegraph Group Limited for the articles on pages 5, 14 and 224; *The Daily Express* for the article on page 6; *The Guardian* for the article on page 48 © Guardian News & Media Ltd 1995; picture on page 118 © Andrew Holt/Alamy; picture on page 149 © Arthur Turner/Alamy; picture on page 186 © Photofusion Picture Library/Alamy; picture on p 210 © Dan Atkin/Alamy; extracts on p 212 by Finola Farrant and Joe Leverson and page 239 from New Law Journal by permission of LexisNexis Butterworths; picture on page 242 © Michael Stephens/PA Wire/PA Photos; picture on page 259 © PA Archive/PA Photos; picture on page 323 © John Edward Linden/Arcaid/Corbis. © Crown copyright material is reproduced with permission of the Controller of HMSO.

Every effort has been made to trace and acknowledge ownership of copyright. The publishers will be glad to make suitable arrangements with any copyright holders whom it has not been possible to contact.

Table of Acts of Parliament

Table of Cases

Chapter 1

The Rule of Law

1.1 What is law?

Law can affect many aspects of our lives, yet most people living in England and Wales have little understanding of the legal system that operates in these countries. For many their main awareness comes from newspaper articles with headlines such as 'Murderer jailed for life'; 'Young offender goes free'; 'Burglar caught'. This type of headline appears so frequently that it is not surprising that, when law is mentioned, many people only think of the criminal law and the courts that deal with this type of case. In reality the law covers an enormous range of situations and the legal system in England and Wales has a variety of courts and methods for dealing with different types of cases.

1.1.1 Different types of law

Since the law does cover such a wide variety of matters it can be helpful to divide it into different categories. The first distinction is that between international and national (municipal) law; national law can then be classified into public and private law; finally these classifications can be sub-divided into a number of different categories. These divisions are explained below.

International and national law

International law is concerned with disputes between nations; much of this law comes from treaties which have been agreed by the governments of the countries. National law is the law which applies within a country: each country will have its own national law and there are often wide differences between the law of individual countries. This can be shown by the fact that Scotland has its own law and legal system which are quite separate from the law and legal system which operate in England and Wales. For example, while serious criminal cases are tried by jury in both systems, the Scottish jury has 15 members and the decision can be made by a simple majority of 8–7. In contrast the jury in England and Wales has 12 members, at least 10 of whom must agree on the decision.

Public and private law

Within national law there is usually a clear distinction between public and private law. Public law involves the State or government in some way, while private law is concerned with disputes between private individuals or businesses. Both public and private law can be sub-divided into different categories.

Public law

There are three main types of law in this category. These are:

1. **Constitutional law**

   This controls the method of government and any disputes which arise over such matters as who is entitled to vote in an election, or who is allowed to become a Member of Parliament, or whether an election was carried out by the correct procedure.

2. **Administrative law**

   This controls how Ministers of State or other public bodies such as local councils should operate. An important part of this is the right to judicial review of certain decisions. Judicial review allows judges to consider whether a decision (or a refusal to make a decision) is reasonable. If it is not, then the decision is re-considered.

3. **Criminal law**

   This sets out the types of behaviour which are forbidden at risk of punishment. A person who commits a crime is said to have offended against the State, and so the State has the right to prosecute them. This is so even though there is often an individual victim of a crime as well. For example, if a defendant commits the crime of burglary by breaking into a house and stealing, the State prosecutes the defendant for that burglary, although it is also possible for the victim to bring a private prosecution if the State does not take proceedings. However, if there is a private prosecution, the State still has the right to intervene and take over the matter. At the end of the case, if the defendant is found guilty, the court will punish the defendant for the offence, because he or she has broken the criminal law set down by the State. The victim will not necessarily be given any compensation, since the case is not viewed as a dispute between the burglar and the householder. However, the criminal courts have the power to order that the offender pays the victim compensation and can make such an order, as well as punishing the offender.

Private law

This is usually called civil law and has many different branches. The main ones are contract, tort, family law, law of succession, company law and employment law. This book does not deal with the actual legal rules of any of these areas, only with the system for dealing with disputes. However, it is sensible to have some idea of what types of dispute may be involved in these areas of law, so look at the following situations:

- A family complain that their package holiday did not match what was promised by the tour operator and that they were put into a lower grade hotel than the one they had paid for
- A woman has bought a new car and discovers the engine is faulty
- A man who bought a new car on hire-purchase has failed to pay the instalments due to the hire-purchase company.

All these situations come under the law of contract. There are, of course, many other situations in which contracts can be involved. Now look at the next list of situations; they are also civil matters, but of a different type.

- A child passenger in a car is injured in a collision (the tort of negligence)
- A family complain that their health is being affected by the noise and dust from a factory which has just been built near their house (the tort of nuisance)
- A woman is injured by faulty machinery at work (the tort of negligence, but may also involve occupiers' liability and/or employer's duty under health and safety regulations)

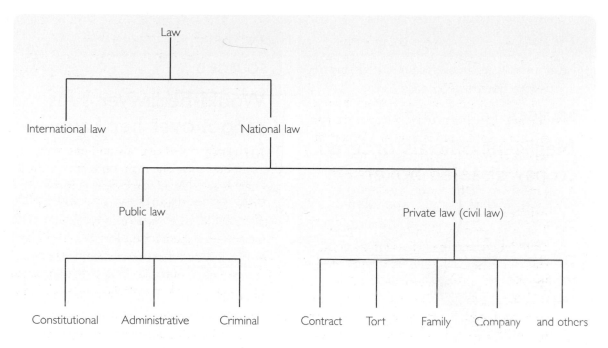

Figure 1.1 *Summary of the different categories of law*

- A man complains that a newspaper has written an untrue article about him, which has affected his reputation (the tort of defamation).

All these cases come under the law of tort. A tort occurs where the civil law holds that, even though there is no contract between them, one person owes a legal responsibility of some kind to another person, and there has been a breach of that responsibility. There are many different types of tort, and the above examples demonstrate only some of them. Many cases arise from road traffic crashes, since drivers owe a duty of care to anyone who might be injured by their negligent driving.

Other divisions of private (civil) law concentrate on particular topics. Family law covers such matters as whether a marriage is valid, what the rules are for divorce and who should have the day-to-day care of any children of the family. The law of succession is concerned both with regulating who inherits property when a person dies without making a will, and also what the rules are for making a valid will. Company law is very important in the business world: it regulates how a company should be formed, sets out formal rules for running companies, and deals with the rights and duties of shareholders and directors. Employment law covers all aspects of employment, from the original formation of a contract of employment to situations of redundancy or unfair dismissal. As well as these areas of private law, there are also laws relating to land, to copyright and patents, to marine law and many other topics, so it can be seen that civil law covers a wide variety of situations.

Differences between civil and criminal law

It is important to realise that civil law is very different from criminal law. The first point is shown in Figure 1.1 above. Criminal law is part of public law while civil law is the separate

Activity

Read the following newspaper articles and answer the questions on page 6.

SOURCE A

Negligent officials ordered to pay disabled boxer

The boxer Michael Watson, who suffered brain damage during a world championship bout with Chris Eubank, won a historic High Court case yesterday, raising questions about the future of the professional sport in this country.

In what was described as a landmark decision, the British Boxing Board of Control was found to have been negligent and liable for compensation for the injuries that left Mr Watson with only half his brain functioning, partially paralysed and confined to a wheelchair . . .

Eight years of litigation have followed Mr Watson's injury on 21 September 1991. The legal costs alone are said to amount to £500,000. In addition there will be financial compensation for Mr Watson . . . The actual amount will be decided by a High Court judge.

Taken from an article by Kim Sengupta in *The Independent*, 24 September 1999

Activity

SOURCE B

Would-be lawyer sues school over her Latin failure

A leading independent school is being sued by its former deputy head girl for £150,000 after she failed to achieve a top grade in her Latin A-level. Katherine Norfolk claims that Hurstpierpoint College in West Sussex is responsible for poor teaching that led to her being given an E grade, which she says will damage her career and salary prospects . . . Miss Norfolk had been a star pupil and had been predicted to gain an A grade in her Latin exam. She had won the school prize for Latin every year, according to papers lodged in the High Court. But when her A-level results came through last autumn she received an A in History, a B in French but a fail in Latin. After being re-marked twice she was awarded an E . . . Miss Norfolk is suing mainly for the loss of potential earnings, but also for the loss of esteem among her peers and for the distress caused by failing to achieve a higher grade.

Adapted from an article by David Brown and John Shaw in *The Times*, 1st October 2001

category of private law. The reason that criminal law is part of public law is that crime is regarded as an action against the state and society as a whole. Civil law is called private law because the issues it deals with are between two individuals. The two types of law have different aims and are dealt with in different courts.

On this page and the next two pages there are five newspaper articles. Some are about civil law and some are about criminal law. Do the activity based on these and then read section 1.1.2 to get a clearer understanding of the differences between the two.

Activity

SOURCE C

Ex-marine jailed for killing PC

A former US marine was jailed for life yesterday for the cold-blooded murder of PC Ian Broadhurst.

David Bieber, a bouncer and steroid abuser wanted in the US for a murder plot, was also convicted of trying to murder two other officers.

PC Broadhurst, 34, was gunned down on Boxing Day last year while checking a stolen car in Leeds. Bieber shot him in the head at point blank range as the officer begged for his life. PCs Neil Roper, 45, and James Bank, 27, were also shot but lived.

A tape played to the jury included PC Broadhurst pleading for his life, before the sound of gunfire and screaming. He was shot in the chest as he and PC Roper tried to handcuff Bieber.

Mr Broadhurst's widow and mother wept after the verdict at Newcastle Crown Court.

Taken from an article by Stephen Deal in
Metro, 3 December 2004

Activity

SOURCE D

£14,000 for girl whose ear-piercing went wrong

A vicar's step-daughter has been awarded almost £14,000 compensation after an ear-piercing left her disfigured. Katrina Healey, now 15, lost part of her ear after a piercing gun was used instead of a specialist needle to insert a gold stud near the top of her ear.

... Katrina defied her parents to have her ear pierced when she was 12, getting a friend over the age of 18 to sign the consent form in H Warner and Sons jewellers' shop in Barnsley, South Yorks. Afterwards she underwent three hospital operations after her ear swelled and she developed an abscess. A judge at Barnsley County Court has awarded her £13,900 in damages after her parents sued the jewellers.

Adapted from an article by Paul Stokes in
The Daily Telegraph, 6 October 2001

Activity

SOURCE E

Floyd's drink-drive shame

TV Chef Keith Floyd was yesterday banned from driving for 32 months following a drink-drive smash.

A court heard he was so drunk that police held him in cells for 10 hours before he sobered up.

Floyd, 60, was arrested after his Peugeot 806 people carrier hit a Land Rover Discovery at a bridge.

He failed two breath tests – one at the scene and one while in custody, and was charged with driving while one-and-a-half times over the limit.

Floyd, behind the wheel for the first time in four months, claimed to have had just two whiskies before the crash.

But the court heard that he had 120 microgrammes of alcohol per 100 millilitres of breath. The legal limit is 80.

As well as the driving ban, magistrates in Swindon, Wiltshire, fined him £1,500.

Taken from an article by Geoff Marsh in
The Daily Express, 24 November 2004

Questions

1. Identify which of these articles is referring to civil cases and which to criminal cases. (If you wish to check that you are right before continuing with the rest of the questions, turn to the start of Appendix 1 at the back of the book.)

2. Look at the articles which you have identified as criminal cases and state in which courts the defendants were tried.

3. Look at the articles which you have identified as civil cases and state which courts are mentioned.

4. In the criminal cases the defendants all received some form of punishment. List the different punishments used in the cases.

5. Two of the civil cases have been decided. Identify these and, for each, state how long the time delay is between the incident which caused the claim and the actual decision.

6. What do the people in the civil cases hope to receive as a result of their claim?

1.1.2 Distinctions between criminal cases and civil cases

There are many differences between criminal cases and civil cases (you should already have noticed some from the articles):

- **The cases take place in different courts.** In general, criminal cases will be tried in either the Magistrates' Court or the Crown Court, while civil cases are heard in the High Court or the County Court. (Note that some civil matters, especially family cases, can be dealt with in the Magistrates' Court – see sections 13.1 and 17.5 for further details.)
- **The person starting the case is given a different name.** In criminal cases they are referred to as the prosecutor, while in civil cases they are called the claimant (pre-1999, the plaintiff). As already stated, the criminal case is taken on behalf of the State and there is a Crown Prosecution Service responsible for conducting cases, though there are other State agencies who may prosecute certain types of crime, for example, the Environment Agency or Customs and Excise Civil cases are started by the person (or business) who is making the claim
- **The terminology used is different.** A defendant in a criminal case is found guilty or not guilty (an alternative way of putting it is to say the defendant is convicted or acquitted), whereas a defendant in a civil case is found liable or not liable. At the end of a criminal case those who are found guilty of breaking the law may be punished, while at the end of a civil case anyone found liable will be ordered to put right the matter as far as possible. This is usually done by an award of money in compensation, known as damages, though the court can make other

Activity

Judgment overtakes Brink's-Mat accused 11 years later

Eleven years after a man was acquitted of the £26 million Brink's-Mat bullion robbery, a High Court judge ruled that he was involved and must repay the value of the gold.

Anthony White, acquitted at the Old Bailey in 1984 of taking part in Britain's biggest gold robbery, was ordered to repay the £26,369,778 value and £2,188,600 in compensation. His wife Margaret was ordered to pay £1,084,344. Insurers for Brink's-Mat had sued the couple for the value of the proceeds.

Mr Justice Rimmer told Mr White that his acquittal did not mean that the Old Bailey jury had been satisfied he was innocent; only that he was not guilty according to the standard of proof required in criminal cases . . .

The case against the Whites is the latest and almost the last in a series of actions since the 1983 robbery brought by insurers for Brink's-Mat against people either convicted or suspected of taking part in the robbery and of handling the proceeds.

Using the lower standards of proof in civil courts and in actions for seizure of assets, lawyers believe that they will recoup at least £20 million.

Taken from an article by Stewart Tendler in *The Times*, 2 August 1995

	CIVIL CASES	CRIMINAL CASES
Purpose of the law	To uphold the rights of individuals	To maintain law and order; to protect society
Person starting the case	The individual whose rights have been affected	Usually the State through the police and Crown Prosecution Service
Legal name for that person	Claimant	Prosecutor
Courts hearing cases	County Court or High Court Some cases dealt with in tribunals	Magistrates' Court or Crown Court
Standard of proof	The balance of probability	Beyond reasonable doubt
Person/s making the decision	Judge Very rarely a jury	Magistrates OR jury
Decision	Liable or not liable	Guilty or not guilty
Powers of the court	Usually an award of damages, also possible: injunction, specific performance of a contract, rescission or rectification	Prison, fine, community sentence, discharge, etc (see Chapter 14)

Figure 1.2 *Distinctions between civil and criminal cases*

orders such as an injunction to prevent similar actions in the future, or an order for specific performance where the defendant who broke a contract is ordered to complete that contract

- **The standard of proof is different.** Criminal cases must be proved 'beyond reasonable doubt'. This is a very high standard of proof, and is necessary since a conviction could result in a defendant serving a long prison sentence. Civil cases have only to be proved 'on the balance of probabilities', a lower standard in which the judge decides who is most likely to be right. This difference in the standard to which a case has to be proved means that even though a defendant in a criminal case has been acquitted, a civil case based on the same facts against that defendant can still be successful. Such situations are not common, but one is illustrated in the article on the previous page.

It is more common for a civil action to follow a successful criminal case, especially in road accident cases. A defendant may be found guilty of a driving offence, such as going through a red traffic light or driving without due care and attention; this is a criminal case. Anyone who was injured or had property damaged as a result of the incident could bring a civil action to claim compensation. The fact that the defendant had already been convicted of a driving offence will make it easier to prove the civil case.

In the English legal system an understanding of these basic distinctions between civil and criminal cases is important. To help you, a chart of the main differences is provided in Figure 1.2.

1.1.3 Definition of 'law'

So far we have only considered some divisions of law, and briefly introduced the system which applies in England and Wales. It is now necessary to look more widely at, and to discuss what is meant by, law in general terms and to compare it with concepts of morality and justice.

It is not easy to give a simple one sentence definition of law – however, legal theorists have tried to provide such a definition. John Austin, writing in the early nineteenth century, defined law as being a command issued from a superior (the State) to an inferior (the individual) and enforced by sanctions. This definition, however, does not truly apply to regulatory law such as that setting out how a will should be made; nor does it cover the concept of judicial review, where individuals may challenge the 'command' made by a Minister of State. Austin was writing at a time when the law was much less developed than it is today, so it is not surprising that his definition does not cover all types of law today.

Sir John Salmond defined law as being 'the body of principles recognised and applied by the state in the administration of justice'. This is a much broader definition than Austin's and is probably the nearest that one can get to a workable 'one sentence' definition. Law could also be described as a formal mechanism of social control. It is formal because the rules set down in the law can be enforced through the courts and legal system, while in a broad sense all law could be said to be involved in some area of social control.

Law and rules

Law applies throughout a country to the people generally. There are other rules that apply only to certain groups or in limited situations: for example all sports have a set of rules to be followed, and the sanction applied for breaking the rules may be that a free kick is given to the other side, or that a player is sent off, or in serious cases a player is banned from competing for a certain number of weeks or months.

There are also unwritten 'rules' within communities. These come from local custom or practice, or they may be connected to religious beliefs. They enforce what is regarded by the community as the norm for behaviour. If you break such rules, others in the community may disapprove of your behaviour, but there is no legal sanction to force you to comply or to punish you if you refuse to do so. Such normative values are often connected with sexual behaviour and the concept of morality. The relationship of law and morality is explored in the next section of this chapter.

Codes of law

In some civilisations or countries, an effort has been made to produce a complete set of rules designed to deal with every possible situation that might arise. Some of the early major civilisations attempted this, notably the code of Justinian in Roman times. In the eighteenth century, Frederick the Great of Prussia compiled a code of 17,000 'rules' which he saw as a complete and ideal set of laws. In France, Napoleon also codified the law, and this Napoleonic Code is still the basis of French law today. In theory this idea of a complete code is attractive. It makes the law more accessible so that everyone knows exactly what their rights and duties are; however, law needs to be able to change and develop with the needs of society, and a fully codified system would prevent any such change.

1.2 Law and morality

The moral values of communities lay down a framework for how people should behave. Concepts of morality differ from culture to culture, although most will outlaw extreme behaviour such as murder. Often morality is based on religious ideas: the Bible teachings provide a moral code for Christian communities, and the teachings in the Koran for Muslims. The law of a country will usually reflect the moral values accepted by the majority of the country, but the law is unlikely to be exactly the same as the common religious moral code. One example is adultery: this is against the moral code for both Christians and Muslims but is not considered a crime in Christian countries; however, in some Muslim countries (though not all) it is against the criminal law.

The moral standards of a community are recognised as having a profound influence on the development of law, but in complex societies, morality and law are never likely to be co-extensive. Major breaches of a moral code (such as murder and robbery) will also be against the law, but in other matters there may not be consensus.

In England and Wales there has been a move away from religious belief and the way that the law has developed reflects this. Abortion was legalised in 1967, yet many people still believe it is morally wrong. A limited form of euthanasia has been accepted as legal with the ruling in *Airedale NHS Trust* v *Bland* (1993), where it was ruled that medical staff could withdraw life support systems from a patient who could breathe unaided, but who was in a persistent vegetative state. This ruling meant that they could withdraw the feeding tubes of the patient, despite the fact that this would inevitably cause him to die. Again, many groups believe that this is immoral as it denies the sanctity of human life.

Activity

In *Re A (Conjoined twins)* (2000) the Court of Appeal had to decide whether doctors should operate to separate Siamese twins when it was certain that the operation would kill one twin as she could not exist without being linked to her twin.

a   Search on the Internet for a report of this case. Try *www.bailii.org* and look under the England and Wales reports – the Court of Appeal (Civil Division) for September 2000. The case is likely to be indexed as *A (children), Re* with a reference of EWCA (Civ) 254.

b   Discuss:

1. Whether this sort of decision should be made by judges.

2. Whether you think that, knowing one child would die, it was right for the operation to go ahead.

Differences between law and morality

There are also differences between law and morality in the way the two develop and the sanctions imposed. The following is a suggested list of such differences.

1. Morality cannot be deliberately changed; it evolves slowly and changes according to the will of the people. Law can be altered deliberately by legislation: this means that behaviour which was against the law can be 'de-criminalised' overnight. Equally, behaviour which was lawful can be declared unlawful.

2. Morality is voluntary with consequences, but generally carrying no official sanction (though some religions may 'excommunicate'); morality relies for its effectiveness on the individual's sense of shame or guilt. Law makes certain behaviour obligatory with legal sanctions to enforce it.

3. Breaches of morality are not usually subject to formal adjudication; breaches of law will be ruled on by a formal legal system.

1.3 Law and justice

It is often said that the law provides justice, yet this is not always so. Justice is probably the ultimate goal towards which the law should strive, but it is unlikely that law will ever produce 'justice' in every case.

First there is the problem of what is meant by 'justice'. The difficulty of defining justice was commented on by Lord Wright, who said:

'the guiding principle of a judge in deciding cases is to do justice; that is justice according to the law, but still justice. I have not found any satisfactory definition of justice . . . what is just in a particular case is what appears just to the just man, in the same way as what is reasonable appears to be reasonable to the reasonable man.'

In some situations people's concept of what is justice may not be the same. Justice can be seen as applying the rules in the same way to all people, but even this may lead to perceived injustices – indeed rigid application of rules may actually produce injustice.

An area in which there has been a lot of discussion is the amount of force that a householder can use on a burglar who enters that person's home. What is fair and just for both parties? Should the householder be allowed to seriously injure, or even kill, the burglar? Should the burglar be able to claim compensation for any injuries suffered?

The following activity is based on a similar situation.

Activity

Read the facts of the following case and use the case and the questions below as the basis of a discussion on the concept of justice.

Case *Revill* v *Newbery* (1996)

Facts Mark Revill, aged 21, with another man attempted to break into a brick shed on William Newbery's allotment at about 2 o'clock in the morning. Mr Revill and his companion had already that night stolen cars and caused criminal damage elsewhere, and intended to steal items from the shed. Mr Newbery, who was aged 76, was sleeping in the shed in order to protect his property after earlier thefts and vandalism. He had with him an air rifle and a single barrelled 12-bore shotgun and ammunition for both guns. When he was awakened by the noise of the two men trying to break in, he loaded the shotgun, poked it through a small hole in the door and fired. The shot hit Mr Revill on the right upper arm and chest.

Criminal proceedings Mr Revill was prosecuted for various criminal offences he had committed that night, pleaded guilty and was sentenced. Mr Newbery was prosecuted for wounding Mr Revill, but was found not guilty by the jury at the Crown Court.

Civil proceedings Mr Revill then brought a civil case against Mr Newbery claiming damages for the injuries he had suffered from the shotgun blast. In this case the judge awarded Mr Revill damages of £12,100 but reduced the amount to £4,033 because the judge held that Mr Revill was two-thirds to blame for what had happened. This meant that Mr Newbery was ordered to pay Mr Revill £4,033.

Mr Newbery appealed against this order but the Court of Appeal dismissed his appeal saying that his conduct was 'clearly dangerous and bordered on the reckless'. One of the judges pointed out that: 'Violence may be returned with necessary violence but the force used must not exceed the limits of what is reasonable in the circumstances.'

Questions

1. Should a criminal be able to use the legal rules to claim for injuries caused by another person? Is it justice to award damages to someone who was injured while carrying out criminal activities?
2. Bearing in mind the fact that Mr Newbery had fired without warning, was the decision in the civil case brought by Mr Revill, that Mr Newbery should pay a reduced amount of damages to Mr Revill for the injuries, a just one?
3. Mr Newbery was found not guilty of a criminal charge of wounding Mr Revill. Was this a 'just' decision?

Conclusion

From sections 1.2 and 1.3 it is clear that the three concepts of law, morality and justice are quite distinct. There is, however, a large overlap between law and morality, law and justice and also morality and justice. This idea of the overlapping of the three is illustrated in diagram form in Figure 1.3.

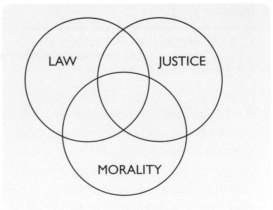

Figure 1.3 *Diagram of the relationship of law, morality and justice*

1.4 Rights and duties

The law gives rights to individuals and methods of enforcing those rights. Quite often the law is involved in a balancing act, trying to ensure that one person's rights do not affect another person's rights. In order to keep the balance the law also imposes duties on people.

This is more easily understood by looking at examples. In the law of contract, where one person buys a digital television from a shop each party will have rights and duties under this contract. For example, the shop has the right to be paid the agreed price for the TV, while the buyer has the right to have a set which is in working order.

The idea of rights and duties can also be seen clearly in employment law. An employer has a duty to pay wages to the employee, while the employee has the right to sue for any wages which are owed. An employee has a duty to obey reasonable lawful orders while an employer has a right to expect this and may be able to dismiss the employee if there is a serious breach. An employer has a duty to provide a safe system of work for all employees, while an employee has the right to claim compensation if he is injured because the employer has broken this duty. These are just a few of the rights and duties of employers and employees and this balancing of their rights and duties is also shown in Figure 1.4.

Even where there is no contract or agreement between the parties, the law can impose rights and duties on people. An example of this is the right to use one's own land (this includes a house or a flat) as one wants to. The law recognises that people have the right to enjoy the use of their own property, but this right is balanced by the right of other land users to enjoy the use of their properties. So the tort of nuisance allows a claim to be made if one's enjoyment of land is affected by too much noise, smoke, smells or other nuisances coming from another person's land.

Even in the criminal law this idea of rights and duties can be seen. The criminal law imposes a duty on all citizens to obey the law or face possible punishment. This duty is imposed to protect other citizens or society as a whole. In this way the law upholds the rights of people not to be assaulted or to have their possessions stolen or whatever else the particular crime involves.

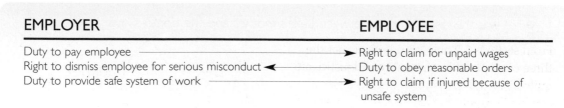

EMPLOYER	EMPLOYEE
Duty to pay employee ⟶	Right to claim for unpaid wages
Right to dismiss employee for serious misconduct ⟵	Duty to obey reasonable orders
Duty to provide safe system of work ⟶	Right to claim if injured because of unsafe system

Figure 1.4 *Balancing rights and duties in employment law*

Activity

The case in the following extract from *The Daily Telegraph* involves issues of morality, justice and the rights of the child and his parents. In fact, Baby Luke died three weeks after this judgment was made. Read the extract and answer the questions below.

High Court gives doctors right to let baby Luke die

Doctors treating a terminally-ill baby with a rare genetic disorder won the right yesterday to deny him life-saving treatment.

Luke Winston-Jones, eight months, has never left hospital and cannot recover from his illness, but his mother asked the High Court to rule that doctors must resuscitate her son if his condition deteriorates. His doctors said he should be allowed to die.

Mrs Winston-Jones argued that her son had defied all the odds to remain alive and, although she knew he was bound to die, she wanted him to do so at the right moment and not before.

Dame Elizabeth [Butler-Sloss], the president of the High Court family division, ruled yesterday that doctors were legally entitled not to put Luke on a ventilator. She said the procedure carried the risk of the baby then becoming dependent on a ventilator, which would deprive him of his close relationship with his mother during the last weeks or months of his life. His life 'would not be worth living', the judge said.

She ruled, however, that heart massage as a means of keeping Luke alive should remain an option.

Taken from an article by Sally Pook in *The Daily Telegraph*, 23 October 2004

Questions

1. What was the disagreement between Luke's mother and the doctors over Luke's treatment?

2. In which division of the High Court was the case heard?

3. What was the judge's decision?

4. Where there is disagreement over treatment, who do you think should make the decision over the type of treatment that a baby receives? Should it be:

   (a) the parents of baby

   (b) the doctors

   (c) the court?

   Give reasons for your answers.

1.5 Human rights and the English Legal System

Under the Human Rights Act 1998, the European Convention on Human Rights was incorporated into our law. This has affected many areas of the English Legal System. This section gives a brief summary of some of the key affects. There is fuller detail about the European Convention and the Human Rights Act 1998 in Chapter 20.

Precedent

Section 2(1)(a) of the Human Rights Act states that our courts must take into account any judgment or decision of the European Court of Human Rights. This means that judges when deciding a case must look at human rights cases, as well as our own English law.

Statutory interpretation

Section 3 of the Act states that, so far as it is possible to do so, all legislation (that is Acts of Parliament and other laws made in this country) must be given effect so that it is compatible with the European Convention. For example, if the wording of an Act of Parliament has two possible meanings, then the meaning which fits with the European Convention is the one that must be used.

Trials

Article 6 of the European Convention gives the right to a fair trial. This means that all aspects of the trial must be fair. For example, the way in which juvenile offenders are tried was changed after the case of *T* v *United Kingdom; V* v *United Kingdom* (1999). In this case a boy of 10 and a boy of 11 were tried for murder in the Crown Court. The European Court of Human Rights held the formality of a Crown Court trial would have made it difficult for the boys to understand what was happening. This meant that the trial was not fair and there was a breach of the European Convention.

Sentencing

Where an offender is sentenced to prison for life, it usual to set a minimum period which must be served before the offender can be considered for parole. This minimum sentence used to be set by the Home Secretary (a Government Minister). The European Court of Human Rights held that this was a breach of the European Convention. This has been changed so that judges are now responsible for setting any minimum period.

Judicial appointment

Part-time judges in this country used to be appointed for a period of three years. After this time they could then be appointed for further periods of three years. In addition, the appointment was by the Lord Chancellor (a Government Minister). The length of appointment was changed to five years, as it was thought that the shorter period meant that there was a risk of the judges not being sufficiently independent from the Government. This would have been a breach of the European Convention.

Conclusion

The above points are not the only way in which the English Legal System has been affected by the European Convention on Human Rights. However, they are an illustration of how wide-ranging the effect on our legal system has been.

Examination Questions

(a) What is meant by the Rule of Law?   *[11 marks]*

   and

(b) To what extent if at all is the Rule of Law applied in the English and
   Welsh legal system?   *[14 marks]*

LW2 June 2003, WJEC

Chapter 2

The development of law

The law of England and Wales has been built up very gradually over the centuries. There is not just one way of creating or developing law; there have been, and still are, a number of different ways. These methods of developing law are usually referred to as sources of law. Historically, the most important ways were custom and decisions of judges. Then, as Parliament became more powerful in the eighteenth and early nineteenth centuries, Acts of Parliament were the main source of new laws, although judicial decisions were still important as they interpreted the Parliamentary law and filled in gaps where there was no statute law (statute law is explained in Chapter 4). During the twentieth century, statute law and judicial decisions continued to be the major sources of law but, in addition, two new sources of law became increasingly important: these were delegated legislation and European law. All these sources of law have combined to make our present day law as indicated by Figure 2.1

All these sources of law are examined in turn in this chapter and Chapters 3, 4, 5 and 6.

2.1 Customs

These are rules of behaviour which develop in a community without being deliberately invented. There are two main types of custom: general customs and local customs.

2.1.1 General customs

Historically these are believed to have been very important in that they were, effectively, the basis of our Common law (see section 2.2). It is thought that following the Norman conquest (as the country was gradually brought under centralised government) the judges appointed by the kings to travel around the land making decisions in the King's name based at least some of their decisions on the common customs. This idea caused Lord Justice Coke in the seventeenth century to describe these customs as being 'one of the main triangles of the laws of England'. However, other commentators dispute this theory.

Today, Michael Zander writes that probably a high proportion of the so-called customs were almost certainly invented by the judges. In any event, it is accepted that general customs have long since been absorbed into legislation or case law and are no longer a creative source of law.

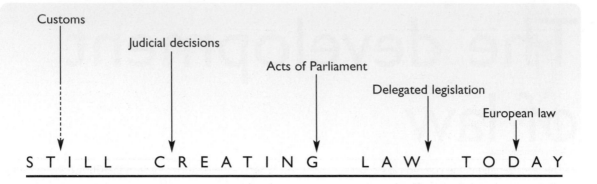

Figure 2.1 *Historical development of sources of law*

2.1.2 Local customs

This is the term used where a person claims that he is entitled to some local right, such as a right of way or a right to use land in a particular way, because this is what has always happened locally. Such customs are an exception to the general law of the land, and will only operate in that particular area.

Since there were (or still are) exceptions to the general common law, the judges, from the earliest times, established a series of rigorous tests or hurdles that had to be passed before they recognised any local custom. These tests still exist today and are used on the rare occasions that a claim to a right comes before the courts because of a local custom. The tests are as follows:

- The custom must have existed since 'time immemorial'
- The custom must have been exercised peaceably, openly and as of right
- The custom must be definite as to locality, nature and scope
- The custom must be reasonable.

It is very unusual for a new custom to be considered by the courts today and even rarer for the courts to decide that it will be recognised as a valid custom, but there have been some such cases. For example in *Egerton*

v *Harding* (1974) the court decided that there was a customary duty to fence land against cattle straying from the common. Another case was *New Windsor Corporation* v *Mellor* (1974) where a local authority was prevented from building on land because the local people proved there was a custom that they had the right to use the land for lawful sports. Although customs may develop, they are not part of the law until recognised by the courts; it is the judges who decide which customs will be recognised as enforceable at law.

2.2 Common law

Clearly the legal system in England and Wales could not rely only on customs. Even in Anglo-Saxon times there were local courts which decided disputes, but it was not until after the Norman conquest in 1066 that a more organised system of courts emerged. This was because the Norman kings realised that control of the country would be easier if they controlled, among other things, the legal system. The first Norman king, William the Conqueror, set up the Curia Regis (the King's Court) and appointed his own judges. The nobles who had a dispute were encouraged to apply to have the king (or his judges) decide the matter.

COMMON LAW

Different meanings	Distinguishes it from:
The law developed by the early judges to form a 'common' law for the country	The local laws used prior to the Norman conquest
The law which has continued to be developed by the judges through the doctrine of judicial precedent Judge-made law	Laws made by a legislative body, such as Acts of Parliament or delegated legislation
The law operated in the common law courts before the reorganisation of the courts in 1873–75	Equity – the decisions made in the Chancery courts

Figure 2.2 *Different meanings of the term 'common law'*

2.2.1 Development of common law

As well as this central court, the judges were sent to major towns to decide any important cases. This meant that judges travelled from London all round the country that was under the control of the king. In the time of Henry II (1154–89) these tours became more regular and Henry divided up the country into 'circuits' or areas for the judges to visit. Initially the judges would use the local customs or the old Anglo-Saxon laws to decide cases, but over a period of time it is believed that the judges on their return to Westminster in London would discuss the laws or customs they had used, and the decisions they had made, with each other. Gradually, the judges selected the best customs and these were then used by all the judges throughout the country. This had the effect that the law became uniform or 'common' through the whole country, and it is from here that the phrase 'common law' seems to have developed.

2.2.2 Definitions of common law

Common law is the basis of our law today: it is unwritten law that developed from customs and judicial decisions. The phrase 'common law' is still used to distinguish laws that have been developed by judicial decisions, from laws that have been created by statute or other legislation (see Figure 2.2). For example, murder is a common law crime while theft is a statutory crime. This means that murder has never been defined in any Act of Parliament, but theft is now defined by the Theft Act 1968.

Common law also has another meaning, in that it is used to distinguish between rules that were developed by the common law courts (the King's courts) and the rules of Equity which were developed by the Lord Chancellor and the Chancery courts.

2.3 Equity

Historically this was an important source and it still plays a part today with many of our legal concepts having developed from equitable principles. The word 'equity' has a meaning of 'fairness', and this is the basis on which it operates, when adding to our law.

2.3.1 The development of equity

Equity developed because of problems in the common law. Only certain types of case were recognised. The law was also very technical; if there was an error in the formalities the person making the claim would lose the case.

Another major problem was the fact that the only remedy the common law courts could give was 'damages' – that is an order that the defendant pay a sum of money to the plaintiff (now claimant) by way of compensation. In some cases this would not be the best method of putting matters right between the parties. For example, in a case of trespass to land, where perhaps the defendant had built on his neighbour's land, the building would still be there and the plaintiff would have lost the use of that part of his land. In such a situation the plaintiff would probably prefer to have the building removed, rather than be given money in compensation.

People who could not obtain justice in the common law courts appealed directly to the king. Most of these cases were referred to the king's Chancellor, who was both a lawyer and a priest, and who became known as the keeper of the king's conscience. This was because the Chancellor based his decisions on principles of natural justice and fairness, making a decision on what seemed 'right' in the particular case rather than on the strict following of previous precedents. He was also prepared to look beyond legal documents, which were considered legally binding by the common law courts, and to take account of what the parties had intended to do.

To ensure that the decisions were 'fair' the Chancellor used new procedures such as subpoenas, which ordered a witness to attend court or risk imprisonment for refusing to obey the Chancellor's order. He also developed new remedies which were able to compensate plaintiffs more fully than the common law remedy of damages. The main equitable remedies were: injunctions; specific performance; rescission; and rectification. These are all still used today and are explained more fully in Chapter 9.

Eventually a Court of Chancery under the control of the Chancellor came into being which operated these rules of fairness or equity. Equity was not a complete system of law; it merely filled the gaps in the common law and softened the strict rules of the common law.

Conflict between equity and common law

The two systems of common law and equity operated quite separately, so it was not surprising that this overlapping of the two systems led to conflict between them. One of the main problems was that the common law courts would make an order in favour of one party and the Court of Chancery an order in favour of the other party. The conflict was finally resolved in the *Earl of Oxford's case* (1615) when the king ruled that equity should prevail; in other words, the decision made in the Chancery court was the one which must be followed by the parties. This ruling made the position of equity stronger and the same rule was subsequently included in section 25 of the Judicature Act 1873.

2.3.2 The relevance of equity today

Equitable rights, interests and remedies remain important in the law today. Concepts such as mortgages and trusts are founded on the idea that one person owns the legal interest in property but has to use that property for the benefit of another. This other person is said to have an equitable interest in the property. It is difficult to imagine life today without mortgages – the vast majority of homeowners buy their property with the aid of a mortgage. Trusts are widely used in setting up such matters as pension funds, as well as within families when property is settled on younger members of the family or between husband and wife.

Modern use of equitable remedies

Equitable remedies are still important and used in a variety of circumstances.

For example, injunctions are often ordered in cases of domestic violence as a protection for the abused partner. Such an injunction often forbids the violent partner from entering the premises where the other partner is living or even going with a certain distance of the place.

Injunctions are also used to prevent trespass to land or to prevent excessive noise, or smoke or other nuisances. They are used in employment law in various situations. For example, a former employee can be prevented from disclosing trade secrets to anyone, or an injunction may be granted against a trade union to prevent unlawful industrial action.

Examination Questions

(a) Outline the development of common law and equity.   [11 marks]
    and
(b) What has been the impact of modern equity upon the common law?   [14 marks]

LW2 June 2004, WJEC

Chapter 3

Judicial precedent

Judicial precedent refers to the source of law where past decisions of the judges create law for future judges to follow. This source of law is also known as case-law. It is a major source of law, both historically and today.

3.1 The doctrine of precedent

The English system of precedent is based on the Latin maxim *stare decisis et non quieta movere* (usually shortened to *stare decisis*) which loosely translated means: 'stand by what has been decided and do not unsettle the established'. This supports the idea of fairness and provides certainty in the law.

3.1.1 *Ratio decidendi*

Precedent can only operate if the legal reasons for past decisions are known, therefore at the end of a case there will be a judgment – a speech made by the judge giving the decision and, more importantly, explaining the reasons for that decision. In a judgment the judge is likely to give a summary of the facts of the case, review the arguments put to him by the advocates in the case, and then explain the principles of law he is using to come to the decision. These principles are the important part of the judgment and are known as the

ratio decidendi which means the reason for deciding (and is pronounced 'ray-she-o des-id-end-i'). This is what creates a precedent for judges to follow in future cases. Sir Rupert Cross defined the *ratio decidendi* as 'any rule expressly or impliedly treated by the judge as a necessary step in reaching his conclusion'.

3.1.2 *Obiter dicta*

The remainder of the judgment is called *obiter dicta* ('other things said') and judges in future cases do not have to follow it. Sometimes a judge will speculate on what his decision would have been if the facts of the case had been different. This hypothetical situation is part of the *obiter dicta* and the legal reasoning put forward may be considered in future cases, although, as with all *obiter* statements, it is not binding precedent. A major problem when looking at a past judgment is to divide the *ratio decidendi* from the *obiter dicta*, as the judgment is usually in a continuous form, without any headings specifying what is meant to be part of the *ratio decidendi* and what is not.

3.1.3 Judgments

It is also worth realising that there can be more than one speech at the end of a case, depending on the number of judges hearing the case. In courts of first instance there will be only one judge and therefore one judgment. However, in the appeal courts (the Divisional Courts, the Court of Appeal and the House of Lords) cases are heard by at least two judges and up to a maximum of seven judges in the House of Lords. So for these courts there can be more than one judgment. The fact that there are two or more judges does not mean that there will always be several judgments as it is quite common for one judge to give the judgment and the other judge/judges simply to say 'I agree'! However, in cases where there is a particularly important or complicated point of law, more than one judge may want to explain his legal reasoning on the point. This can cause problems in later cases as each judge may have had a different reason for his decision, so there will be more than one *ratio decidendi*. (By the way, the plural of *ratio* is *rationes*.) As well as learning the Latin phrases *ratio decidendi*, *obiter dicta* and *stare decisis* there are some English phrases which are important for understanding the concept of judicial precedent. These are original or declaratory precedent, binding precedent and persuasive precedent.

3.1.4 Original precedent

If the point of law in a case has never been decided before, then whatever the judge decides will form a new precedent for future cases to follow, i.e. it is an original precedent. As there are no past cases for the judge to base his decision on, he is likely to look at cases which are the closest in principle and he may decide to use similar rules. This way of arriving at a judgment is called reasoning by analogy. Some legal commentators used to hold that the judge is only declaring what the law is (that is, the law has always been there, but it is the first time a judge has had to decide it). This view holds that judges do not create law, they merely declare what it has always been. Nowadays it is accepted that judges do have a law-making role in these situations – when a new point has to be decided, the judge is creating new law.

This idea of creating new law by analogy can be seen in *Hunter and others* v *Canary Wharf Ltd and London Docklands Development Corporation* (1995). Part of the decision involved whether the interference with television reception by a large building was capable of constituting an actionable private nuisance. The facts of the case were that in 1990 a tower known as the Canary Wharf Tower was built by the first defendant in an enterprise zone in East London. The tower was about 250 metres high and over 50 metres square. The claimant, and hundreds of others suing with her, claimed damages from the first defendant for interference over a number of years with reception of television broadcasts at their homes in East London. The interference was claimed to have been caused by the tower.

3.1.5 Binding precedent

This is a precedent from an earlier case which must be followed even if the judge in the later case does not agree with the legal principle. A binding precedent is only created when the facts of the second case are sufficiently similar to the original case and the decision was made by a court which is senior to (or in some cases the same level as) the court hearing the later case.

Activity

Read the following extract from the judgment in this case of *Hunter and others v Canary Wharf Ltd and London Docklands Development Corporation*. Then answer the questions below.

When the case was heard on appeal in the Court of Appeal, Lord Justice Pill giving judgment said:

'Lord Irving (counsel for the defendants) submits that interference with television reception by reason of the presence of a building is properly to be regarded as analogous to loss of aspect (view). To obstruct the receipt of television signals by the erection of a building between the point of receipt and the source is not in law a nuisance. In Aldred's Case (1611) Wray CJ cited what he had said in Bland v Moselely:

"for prospect, which is a matter only of delight and not of necessity, no action lies for stopping thereof, and yet it is a great recommendation of a house if it has a long and large prospect . . . But the law does not give an action for such things of delight".

I accept the importance of television in the lives of very many people. However, in my judgment the erection or presence of a building in the line of sight between a television transmitter and other properties is not actionable as an interference with the use and enjoyment of land. The analogy with loss of prospect is compelling. The loss of a view, which may be of the greatest importance to many householders, is not actionable and neither is the mere presence of a building in the sight line to the television transmitter.'

Questions

1. In respect of the interference with television reception, with what did Lord Justice Pill draw an analogy?

2. Do you think that the judge was correct to make an analogy between the two situations? Give reasons for your answer.

3. By drawing this analogy does it mean that the claimant won or lost the case?

3.1.6 Persuasive precedent

This is a precedent that is not binding on the court, but the judge may consider it and decide that it is a correct principle so he is persuaded that he should follow it. Persuasive precedent comes from a number of sources as explained below:

Courts lower in the hierarchy

Such an example can be seen in *R v R* (1991) where the House of Lords agreed with and followed the same reasoning as the Court of Appeal in deciding that a man could be guilty of raping his wife.

Decisions of the Judicial Committee of the Privy Council

This court is not part of the court hierarchy in England and Wales and so its decisions are not binding, but, since many of its judges are also members of the House of Lords, their judgments are treated with respect and may often be followed. An example of this can be seen in the law on remoteness of damages in the law of tort and the decision made by the Privy Council in the case of *The Wagon Mound (No 1)* (1961). In later cases courts in England and Wales followed the decision in this case.

This also happened in *A-G for Jersey* v *Holley* (2005) when the majority of the Privy Council (six out of nine judges) ruled that in the defence of provocation, a defendant is to be judged by the standard of a person having ordinary powers of self-control. This was contrary to an earlier judgment of the House of Lords. As a result, there were conflicting decisions from the House of Lords and the Privy Council. Although a decision by the Privy Council is not binding on English courts, in *R* v *Mohammed* (2005) the Court of Appeal followed *Holley* rather than the decision in *Smith*. Then in *R* v *James*; *R* v *Karimi* (2006), a five-member Court of Appeal confirmed that the decision in *Holley* should be followed by courts in England and Wales.

Statements made obiter dicta (particularly where the comment was made in a House of Lords decision)

This is clearly seen in the law on duress as a defence to a criminal charge, where the House of Lords in *R* v *Howe* (1987) ruled that duress could not be a defence to a charge of murder. In the judgment the Lords also commented, as an obiter statement, that duress would not be available as a defence to someone charged with attempted murder. When, later, in *R* v *Gotts* (1992) a defendant charged with attempted murder tried to argue that he could use the defence of duress, the *obiter* statement from *Howe* was followed as persuasive precedent by the Court of Appeal.

A dissenting judgment

Where a case has been decided by a majority of judges (for example, 2–1 in the Court of Appeal), the judge who disagreed will have explained his reasons. If that case goes on appeal to the House of Lords, or if there is a later case on the same point which goes to the House of Lords, it is possible that the House of Lords may prefer the dissenting judgment and decide the case in the same way. The dissenting judgment has persuaded them to follow it.

Decisions of courts in other countries

This is especially so where the other country uses the same ideas of common law as in our system. This applies to Commonwealth countries such as Canada, Australia and New Zealand.

3.2 The hierarchy of the courts

In England and Wales our courts operate a very rigid doctrine of judicial precedent which has the effect that:

- Every court is bound to follow any decision made by a court above it in the hierarchy
- In general, appellate courts (courts which hear appeals) are bound by their own past decisions

So the hierarchy of the courts is the next important point to get clear. Which courts come where in the hierarchy? Figure 3.1 shows this in the form of a cascade model and Figure

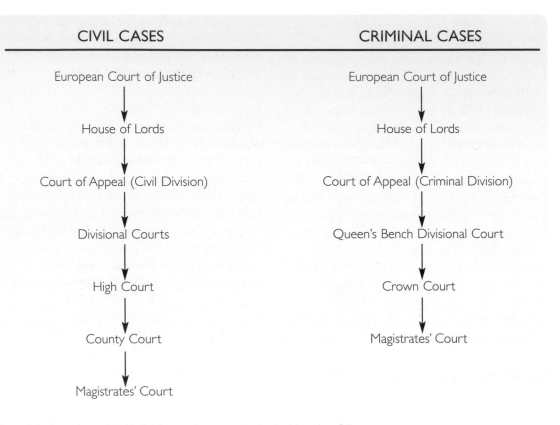

Figure 3.1 *Cascade model of judicial precedent operating in the hierarchy of the courts*

3.2 gives each court and its position in respect of the other courts. The position of each court is also considered in this section and in sections 3.3 and 3.4.

3.2.1 Appellate courts

Appellate courts are those that hear appeals.

The European Court of Justice

Since 1973 the highest court affecting our legal system is the European Court of Justice. For points of European law, a decision made by this court is binding on all other courts in England and Wales. However, there are still laws which are unaffected by European Union law and for these the House of Lords is the supreme court. An important feature of the European Court of Justice is that it is prepared to overrule its own past decisions if it feels it is necessary. This flexible approach to past precedents is seen in other legal systems in Europe, and is a contrast to the more rigid approach of our national courts.

House of Lords

The most senior national court is the House of Lords and its decisions bind all other courts in the English legal system. The House of Lords is not bound by its own past decisions, although it will generally follow them. This point is discussed in detail in section 3.3.

Court of Appeal

At the next level down in the hierarchy is the Court of Appeal which has two divisions: Civil

COURT	COURTS BOUND BY IT	COURTS IT MUST FOLLOW
European Court	All courts	None
House of Lords	All other courts in the English legal system	European Court
Court of Appeal	Itself (with some exceptions) Divisional Courts All other lower courts	European Court House of Lords
Divisional Courts	Itself (with some exceptions) High Court All other lower courts	European Court House of Lords Court of Appeal
High Court	County Court Magistrates' Court	European Court House of Lords Court of Appeal Divisional Courts
Crown Court	Possibly Magistrates' Court	All higher courts

County Court and Magistrates' Court do not create precedent and are bound by all higher courts

Figure 3.2 *The courts and precedent*

and Criminal. Both divisions of the Court of Appeal are bound to follow decisions of the European Court of Justice and the House of Lords. In addition they must usually follow past decisions of their own; although there are some limited exceptions to this rule, and the Court of Appeal (Criminal Division) is more flexible where the point involves the liberty of the subject. The position of the two divisions is discussed in detail in section 3.4.

Divisional Courts

The three Divisional Courts (Queen's Bench, Chancery and Family) are bound by decisions of the European Court of Justice, the House of Lords and the Court of Appeal. In addition the Divisional Courts are bound by their own past decisions, although they operate similar exceptions to those operated by the Court of Appeal.

3.2.2 Courts of first instance

The term court of first instance means any court where the original trial of a case is held. The appellate courts considered in section 3.2.1 do not hear any original trials. They only deal with appeals from decisions of other courts. Quite often an appeal will be about a point of law. This allows the appellate courts to decide the law and this is why the appellate courts are much more important than courts of first instance when it comes to creating precedent.

Courts of first instance rarely create precedent. They must follow the decisions of the courts above them.

The High Court

This is bound by decisions of all the courts above and in turn it binds the lower courts. High Court judges do not have to follow each others' decisions but will usually do so. In *Colchester Estates (Cardiff)* v *Carlton Industries plc* (1984) it was held that where there were two earlier decisions which conflicted, then, provided the first decision had been fully considered in the later case, that later decision should be followed.

Inferior courts

These are the Crown Court, the County Court and the Magistrates' Court. They are bound to follow decisions by all higher courts and it is unlikely that a decision by an inferior court can create precedent. The one exception is that a ruling on a point of law by a judge in the Crown Court technically creates precedent for the Magistrates' Court. However, since such rulings are rarely recorded in the law reports, this is of little practical effect.

3.3 The House of Lords

The main debate about the House of Lords is the extent to which it should follow its own past decisions and the ideas on this have changed over the years. Originally the view was that the House of Lords had the right to overrule past decisions, but gradually during the nineteenth century this more flexible approach disappeared. By the end of that century, in *London Street Tramways* v *London County Council* (1898), the House of Lords held that certainty in the law was more important than the possibility of individual hardship being caused through having to follow a past decision.

So from 1898 to 1966 the House of Lords regarded itself as being completely bound by its own past decisions unless the decision had been made *per incuriam*, that is 'in error'. However, this idea of error referred only to situations where a decision had been made without considering the effect of a relevant statute.

This was not felt to be satisfactory, as the law could not alter to meet changing social conditions and opinions, nor could any possible 'wrong' decisions be changed by the courts. If there was an unsatisfactory decision by the House of Lords, then the only way it could be changed was by Parliament passing a new Act of Parliament. This happened in the law about intention as an element of a criminal offence. The House of Lords in *DPP* v *Smith* (1961) had ruled that an accused could be guilty of murder if a reasonable person would have foreseen that death or very serious injury might result from the accused's actions. This decision was criticised as it meant that the defendant could be guilty even if he had not intended to cause death or serious injury, nor even realised that his actions might have that effect. Eventually Parliament changed the law by passing the Criminal Justice Act 1967.

3.3.1 The Practice Statement

It was realised that the House of Lords should have more flexibility. For today's system of judicial precedent the critical date is 1966, when the Lord Chancellor issued a Practice Statement announcing a change to the rule in *London Street Tramways* v *London County Council*. The Practice Statement said:

'Their Lordships regard the use of precedent as an indispensable foundation upon which to decide what is the law and its application to individual cases. It provides at least some degree of certainty upon which individuals can rely in the conduct of their affairs, as well as a basis for orderly development of legal rules.

Their Lordships nevertheless recognise that the rigid adherence to precedent may lead to injustice in a particular case and also unduly restrict the proper development of the law. They propose, therefore, to modify their present practice and while treating former decisions of this House as normally binding, to depart from a previous decision when it appears right to do so.

Key Facts		
1898	House of Lords decides in the case of *London Street Tramways* that it is bound to follow its own previous decisions	
1966	Issue of the Practice Statement House of Lords will depart from previous decisions when 'it is right to do so'	
1968	First use of Practice Statement in *Conway v Rimmer* Only involves technical law on discovery of documents	
1972	First major use of Practice Statement in *Herrington v British Railways Board* on the duty of care owed to child trespassers	
1980s and 1990s	House of Lords shows an increasing willingness to use Practice Statement to overrule previous decisions, eg *R v Shivpuri* (criminal attempts); *Pepper v Hart* (use of *Hansard* in statutory interpretation)	
2003	Practice statement used to overrule the decision in *Caldwell* on recklessness in the criminal law	

Figure 3.3 *Key fact chart for the operation of judicial precedent in the House of Lords*

In this connection they will bear in mind the danger of disturbing retrospectively the basis on which contracts, settlement of property and fiscal arrangements have been entered into and also the especial need for certainty as to the criminal law. This announcement is not intended to affect the use of precedent elsewhere than in this House.'

3.3.2 Use of the Practice Statement

Since 1966, this Practice Statement has allowed the House of Lords to change the law if it believes that an earlier case was wrongly decided. It has the flexibility to refuse to follow an earlier case when 'it appears right to do so'. This phrase is, of course, very vague and gives little guidance as to when the House of Lords might overrule a previous decision. In fact the House of Lords has been reluctant to use this power, especially in the first few years after 1966. The first case in which the Practice Statement was used was *Conway v Rimmer* (1968), but this only involved a technical point

on discovery of documents.

The first major use did not occur until 1972 in *Herrington* v *British Railways Board* (1972), which involved the law on the duty of care owed to a child trespasser. The earlier case of *Addie* v *Dumbreck* (1929) had decided that an occupier of land would only owe a duty of care for injuries to a child trespasser, if those injuries had been caused deliberately or recklessly. In *Herrington* the Lords held that social and physical conditions had changed since 1929, and the law should also change.

There was still great reluctance in the House of Lords to use the Practice Statement, as can be seen by the case of *Jones* v *Secretary of State for Social Services* (1972). This case involved the interpretation of the National Insurance (Industrial Injuries) Act 1946 and four out of the seven judges hearing the case regarded the earlier decision in *Re Dowling* (1967) as being wrong. Despite this the Lords refused to overrule that earlier case, preferring to keep to the idea that certainty was the most important feature of precedent. The same attitude was shown in *Knuller* v *DPP* (1973) when Lord Reid said:

'Our change of practice in no longer regarding previous decisions of this House as absolutely binding does not mean that whenever we think a previous precedent was wrong we should reverse it. In the general interest of certainty in the law we must be sure that there is some very good reason before we so act.'

From the mid-1970s onwards the House of Lords showed a little more willingness to make use of the Practice Statement. For example, in *Miliangos* v *George Frank (Textiles) Ltd* (1976) the House of Lords used the Practice Statement to overrule a previous judgment that damages could only be awarded in sterling. More recently in *Murphy* v *Brentwood District Council* (1990), the House of Lords overruled the decision in *Anns* v *Merton London Borough* (1977) regarding the test for negligence in the law of tort. Another major case was *Pepper* v *Hart* (1993) where the previous ban on the use of *Hansard* in statutory interpretation was overruled.

In *Horton* v *Sadler and another* (2006) the House of Lords used the Practice Statement to depart from a previous decision of its own. The case involved a personal injury claim, but the point of law being decided was about the power to allow service out of time under s 33 of the Limitation Act 1980. The House of Lords departed from their decision in *Walkley* v *Precision Forgings Ltd* (1979).

The Law Lords departed from *Walkley* for three reasons:

- It unfairly deprived claimants of a right that Parliament had intended them to have
- It had driven the Court of Appeal to draw distinctions which were correct but were so fine as to reflect no credit on the area of law and
- It went against the clear intention of Parliament.

Lord Bingham in his speech considered the issue of departing from a previous decision. He pointed out that the case was not one in which contracts, settlements of property or fiscal arrangements had been entered into, nor did it involve the criminal law where certainty was particularly important. Also, there would not be any detriment to public administration caused by departing from the previous decision.

3.3.3 The Practice Statement in criminal law

The Practice Statement stressed that criminal law needs to be certain, so it was not surprising that the House of Lords did not rush to overrule any judgments in criminal cases. The first use in a criminal case was in *R* v *Shivpuri* (1986) which overruled the decision in *Anderton* v *Ryan* (1985) on attempts to do the impossible. The interesting point was that the decision in *Anderton* had been made less than a year before, but it had been severely criticised by academic lawyers. In *Shivpuri* Lord Bridge said:

'I am undeterred by the consideration that the decision in Anderton v Ryan *was so recent. The Practice Statement is an effective abandonment of our pretention to infallibility. If a serious error embodied in a decision of this House has distorted the law, the sooner it is corrected the better.'*

In other words, the House of Lords recognised that they might sometimes make errors and the most important thing then was to put the law right. Where the Practice Statement is used to overrule a previous decision, that past case is then effectively ignored. The law is now that which is set out in the new case.

3.3.4 Conclusion

Another important case on the use of the Practice Statement is *R* v *R and G* (2003). In

Activity

Read the following passage which comes from an extra explanatory note which was given to the press when the Practice Statement was issued and answer the questions below.

'The statement is one of great importance, although it should not be supposed that there will frequently be cases in which the House thinks it right not to follow their own precedent. An example of a case in which the House might think it right to depart from a precedent is where they consider that the earlier decision was influenced by the existence of conditions which no longer prevail, and that in modern conditions the law ought to be different.

One consequence of this change is of major importance. The relaxation of the rule of judicial precedent will enable the House of Lords to pay greater attention to judicial decisions reached in the superior courts of the Commonwealth, where they differ from earlier decisions of the House of Lords. That could be of great help in the development of our own law. The superior courts of many other countries are not rigidly bound by their own decisions and the change in the practice of the House of Lords will bring us more into line with them.'

Questions

1. Why is the Practice Statement of great importance?
2. Does the note suggest that the Practice Statement is likely to be used often?
3. Do you agree that 'in modern conditions the law ought to be different'? Give reasons and examples to support your answer.
4. Why should the House of Lords want to consider decisions from Commonwealth countries? What authority do such decisions have in the English legal system?

this case the House of Lords used the Practice Statement to overrule the earlier decision of *Caldwell* (1982) on the law of criminal damage. In *Caldwell* the House of Lords had ruled that recklessness included the situation where the defendant had not realised the risk of his actions causing damage, but an ordinary careful person would have realised there was a risk. In *R v R and G* it was held that this was the wrong test to use. The Law Lords overruled *Caldwell* and held that a defendant is only reckless if he realises that there is a risk of damage and goes ahead and takes that risk.

This case shows that the House of Lords is becoming more prepared to use the Practice Statement where they think it is 'right to do so'.

3.4 The Court of Appeal

As already stated there are two divisions of this court, the Civil Division and the Criminal Division, and the rules for precedent are not quite the same in these two divisions.

3.4.1 Decisions of courts above it

Both divisions of the Court of Appeal are bound by decisions of the European Court of Justice and the House of Lords. This is true even though there have been attempts in the past, mainly by Lord Denning, to argue that the Court of Appeal should not be bound by the House of Lords. In *Broome* v *Cassell & Co Ltd* (1971) Lord Denning refused to follow the earlier decision of the House of Lords in *Rookes* v *Barnard* (1964) on the circumstances in which exemplary damages could be awarded.

Again in the cases of *Schorsch Meier GmbH* v *Henning* (1975) and *Miliangos* v *George Frank (Textiles) Ltd* (1976) the Court of Appeal refused to follow a decision of the House of Lords in *Havana Railways* (1961) which said that damages could only be awarded in sterling (English money). Lord Denning's argument for refusing to follow the House of Lords' decision was that the economic climate of the world had changed, and sterling was no longer a stable currency; there were some situations in which justice could only be done by awarding damages in another currency. The case of *Schorsch Meier GmbH* v *Henning* was not appealed to the House of Lords, but *Miliangos* v *George Frank (Textiles) Ltd* did go on appeal to the Lords, where it was pointed out that the Court of Appeal had no right to ignore or overrule decisions of the House of Lords. The more unusual feature of *Miliangos* was that the House of Lords then used the Practice Statement to overrule its own decision in *Havana Railways*.

Comment

Should the Court of Appeal have to follow House of Lords' decisions?

The main argument in favour of the Court of Appeal being able to ignore House of Lords' decisions is that very few cases reach the House of Lords, so that if there is an error in the law it may take years before a suitable case is appealed all the way to the House of Lords. The cases of *Schorsch Meier* and *Miliangos* illustrate the potential for injustice if there is no appeal to the House of Lords. What would have happened if the Court of Appeal in *Schorsch Meier* had decided that it had to follow the House of Lords' decision in *Havana Railways*? It is quite possible that the later case of *Miliangos* would not have even been appealed to the Court of Appeal. After all, why waste money on an appeal when there have been previous cases in both the Court of Appeal and the House of Lords ruling on that point of law? The law would have been regarded as fixed and it might never have been changed.

On the other hand, if the Court of Appeal could overrule the House of Lords, the system of precedent would break down and the law would become uncertain. There would be two conflicting precedents for lower courts to choose from. This would make it difficult for the judge in the lower court. It would also make the law so uncertain that it would be difficult for lawyers to advise clients on the law. However, since the case of *Miliangos*, there has been no further challenge by the Court of Appeal to this basic idea (in our system of judicial precedent) that lower courts must follow decisions of courts above them in the hierarchy.

3.4.2 Human rights cases

Section 2(1)(a) of the Human Rights Act 1998 states that courts must take into account any judgment or decision of the European Court of Human Rights. In the case of *Re Medicaments (No 2), Director General of Fair Trading* v *Proprietary Association of Great Britain* (2001) the Court of Appeal refused to follow the decision of the House of Lords in *R* v *Gough* (1993) because it was slightly different to decisions of the European Court of Human Rights.

The *Director General* case was about whether a decision should be set aside because of the risk of bias on the part of one of the panel. In *Gough* the test for bias included the appeal court deciding whether there was a real danger that the tribunal was biased. The Court of Appeal said that in the European Court of Human Rights cases the emphasis was on the impression which the facts would give on an objective basis. This they claimed was a 'modest adjustment' of the test in *Gough*. However, this appears to be one situation in which the Court of Appeal need not follow a House of Lords decision.

3.4.3 The Court of Appeal and its own decisions

The first rule is that decisions by one division of the Court of Appeal will not bind the other division. However, within each division, decisions are normally binding, especially for the Civil Division. This rule comes from the case of *Young* v *Bristol Aeroplane Co Ltd* (1944) and the only exceptions allowed by that case are:

- Where there are conflicting decisions in past Court of Appeal cases, the court can choose which one it will follow and which it will reject

- Where there is a decision of the House of Lords which effectively overrules a Court of Appeal decision the Court of Appeal must follow the the decision of the House of Lords
- Where the decision was made *per incuriam*, that is carelessly or by mistake because a relevant Act of Parliament or other regulation has not been considered by the court.

The Civil Division of the Court of Appeal under Lord Denning tried to challenge the rule in *Young's* case, claiming that as it had made the earlier decision it could change it. As Lord Denning said in *Gallie* v *Lee* (1969): 'It was a self-imposed limitation and we who imposed it can also remove it.' This view was not shared by the other judges in the Court of Appeal, as is shown by the statement of Russell LJ in the same case of *Gallie* v *Lee* where he said: 'The availability of the House of Lords to correct errors in the Court of Appeal makes it, in my view, unnecessary for the court to depart from its existing discipline.'

However, in *Davis* v *Johnson* (1979) the Court of Appeal refused to follow a decision made only days earlier regarding the interpretation of the Domestic Violence and Matriminial Proceedings Act 1976. The case went to the House of Lords on appeal where the Law Lords, despite agreeing with the actual interpretation of the law, ruled that the Court of Appeal had to follow its own previous decisions and said that they 'expressly, unequivocally and unanimously reaffirmed the rule in *Young* v *Bristol Aeroplane*'.

Since this case and, perhaps more especially since the retirement of Lord Denning, the Court of Appeal has not challenged the rule in *Young's* case, though it has made some use of the *per incuriam* exception allowed by *Young's* case. For example in *Williams* v *Fawcett* (1986) the Court refused to follow previous decisions because these had been based on a misunderstanding of the County Court rules dealing with procedure for committing to prison those who break court undertakings. In *Rickards* v *Rickards* (1989) the court refused to follow a case it had decided in 1981. This was because of the fact that, in the previous case, it had misunderstood the effect of a House of Lords' decision. Even though the court did not follow its own previous decision Lord Donaldson said that it would only be in 'rare and exceptional cases' that the Court of Appeal would be justified in refusing to follow a previous decision. *Rickards* v *Rickards* was considered a 'rare and exceptional' case because the mistake was over the critical point of whether the court had power to hear that particular type of case. Also it was very unlikely that the case would be appealed to the House of Lords.

3.4.4 The Court of Appeal (Criminal Division)

The Criminal Division, as well as using the exceptions from *Young's* case, can also refuse to

Activity

Read the following comments by Lord Scarman in his judgment in *Tiverton Estates Ltd* v *Wearwell Ltd* (1975) and answer the questions below.

'The Court of Appeal occupies a central, but intermediate position in our legal system. To a large extent, the consistency and certainty of the law depend upon it . . . If, therefore, one division of the court should refuse to follow another because it believed the other's decision to be wrong, there would be a risk of confusion and doubt arising where there should be consistency and certainty.

The appropriate forum for the correction of the Court of Appeal's errors is the House of Lords, where the decision will at least have the merit of being final and binding, subject only to the House's power to review its own decisions. The House of Lords as the court of last resort needs this power of review; it does not follow that an intermediate court needs it.'

Questions

1. Why did Lord Scarman describe the Court of Appeal as occupying 'a central but intermediate position'?

2. Do you agree with his view that there would be a 'risk of confusion and doubt' if the Court of Appeal was not obliged to follow its own past decisions?

3. Describe the situations in which the Court of Appeal may refuse to follow its own past decisions.

4. Why does the House of Lords need the power of review?

Key Facts

General rules for Court of Appeal	Comment
Bound by European Court of Justice	Since 1972 all courts in England and Wales are bound by the European Court of Justice.
Bound by House of Lords	This is because the House of Lords is above the Court of Appeal in the court hierarchy. Also necessary for certainty in the law. Court of Appeal tried to challenge this rule in *Broome* v *Cassell* (1971) and also in *Miliangos* (1976). The House of Lords rejected this challenge. The Court of Appeal must follow decisions of the House of Lords.
Bound by its own past decisions	Decided by the Court of Appeal in *Young's case* (1944), though there are minor exceptions (see below). In *Davis* v *Johnson* (1979) the Court of Appeal tried to challenge this rule but the House of Lords confirmed that the Court of Appeal had to follow its own previous decisions.
Exceptions	**Comment**
Exceptions in Young's case	Court of Appeal need not follow its own previous decisions where: • there are conflicting past decisions • there is a House of Lords' decision which effectively overrules the Court of Appeal decision • the decision was made per incuriam (in error)
Limitation of *per incuriam*	Only used in 'rare and exceptional cases' (*Rickards* v *Rickards* (1989)).
Special exception for the Criminal Division	If the law has been 'misapplied or misunderstood' (*R* v *Gould* (1968)).

Figure 3.4 *Key fact chart for the Court of Appeal and the doctrine of precedent*

follow a past decision of its own if the law has been 'misapplied or misunderstood'. This extra exception arises because in criminal cases people's liberty is involved. This idea was recognised in *R* v *Taylor* (1950). The same point was made in *R* v *Gould* (1968). Also in *R* v *Spencer* (1985) the judges said that there should not in general be any difference in the way that precedent was followed in the Criminal Division and in the Civil Division, 'save that we must remember that we may be dealing with the liberty of the subject and if a departure from authority is necessary in the interests of justice to an appellant, then this court should not shrink from so acting'.

3.5 The Judicial Committee of the Privy Council

The Judicial Committee of the Privy Council hears appeals from some Commonwealth countries and from places such as the Channel Islands.

3.5.1 Judges

The judges include the Law Lords and also judges who have held high judicial office in countries which still use it as their final court of appeal. Normally a panel of five judges sits to hear an appeal. There can, however, be more judges on the panel where the case is particularly important.

3.5.2 The Privy Council and Precedent

The Judicial Committee of the Privy Council is not part of the English Legal System and its decisions are not binding on English courts.

However, its decisions are persuasive precedent which courts in England and Wales may decide to follow.

Normally the Judicial Committee of the Privy Council will follow decisions of the House of Lords. The exception to this is where the point of law has developed differently in the country from which the appeal has come. In such a situation the court is not bound by House of Lords' decisions and can decide to follow the law of the particular country.

An unusual case was *A-G for Jersey* v *Holley* (2005), which was an appeal from Jersey on the law of provocation (a special partial defence to murder). An extra large panel of nine judges, all of whom were also Law Lords, was used to decide the case. They refused, by a majority of six judges to three, to follow a previous decision by the House of Lords in *R* v *Smith (Morgan James)* (2000), even though the law in Jersey was the same as in England. The judges in the majority actually said that the decision in *Smith* was wrong.

This created problems when the same point of law came before the Court of Appeal (Criminal Division) in a later case. Should the Court of Appeal follow the House of Lords' decision in *Smith* or should it follow the Privy Council decision in *Holley*? Normally the Court of Appeal would be bound by any decision of the House of Lords. However, the Court of Appeal took the unusual decision to follow the ruling by the Privy Council rather than that of the House of Lords. This was mainly because the decision in *Holley* was made by six judges from the House of Lords, even though the case was actually dealt with by the Privy Council.

3.6 Distinguishing, overruling and reversing

3.6.1 Distinguishing

This is a method which can be used by a judge to avoid following a past decision which he would otherwise have to follow. It means that the judge finds that the material facts of the case he is deciding are sufficiently different for him to draw a distinction between the present case and the previous precedent. He is not then bound by the previous case.

Two cases demonstrating this process are *Balfour* v *Balfour* (1919) and *Merritt* v *Merritt* (1971). Both cases involved a wife making a claim against her husband for breach of contract. In *Balfour* it was decided that the claim could not succeed because there was no intention to create legal relations; there was merely a domestic arrangement between a husband and wife and so there was no legally binding contract. The second case was successful because the court held that the facts of the two cases were sufficiently different in that, although the parties were husband and wife, the agreement was made after they had separated. Furthermore the agreement was made in writing. This distinguished the case from *Balfour*; the agreement in *Merritt* was not just a domestic arrangement but meant as a legally enforceable contract.

3.6.2 Overruling

This is where a court in a later case states that the legal rule decided in an earlier case is wrong. Overruling may occur when a higher court overrules a decision made in an earlier case by a lower court, for example, the House of Lords overruling a decision of the Court of Appeal. It can also occur where the European Court of Justice overrules a past decision it has made; or when the House of Lords uses its power under the Practice Statement to overrule a past decision of its own.

An example of this was seen in *Pepper* v *Hart* (1993) when the House of Lords ruled that *Hansard* (the record of what is said in Parliament) could be consulted when trying to decide what certain words in an Act of Parliament meant. This decision overruled the earlier decision in *Davis* v *Johnson* (1979) when the House of Lords had held that it could not consult *Hansard*.

3.6.3 Reversing

This is where a court higher up in the hierarchy overturns the decision of a lower court on appeal in the same case. For example, the Court of Appeal may disagree with the legal ruling of the High Court and come to a different view of the law; in this situation they reverse the decision made by the High Court.

3.7 Judicial law-making

Although there used to be a school of thought that judges did not actually 'make' new law but merely declared what the law had always been, today it is well recognised that judges do use precedent to create new law and to extend old principles. There are many areas of law which owe their existence to decisions by the judges.

Law of contract

Nearly all the main rules which govern the formation of contracts come from decided cases. Many of the decisions were made in the nineteenth century, but they still affect the law today.

Key Facts

Concept	Definition	Comment
stare decisis	Stand by what has been decided	Follow the law decided in previous cases for certainty and fairness
ratio decidendi	Reason for deciding	The part of the judgment which creates the law
obiter dicta	Others things said	The other parts of the judgment – these do not create law
binding precedent	A previous decision which has to be followed	Decisions of higher courts bind lower courts
persuasive precedent	A previous decision which does not have to be followed	The court may be 'persuaded' that the same legal decision should be made
original precedent	A decision in a case where there is no previous legal decision or law for the judge to use	This leads to judges 'making' law
distinguishing	A method of avoiding a previous decision because facts in the present case are different	e.g. *Balfour* v *Balfour* not followed in *Merritt* v *Merritt*
overruling	A decision which states that a legal rule in an earlier case is wrong	e.g. in *Pepper* v *Hart* the House of Lords overruled *Davis* v *Johnson* on the use of *Hansard*
reversing	Where a higher court in the same case overturns the decision of the lower court	This can only happen if there is an appeal in the case

Figure 3.6 *Key fact chart for the basic concepts of judicial precedent*

Tort of negligence

The law of negligence in the law of tort is another major area which has been developed and refined by judicial decisions. An important starting point in this area of law was the case of *Donoghue* v *Stevenson* (1932) in which the House of Lords, when recognising that a manufacturer owed a duty of care to the 'ultimate consumer', created what is known as the 'neighbour test'. Lord Atkin in his judgment in the case said: 'You must take reasonable care to avoid acts or omissions which you can reasonably foresee would be likely to injure your neighbour'. This concept has been applied by judges in several different situations, so that the tort of negligence has developed into a major tort. An interesting extension was in the case of *Ogwo* v *Taylor* (1987) where it was held that a man, who negligently started a fire in his roof when trying to burn off paint with a blow torch, owed a duty of care to a fireman who was injured trying to put out the fire.

There have also been major developments in case-law on liability for nervous shock where there has been negligence. The House of Lords laid down the guidelines for this area of law in the case of *Alcock* v *Chief Constable of South Yorkshire* (1991) which involved claims made by people who had lost relatives in the Hillsborough tragedy.

Criminal law

In the criminal law the judges have played a major role in developing the law on intention. For example, it is only because of judicial decisions that the intention for murder covers not only the intention to kill but also the intention to cause grievous bodily harm. Judicial decisions have also effectively created new crimes, as in *Shaw* v *DPP* (1962) which created the offence of conspiracy to corrupt public morals and *R* v *R* (1991) when it was decided that rape within marriage could be a crime.

However, there have been cases in which the House of Lords has refused to change the law, saying that such a change should only be made by Parliament. This happened in *C* v *DPP* (1995) when it refused to abolish the presumption that children between 10 and 14 were incapable of having the necessary intention to commit a crime. (This presumption meant that there always had to be evidence that the child knew he or she was doing something which was seriously wrong.) In fact the Government did change the law later in the Crime and Disorder Act 1998.

Comment

Should judges make law?

It is argued that it is wrong for judges to make law. Their job is to apply the law. It is for Parliament to make the law. Parliament is elected to do this but judges are not. This means that law-making by judges is undemocratic.

But, in reality judges have to make law in some situations. The first is where a case involves a legal point which has never been decided before. As there is no law on it, the judge in the case has to make a decision. After all, the parties in the case would not want the judge to refuse to deal with the case; they want the matter decided.

The second area is more controversial. This is where judges overrule old cases and in doing so create new law. It is important for the law to be updated in this way. Law for the twenty first century needs to be based on today's society and values. Law decided a hundred years or more ago may no longer be suitable. Ideally, Parliament should reform the law, but Parliament is sometimes slow to do this. If judges never overruled old cases, then the law might be 'out of date'.

An example of this is the case of *R* v *R* (1991). In this case a man was charged with raping his wife. The point the court had to decide was whether, by being married, a woman automatically consented to sex with her husband and could never say 'no'. The old law dated back to 1736 when it was said that 'by their mutual matrimonial consent the wife hath given up her herself in this kind to her husband, which she cannot retract'. In other words, once married, a woman was always assumed to consent and could not go back on this. This was still held to be the law in *R* v *Miller* (1954), even though the wife had already started divorce proceedings.

Parliament had not done anything to reform this law.

So, when the case of *R* v *R* came before the courts, the judges had to decide whether to follow the old law, or whether they should change the law to match the ideas of the late twentieth century. In the House of Lords, the judges pointed out that 'the status of women and the status of a married woman in our law have changed quite dramatically. A husband and wife are now for all practical purposes equal partners in marriage'. As a result it was decided that if a wife did not consent to sex then her husband could be guilty of rape. The House of Lords stated that the common law (judge-made law) 'is capable of evolving in the light of changing social, economic and cultural developments'. This clearly recognises that judges in the House of Lords can, and will, change the law if they think it necessary.

3.8 The effect of an Act of Parliament

Although judges can and do make law, precedent is subordinate to statute law, delegated legislation and European regulations. This means that if (for example) an Act of Parliament is passed and that Act contains a provision which contradicts a previously decided case, that case decision will cease to have effect; the Act of Parliament is now the law on that point. This happened when Parliament passed the Law Reform (Year and a Day Rule) Act in 1996. Up to then judicial decisions meant that a person could only be charged with murder or manslaughter if the victim died within a year and a day of receiving his injuries. The Act enacted that there was no time limit, and a person could be guilty even if the victim died several years

later, so cases after 1996 follow the Act and not the old judicial decisions.

3.9 Comparison with other legal systems

3.9.1 Codes of law

Most countries have some system of considering past case decisions, but these are rarely as rigid as the system of judicial precedent followed in England and Wales. In countries which have a code of law, precedent plays a much less important part. This civil system is operated in many continental countries; the judges are less likely to make law, the code should provide for all situations and so the judge's task is to interpret the code. Since the code is the fountain of the law, judicial decisions are not followed so closely. Even judges in lower courts can refuse to follow a decision by another court if they feel that the code was not correctly interpreted.

3.9.2 Less rigid precedent

Even in other countries which have a common law system similar to England's where case decisions form a major part of the law, the doctrine of precedent is not applied so strictly. For example, in the United States of America a previous precedent is likely to be ignored if it fails to meet with academic approval: if there is considerable criticism of the decision by leading academic lawyers, judges in later cases are likely to take note of that criticism and rule differently. This has happened in England in the case of *R* v *Shivpuri* (1986), but this is a rare happening, while in America it occurs more frequently.

Also in America, cases where the panel of judges disagreed (so that the decision may have been by three judges to two) are likely to be overruled in the future. In England, the fact that the majority was so slender does not make the precedent less valuable.

3.9.3 Prospective overruling

The other difference is that in America the concept of prospective overruling is used. This means that the law is not changed in the case being decided by the court, but it is changed for the future. In England, the judges cannot do this; if their decision changes the law then it is changed in the actual case. This has been described as 'dog's law'; that is you do not know you have done wrong until the court changes the law in your case, in just the way that a dog does not know it has done wrong until you punish him. This is what happened in the case of *R* v *R* (1991) when it was

decided that rape within marriage could be a crime. Until that case, previous decisions had held that this was not a crime. This can be viewed as unfair to the parties in a case. The American use of prospective overruling is preferable in such cases.

3.10 Advantages and disadvantages of precedent

As can be seen from the previous sections there are both advantages and disadvantages to the way in which judicial precedent operates in England and Wales. In fact it could be said that every advantage has a corresponding disadvantage.

3.10.1 Advantages

The main advantages are:

1. **Certainty**
    Because the courts follow past decisions, people know what the law is and how it is likely to be applied in their case; it allows lawyers to advise clients on the likely outcome of cases; it also allows people to operate their businesses knowing that financial and other arrangements they make are recognised by law. The House of Lords' Practice Statement points out how important certainty is.

2. **Consistency and fairness in the law**
    It is seen as just and fair that similar cases should be decided in a similar way, just as in any sport it is seen as fair that the rules of the game apply equally to each side. The law must be consistent if it is to be credible.

3. **Precision**
    As the principles of law are set out in actual cases the law becomes very precise; it is

well illustrated and gradually builds up through the different variations of facts in the cases that come before the courts.

4. **Flexibility**

   There is room for the law to change as the House of Lords can use the Practice Statement to overrule cases. The ability to distinguish cases also gives all courts some freedom to avoid past decisions and develop the law.

5. **Time-saving**

   Precedent can be considered a useful time saving device. Where a principle has been established, cases with similar facts are unlikely to go through the lengthy process of litigation.

The main advantages have been summed up very neatly as follows:

'The main advantages of the precedent system are said to be certainty, precision and flexibility. Legal certainty is achieved in theory at least, in that if the legal problem raised has been solved before, the judge is bound to adopt that solution. Precision is achieved by the sheer volume of reported cases containing solutions to innumerable factual situations. No code or statute could ever contain as much.

Flexibility is achieved by the possibility of decisions being overruled and by the possibility of distinguishing and confining the operation of decisions which appear unsound.'

3.10.2 Disadvantages

However, there are disadvantages as follows:

1. **Rigidity**

   The fact that lower courts have to follow decisions of higher courts, together with the fact that the Court of Appeal has to follow its own past decisions, can make the law too inflexible so that bad decisions made in the past may be perpetuated. There is the added problem that so few cases go to the House of Lords. Change in the law will only take place if parties have the courage, the persistence and the money to appeal their case.

2. **Complexity**

   Since there are nearly half a million reported cases it is not easy to find all the relevant case law even with computerised databases. Another problem is in the judgments themselves, which are often very long with no clear distinction between comments and the reasons for the decision. This makes it difficult in some cases to extract the *ratio decidendi*; indeed in *Dodd's Case* (1973) the judges in the Court of Appeal said they were unable to find the *ratio* in a decision of the House of Lords.

3. **Illogical distinctions**

   The use of distinguishing to avoid past decisions can lead to 'hair-splitting' so that some areas of the law have become very complex. The differences between some cases may be very small and appear illogical.

4. **Slowness of growth**

   Judges are well aware that some areas of the law are unclear or in need of reform, however they cannot make a decision unless there is a case before the courts to be decided. This is one of the criticisms of the need for the Court of Appeal to follow its own previous decisions, as only about 50 cases go to the House of Lords each year. There may be a long wait for a suitable case to be appealed as far as the House of Lords.

3.11 Law reporting

In order to follow past decisions there must be an accurate record of what those decisions were. Written reports have existed in England

and Wales since the thirteenth century, but many of the early reports were very brief and, it is thought, not always accurate. The earliest reports from about 1275 to 1535 were called Year Books, and contained short reports of cases, usually written in French. From 1535 to 1865 cases were reported by individuals who made a business out of selling the reports to lawyers. The detail and accuracy of these reports varied enormously. However, some are still occasionally used today.

In 1865 the Incorporated Council of Law Reporting was set up – this was controlled by the courts. Reports became accurate, with the judgment usually noted down word for word. This accuracy of reports was one of the factors in the development of the strict doctrine of precedent. These reports still exist and are published according to the court that the case took place in. For example, cases references abbreviated to 'Ch' stand for 'Chancery' and the case will have been decided in the Chancery Division; while 'QB' stands for 'Queen's Bench Division'.

There are also other well established reports today, notably the All England series (abbreviated to All ER) and the Weekly Law Reports (WLR). Newspapers and journals also publish law reports, but these are often abbreviated versions in which the law reporter has tried to pick out the essential parts of the judgment.

3.11.1 Internet law reports

All High Court, Court of Appeal and House of Lords cases are now reported on the Internet. Some websites give the full report free, others give summaries or an index of cases. There are also subscription sites which give a very comprehensive service of law reports.

Activity

Search at least one website address and find a recent law report. Some suggestions for websites are given below.

www.lawreports.co.uk gives summaries of important cases in its Daily Law Notes section

www.parliament.uk gives reports of House of Lords cases

www.bailii.org has cases from the Court of Appeal and below.

Examination Questions

1. Consider each of the following situations and explain if the courts concerned can depart from their own previous decisions:

   (i) A case concerning theft was decided in the Court of Appeal (Criminal Division). A year later a similar case is heard by the same court but the judges are reluctant to apply the same decision.

   (ii) A case concerning domestic violence was decided in the Court of Appeal (Civil Division). Days later a similar case is heard by the same court but the judges now feel that the earlier decision was unjust.

   (iii) A case concerning criminal attempts was decided in the House of Lords. Less than a year later a similar case is heard by the Law Lords who now feel that the previous decision was totally wrong.

   Part of question from 2570, January 2003, OCR

2. (a) What is meant by the doctrine of precedent?   *[10 marks]*

   and

   (b) What effect would the abolition of the doctrine of binding precedent have on the legal system?   *[15 marks]*

   LW2 WJEC, June 2006

Acts of Parliament

In today's world there is often a need for new law to meet new situations. Clearly the method of judicial law-making through precedents is not suitable for major changes to the law, nor is it a sufficiently quick, efficient law-making method for a modern society. The other point to be made is that judges are not elected by the people, and in a democracy, the view is that laws should only be made by the elected representatives of society. So, today, the main legislative body in the United Kingdom is Parliament.

Laws passed by Parliament are known as Acts of Parliament or statutes, and this source of law is usually referred to as statute law. About 60 to 70 Acts are passed each year. In addition to Parliament as a whole enacting law, power is delegated to government ministers and their departments to make detailed rules and regulations, which supplement Acts of Parliament. These regulations are delegated legislation (see Chapter 5) and are called statutory instruments.

4.1 Parliament

Parliament consists of the House of Commons and the House of Lords. Under the normal procedure both Houses must vote in favour of a Bill before it can become a new Act of Parliament.

4.1.1 The House of Commons

The people who sit in the House of Commons are referred to as Members of Parliament (MPs). These members of the House of Commons are elected by the public, with the country being divided into constituencies and each of these returning one Member of Parliament (MP). There must be a general election at least once every five years, though such an election can be called sooner by the Prime Minister. In addition, there may be individual by-elections in constituencies where the MP has died or retired during the current session of Parliament. The Government of the day is formed by the political party which has a majority in the House of Commons.

4.1.2 The House of Lords

At the beginning of 2007 the House of Lords consisted of:

- 92 hereditary peers
- life peers
- the judges who are the Law Lords
- the most senior bishops in the Church of England.

Originally most of the members of the House of Lords were hereditary peers. During the twentieth century the awarding of a title for life (a life peerage) became more common. The Prime Minister nominated people who should receive a title for their lifetime, but this title would not pass on to their children. The title was then awarded by the Monarch. In this way people who had served the country and were thought to be suitable members of the House of Lords were able to bring their expertise to the House. Most life peerages were given to former politicians who had retired from the House of Commons. For example, Margaret Thatcher, who had been Prime Minister in the 1980s, was made a life peer.

4.1.3 Reform of the House of Lords

By 1999, there were over 1,100 members of the House of Lords, of whom 750 were hereditary peers. The Labour Government decided that in a modern society an inherited title should not automatically allow someone to participate in making law. They felt that some of the members should be elected and some should be nominated. To help decide exactly what reforms should be made, a Royal Commission (known as the Wakeham Commission) was set up to consider how members of the House of Lords should be selected. In the meantime the right of most of the hereditary peers to sit in

the House of Lords was abolished in November 1999. Only 92 hereditary peers were allowed to continue to be members of the House of Lords.

The Wakeham Commission reported in 2000 and recommended that one-third of the House should be elected. Also, that there should be a limit on the system of political patronage whereby the Prime Minister nominates people to the House of Lords. The Commission recommended that an independent Appointments Commission could reject poorly qualified nominees and also be able to appoint 'people's peers'.

In 2001 some so-called people's peers were appointed to the House of Lords by the Prime Minister. These were supposed to be ordinary people who had been recommended by other ordinary people. However, the list was mainly of already famous people, rather than 'Mr Joe Public'.

This was meant to be a temporary solution while the Government consulted on the final make-up of the House of Lords. However, there have been major disagreements about how many of the House of Lords should be elected by the general public and how many should be nominated (and by whom). As a result the reform of the House of Lords has not been completed.

Judges in the House of Lords

The most senior court in England and Wales is also usually referred to as the House of Lords. In fact its full title is the Judicial Committee of the House of Lords. Only the 12 Law Lords are allowed to sit on this judicial committee. Take care not to confuse the House of Lords in its legislative (law-making) function with the House of Lords as an appeal court.

It is agreed that judges should not sit as part of Parliament. There are plans for a new Supreme Court to replace the Judicial

Committee of the House of Lords. When this court is created, probably in 2009, the judges will cease to be members of the House of Lords and will no longer sit in Parliament.

4.2 Influences on parliamentary law-making

4.2.1 The Government programme

When a Government is formed, it will have a programme of reforms it wishes to carry out. These will have been set out in its party manifesto on which it asked people to vote for it in the General Election. Also, at the start of each parliamentary session, the Government announces (in the Queen's Speech) what particular laws it intends introducing during that session. So most new legislation is likely to arise from Government policy.

4.2.2 European Union Law

However, there are other influences on what law is enacted: European Union law can lead to new Acts of Parliament which are passed in order to bring our law in line with the European law. This may be to implement a specific European Regulation or Directive, as in the case of the Consumer Protection Act 1987, or because a decision of the European Court of Justice has shown that our law does not conform with the Treaty of Rome, as with the Sex Discrimination Act 1986. The effect of European law is considered in more detail in Chapter 7.

4.2.3 Other influences

Other outside influences include proposals for law reform put forward by law reform agencies, commissions or inquiries into the effectiveness of existing law. These law reform agencies are dealt with in detail in Chapter 8. In addition specific events may also play a role in formulating the law. A particularly tragic example was the massacre in March 1996 of 16 young children and their teacher in Dunblane by a lone gunman. After this there was an inquiry into the laws on gun-ownership. By March 1997 Parliament passed the Firearms (Amendment) Act 1997 banning private ownership of most handguns.

Another major example of an event leading to new law was the terrorist attack on the Twin Towers in New York in September 2001. (This is often referred to as 9/11.) Following this our Parliament passed the Anti-Terrorism, Crime and Security Act 2001. One of the provisions of this Act was to allow the detention (without charge) of non-UK citizens where the Home Secretary believes that the person's presence in the UK is a risk to national security and suspects that the person is a terrorist. This provision was held to be a breach of human rights in 2005.

Pressure groups may also cause the Government to reconsider the law on certain areas. This was seen in 1994 when the Government agreed to reduce the age of consent for homosexual acts in private from 21 to 18. Then in 2000 the age of consent was further reduced to 16. Another clear example of the Government bowing to public opinion and the efforts of pressure groups was the introduction of the Disability Discrimination Act 1995. This Act gave disabled people certain rights in relation to employment. It also stated that they should have access to shops and hotels and other services.

The Civil Partnership Act 2004 gave the right to same-sex couples to register their partnership and have a civil ceremony. This was the result of changing attitudes to same-sex partnerships.

4.3 The pre-legislative process

On major matters a Green Paper may be issued by the Minister with responsibility for that matter. A Green Paper is a consultative document on a topic in which the Government's view is put forward with proposals for law reform. Interested parties are then invited to send comments to the relevant Government Department, so that a full consideration of all sides can be made and necessary changes made to the Government's

Activity

Read the following article and answer the questions below

Judge reprieves Dempsey, the harmless pit bull

A High Court judge, who reprieved a pit bull terrier from death row yesterday, savaged the Dangerous Dogs Act (1991) which he said would have sent a 'perfectly inoffensive animal to the gas chamber'.

Dempsey, dubbed Britain's most expensive dog after a long legal battle to save her, will be returned to her overjoyed owner after Lord Justice Staughton and Mr Justice Rougier quashed a destruction order by Ealing Magistrates' Court in 1992.

Dempsey's only crime was being the wrong kind of dog, Judge Rougier said. Magistrates sentenced her to be destroyed after the nephew of her owner, Dianne Fanneran, took her muzzle off in public when she became ill, and she was spotted by a policeman.

Mr Justice Rougier said: 'It seems to me that, while acknowledging the need to protect the public . . . the Dangerous Dogs Act bears all the hallmarks of an ill-thought-out piece of legislation, no doubt drafted in response to another pressure group . . .'

The Act was rushed through in 1991 by the then Home Secretary, Kenneth Baker, after pit bull terriers attacked a man in Lincoln and a 6-year-old girl in Bradford. It requires them to be put down unless they are neutered, tattooed, microchipped, registered, muzzled and kept on a lead in public.

Taken from an article by Clare Dyer in
The Guardian, 23 November 1995

Questions

1. Why was the Dangerous Dogs Act 1991 passed?
2. Why was Dempsey in breach of the Act?
3. What did Mr Justice Rougier say about the Act?
4. How might this problem with the Act have been avoided by the Government when formulating the legislation?

proposals. Following this the Government will publish a White Paper with its firm proposals for new law.

Consultation before any new law is framed is valuable as it allows time for mature consideration. Governments have been criticised for sometimes responding in a 'knee-jerk' fashion to incidents and, as a result, rushing law through that has subsequently proved to be unworkable. This occurred with the Dangerous Dogs Act 1991.

4.4 Introducing an Act of Parliament

The great majority of Acts of Parliament are introduced by the Government — these are initially drafted by lawyers in the civil service who are known as Parliamentary Counsel to the Treasury. Instructions as to what is to be included and the effect the proposed law is intended to have, are given by the government department responsible for it.

4.4.1 Bills

When the proposed Act has been drafted it is published, and at this stage is called a Bill. It will only become an Act of Parliament if it successfully completes all the necessary stages in Parliament. Even at this early stage there are difficulties, as the draftsmen face problems in trying to frame the Bill. It has to be drawn up so that it represents the Government's wishes, while at the same time using correct legal wording so that there will not be any difficulties in the courts applying it. It must be unambiguous, precise and comprehensive. Achieving all of these is not easy, and there may be unforeseen problems with the language used, as discussed in the chapter on statutory interpretation. On top of this there is usually pressure on time, as the Government will have a timetable of when they wish to introduce the draft Bill into Parliament.

4.4.2 Private Members' Bills

Ballot

Bills can also be sponsored by individual MPs. The parliamentary process allows for a ballot each parliamentary session in which 20 private members are selected who can then take their turn in presenting a Bill to Parliament. The time for debate of Private Members' Bills is limited, usually only being debated on Fridays, so that only the first six or seven members in the ballot have a realistic chance of introducing a Bill on their chosen topic. Relatively few Private Members' Bills become law, but there have been some important laws passed as the result of such Bills. A major example was the Abortion Act 1967 which legalised abortion in this country. More recent examples are the Marriage Act 1994, which was introduced by Giles Brandreth, the MP for Chester. This allowed people to marry in any registered place, not only in Register Offices or religious buildings. Another example is the Household Waste Recycling Act 2003 which places local authorities under a duty to recycle waste.

10-minute rule

Backbenchers can also try to introduce a Bill through the '10-minute' rule, under which any MP can make a speech of up to 10 minutes supporting the introduction of new legislation. This method is rarely successful unless there is no opposition to the Bill, but some Acts of Parliament have been introduced in this way, for example the Bail (Amendment) Act 1993 which gave the prosecution the right to appeal against the granting of bail to a defendant. Members of the House of Lords can also introduce Private Members' Bills.

4.4.3 Public and private Bills

A public Bill involves matters of public policy which will affect either the whole country or a large section of it. Most of the Government Bills are in this category, for example, the Powers of Criminal Courts (Sentencing) Act 2000, the Criminal Justice Act 2003 and the Constitutional Reform Act 2005. However, not all Bills are aimed at changing the law for the entire country; some are designed to pass a law which will affect only individual people or corporations. An example of this was the University College London Act 1996 which was passed in order to combine the Royal Free Hospital School of Medicine, the Institute of Neurology and the Institute of Child Health with University College.

4.5 The process in Parliament

In order to become an Act of Parliament, the Bill will usually have to be passed by both Houses of Parliament, and in each House there is a long and complex process (see Figure 4.1). A Bill may start in either the House of Commons or the House of Lords, with the exception of finance Bills which must start in the House of Commons. All Bills must go through the stages explained below:

First Reading

This is a formal procedure where the name and main aims of the Bill are read out. Usually no discussion takes place, but there will be a vote on whether the House wishes to consider the Bill further. The vote may be verbal: this is when the Speaker of the House asks the members as a whole how they vote and the members shout out 'Aye' or 'No'. If it is clear that nearly all members are in agreement, either for or against,

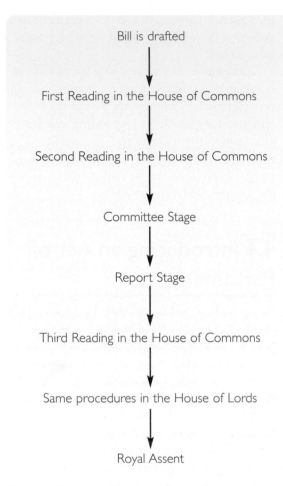

Figure 4.1 *Flow chart of the passing of an Act of Parliament starting in the House of Commons*

there is no need for a more formal vote. If it is not possible to judge whether more people are shouting 'Aye' or 'No' there will be a formal vote in which the members of the House vote by leaving the Chamber and then walking back in through one of two special doors on one side or the other of the Chamber. There will be two 'tellers' positioned at each of these two voting doors to make a list of the Members voting on each side. These tellers count up the number of MPs who voted for and against and declare these numbers to the Speaker in front of the members of the House.

Second Reading

This is the main debate on the whole Bill in which MPs debate the principles behind the Bill. The debate usually focuses on the main principles rather than the smaller details. Those MPs who wish to speak in the debate must catch the Speaker's eye, since the Speaker controls all debates and no-one may speak without being called on by the Speaker. At the end of this a vote is taken in the same way as for the First Reading; obviously there must be a majority in favour for the Bill to progress any further.

Committee Stage

At this stage a detailed examination of each clause of the Bill is undertaken by a committee of between 16 and 50 MPs. This is usually done by what is called a Standing Committee, which, contrary to its name, is a committee chosen specifically for that Bill. The membership of such a committee is decided 'having regard to the qualifications of those members nominated and to the composition of the House'. So, although the Government will have a majority, the opposition and minority parties are represented proportionately to the number of seats they have in the House of Commons. The members of Parliament nominated for each Standing Committee will usually be those with a special interest in, or knowledge of, the subject of the Bill which is being considered. For finance Bills the whole House will sit in committee.

Report Stage

At the Committee stage amendments to various clauses in the Bill may have been voted on and passed, so this report stage is where the committee report back to the House on those amendments. (If there were no amendments at the Committee stage, there will not be a 'Report' stage – instead the Bill will go straight on to the Third Reading.) The amendments will be debated in the House and accepted or rejected. Further amendments may also be added. The Report stage has been described as 'a useful safeguard against a small Committee amending a Bill against the wishes of the House, and a necessary opportunity for second thoughts'.

Third Reading

This is the final vote on the Bill. It is almost a formality since a Bill which has passed through all the stages above is unlikely to fail at this late stage. In fact in the House of Commons there will only be an actual further debate on the Bill as a whole if at least six MPs request it. However, in the House of Lords there may sometimes be amendments made at this stage.

The House of Lords

If the Bill started life in the House of Commons it is now passed to the House of Lords where it goes through the same five stages outlined above and, if the House of Lords makes amendments to the Bill, then it will go back to the House of Commons for it to consider those amendments. If the Bill started in the House of Lords then it passes to the House of Commons.

Royal Assent

The final stage is where the monarch formally gives approval to the Bill and it then becomes an Act of Parliament. This is now a formality and, under the Royal Assent Act 1961, the monarch will not even have the text of the Bills to which she is assenting; she will only have the short title. The last time that a monarch refused assent was in 1707, when Queen Anne refused to assent to the Scottish Militia Bill.

4.5.1 The Parliament Acts 1911 and 1949

The power of the House of Lords to reject a Bill is limited by the Parliament Acts 1911 and 1949. These allow a Bill to become law even if the House of Lords rejects it, provided that the Bill is re-introduced into the House of Commons in the next session of Parliament and passes all the stages again there.

The principle behind the Parliament Acts is that the House of Lords is not an elected body, and its function is to refine and add to the law rather than oppose the will of the democratically elected House of Commons. In fact there have only been four occasions when this procedure has been used to by-pass the House of Lords after they had voted against a Bill. Since 1949 the Parliament Acts have only been used on four occasions. These were for the:

- War Crimes Act 1991
- European Parliamentary Elections Act 1999
- Sexual Offences (Amendment) Act 2000
- Hunting Act 2004.

4.5.2 Commencement of an Act

Following the Royal Assent the Act of Parliament will come in force on midnight of that day, unless another date has been set. However, there has been a growing trend for Acts of Parliament not to be implemented immediately. Instead the Act itself states the date when it will commence or passes responsibility on to the appropriate Minister to fix the commencement date. In the latter case the Minister will bring the Act into force by issuing a commencement order. This can cause problems of uncertainty as it is difficult to discover which sections of an Act have been brought into force. The Criminal Justice Act 2003 is a good example of an Act where the sections have been brought in bit by bit.

The Criminal Justice Act 2003 contains 339 sections as well as several schedules. The commencement section is s 336. It provides that parts of 11 sections (out of the total of 339) come into effect immediately after the Act receives Royal Assent: this was on 19 November 2003. Most of the sections that came into effect immediately were administrative in nature, for example, allowing the relevant minister to create rules ready for parts of the Act to be implemented.

The commencement section then provides that ss 269–277 will come into effect four weeks after the Royal Assent. These sections are about the effects of life sentences and how long must be served in prison. So, these came into effect on 18 December 2003. The commencement section provides that all other sections shall come into effect when the relevant Minister makes an order for this. As a result some sections were brought into force in January 2004, others in February 2004, yet others in April 2004, etc. Some sections have not yet been brought into force.

It may be that some sections or even a whole Act will never become law. An example of this is the Easter Act 1928, which was intended to fix the date of Easter Day. Although this Act passed all the necessary parliamentary stages, and was given the Royal Assent, it has never come into force.

It can be seen that with all these stages it usually takes several months for a Bill to be passed. However, there have been occasions where all parties have thought a new law is needed urgently and an Act has been passed in less than 24 hours. This happened with the Northern Ireland Bill in 1972.

4.5.3 Example of an Act

Figure 4.3 on pages 54 and 55 is a reproduction of the Law Reform (Year and a Day Rule) Act

Key Facts

Green Paper	Consultation document on possible new law
White Paper	Government's firm proposals for new law
First Reading	Formal introduction of Bill into the House of Commons
Second Reading	Main debate on Bill's principles
Committee Stage	Clause by clause consideration of the Bill by a select committee
Report Stage	Committee reports suggested amendments back to the House of Commons
Third Reading	Final debate on the Bill
Repeat of process in the House of Lords	All stages are repeated BUT if the House of Lords votes against the Bill, it can go back to the House of Commons and, under the Parliament Acts 1911 and 1949, become law if the House of Commons passes it for the second time (rare occurrence)
Royal Assent	A formality – normally Acts of Parliament come into force at midnight after receiving the Royal Assent

Figure 4.2 *Key fact chart for the legislative process*

1996. This shows what an Act of Parliament looks like. The name of the Act is given immediately under the Royal coat of arms and underneath the name '1996 CHAPTER 19' means that it was the nineteenth Act to be passed in 1996. Next follows a short statement or preamble about the purpose of the Act. Then there is a formal statement showing that the Act has been passed by both Houses of Parliament and received the Royal Assent; this is included in all Acts. After this comes the body of the Act, which is set out in sections; this is an unusually short Act as it has only three sections.

Section 1 abolishes the 'year and a day rule'. Note that the Act actually refers to it in those terms; this is because the rule was a part of the common law and was never written down in any statute. Section 2 sets out when the consent of the Attorney-General is needed before a prosecution can be started. The last section gives the name by which the Act may be cited and it also sets out that the Act does not apply to cases in which the incident which led to death occurred before the Act was passed.

Activity

Look up a recent Act on the Internet. If you do not know of any try the website *www.opsi.gov.uk*.

Choose an Act and now search for the debates in Parliament on that Act (try *www.parliament.uk*). Don't forget it would be called a Bill before it is passed.

ELIZABETH II   c. **19**

Law Reform (Year and a Day Rule) Act 1996

1996 CHAPTER 19

An Act to abolish the "year and a day rule" and, in consequence of its abolition, to impose a restriction on the institution in certain circumstances of proceedings for a fatal offence. [17th June 1996]

BE IT ENACTED by the Queen's most Excellent Majesty, by and with the advice and consent of the Lords Spiritual and Temporal, and Commons, in this present Parliament assembled, and by the authority of the same, as follows:—

1. The rule known as the "year and a day rule" (that is, the rule that, for the purposes of offences involving death and of suicide, an act or omission is conclusively presumed not to have caused a person's death if more than a year and a day elapsed before he died) is abolished for all purposes.

Abolition of "year and a day rule".

2.—(1) Proceedings to which this section applies may only be instituted by or with the consent of the Attorney General.

Restriction on institution of proceedings for a fatal offence.

(2) This section applies to proceedings against a person for a fatal offence if—

   (a) the injury alleged to have caused the death was sustained more than three years before the death occurred, or

   (b) the person has previously been convicted of an offence committed in circumstances alleged to be connected with the death.

(3) In subsection (2) "fatal offence" means—

   (a) murder, manslaughter, infanticide or any other offence of which one of the elements is causing a person's death, or

   (b) the offence of aiding, abetting, counselling or procuring a person's suicide.

2   c. **19**   *Law Reform (Year and a Day Rule) Act 1996*

(4) No provision that proceedings may be instituted only by or with the consent of the Director of Public Prosecutions shall apply to proceedings to which this section applies.

(5) In the application of this section to Northern Ireland—

(a) the reference in subsection (1) to the Attorney General is to the Attorney General for Northern Ireland, and

(b) the reference in subsection (4) to the Director of Public Prosecutions is to the Director of Public Prosecutions for Northern Ireland.

Short title, commencement and extent.

3.—(1) This Act may be cited as the Law Reform (Year and a Day Rule) Act 1996.

(2) Section 1 does not affect the continued application of the rule referred to in that section to a case where the act or omission (or the last of the acts or omissions) which caused the death occurred before the day on which this Act is passed.

(3) Section 2 does not come into force until the end of the period of two months beginning with the day on which this Act is passed; but that section applies to the institution of proceedings after the end of that period in any case where the death occurred during that period (as well as in any case where the death occurred after the end of that period).

(4) This Act extends to England and Wales and Northern Ireland.

© Crown copyright 1996

PRINTED IN THE UNITED KINGDOM BY MIKE LYNN
Controller and Chief Executive of Her Majesty's Stationery Office
and Queen's Printer of Acts of Parliament

Figure 4.3 The Law Reform (Year and a Day Rule) Act 1996

Section 3 is concerned with the commencement of the Act; this sets the commencement date for s 2 at two months after the Act is passed. As s 1 is not specifically mentioned, the normal rule that an Act comes into effect on midnight of the date on which it receives the Royal Assent applies to that section.

4.6 Criticisms of the legislative process

There are many criticisms which can be made about the legislative process. In fact the Renton Committee on the Preparation of Legislation which reported in 1975 pointed out that there had been criticism for centuries, quoting Edward VI as saying more than 400 years ago: 'I would wish that . . . the superfluous and tedious statutes were brought into one sum together, and made more plain and short, to the intent that men might better understand them.'

The Renton Committee said there were four main categories of complaint:

1. The language used in many Acts was obscure and complex.
2. Acts were 'over-elaborate' because draftsmen tried to provide for every contingency.

3. The internal structure of many Acts was illogical with sections appearing to be out of sequence, making it difficult for people to find relevant sections.

4. There was a lack of clear connection between Acts, so that it was not easy to trace all the Acts on a given topic. In addition, the frequent practice of amending small parts of one Act by passing another increased the difficulty of finding out what the law was.

The Committee made 81 recommendations, but only about half of these have been fully implemented.

4.6.1 Lack of accessibility

Ideally, the laws of the land should be easily accessible to citizens but there are some major problems which create difficulties not only for ordinary citizens, but also for lawyers and even in some cases for the Lord Chancellor! As already mentioned it is difficult to discover which Acts and/or which sections have been brought into force.

An example of problems with knowing what sections are in force is the Criminal Justice Act 2003 which has 339 sections and several schedules. We have already looked at this in section 4.5.2. Only 11 sections came into force when the Royal Assent was given. Some more came into force four weeks after the Royal Assent. Many of other 300-plus sections have been brought into effect a few at a time over a period of time. Three years after the Act was passed, some of the sections had still not been brought into effect.

In fact, there is a special commencement section for s 43 (allowing trial without a jury for complex fraud cases), which states that s 43 can only be brought into effect by a resolution of both Houses of Parliament. When the

Government tried to get such resolution, the House of Lords voted against it. So, in 2006 the Government placed a new Bill before Parliament, the Fraud (Trial Without a Jury) Bill. The aim of this Bill is to repeal the commencement section for s 43 of the Criminal Justice Act 2003, so that s 43 can be brought into effect by an order of the Secretary of State for the Department of Constitutional Affairs.

Where sections are brought into effect at different times, it is difficult to know what the law is. This prevents law from being easily accessible.

Activity

Find the commencement section or schedule in a recent Act of Parliament.

This can be done by looking at a printed copy of an Act in a library or on the Internet at *www.opsi.gov.uk*. There is usually a list of contents at the start of an Act.

4.6.2 Other problems

Many statutes are amended by later statutes so that it is necessary to read two or sometimes more Acts together to make sense of provisions. The law may also be added to by delegated legislation in the form of statutory instruments. All this increases the difficulty of discovering the law that is actually in force.

The language used in Acts is not always easily understood and apart from the obvious difficulties this causes it also results in many cases going to court. In fact about 75 per cent of cases heard by the House of Lords in its judicial capacity each year involve disputes over the interpretation of Acts.

In 1992 the report of a Hansard Society Commission under Lord Rippon underlined five principles for democratic law-making. These were that:

- Laws are made for the benefit of the citizens and all citizens should therefore be involved as fully and openly as possible in the legislative process
- Statute law has to be rooted in the authority of Parliament and thoroughly exposed to democratic scrutiny
- Statute law should be as certain and intelligible as possible
- Statute law has to be as accessible as possible
- Getting the law right is as important as getting it passed quickly.

If these guidelines were to be followed there would be an improvement to the quality of the statute book. In addition, codification and/or consolidation could be used to make the law more accessible. Under this, all the law on one topic could be brought together into one Act of Parliament, making it both more accessible and, hopefully, more comprehensible.

4.7 Parliamentary sovereignty

Parliamentary law is sovereign over other forms of law in England and Wales. This means that an Act of Parliament can completely overrule any custom, judicial precedent, delegated legislation or previous Act of Parliament. This is also referred to as parliamentary supremacy.

The concept of the sovereignty of parliamentary law is based on the idea of democratic law-making. A member of Parliament is elected by the voters in the constituency, so that in theory that MP is participating in the legislative process on the behalf of those voters. However, this is a very simplistic view since:

- MPs usually vote on party lines rather than how their particular constituents wish
- Many MPs are elected by only a very small majority and if there were several candidates in the election, it may well be that the MP was only actually voted for by about 30 per cent or even fewer of the voters
- Parliamentary elections only have to take place once every five years, so that an MP who votes against the wishes of his constituents is not immediately replaced.

In addition, the ideal concept of democracy is lost because much of the drafting of parliamentary law is done by civil servants who are not elected. Finally, there is the point that the House of Lords is not an elected body.

4.7.1 Definition of parliamentary supremacy

The most widely recognised definition of parliamentary supremacy was given by Dicey in the nineteenth century. He made three main points:

1. Parliament can legislate on any subject-matter
2. No Parliament can be bound by any previous Parliament, nor can a Parliament pass any Act that will bind a later Parliament
3. No other body has the right to override or set aside an Act of Parliament.

Legislating on any subject-matter

There are no limits on what Parliament can make laws about. It can make any law it wants. For example, in the past, Parliament changed the rule on who should succeed to the throne. This was in 1700, when Parliament passed the Act of Settlement which stated that the children of King James II (who were the direct line of the monarchy) could not succeed to the throne.

Parliament can also change its own powers. It did this with the Parliament Acts 1911 and 1949, which placed limits on the right of the House of Lords to block a Bill by voting against it (see section 4.5.1).

Cannot bind successor

Each new Parliament should be free to make or change what laws it wishes. Parliament cannot be bound by a law made by a previous Parliament, and can repeal any previous Act of Parliament.

There are, however, some laws that have become such an important part of the British constitution that they cannot realistically be repealed. For example, the Act of Settlement in 1700 changed the line of succession to the throne. It affected who was entitled to become king or queen. Realistically, after 300 years, this cannot now be repealed.

There are other modern limitations which have been self-imposed by Parliament. These are dealt with in section 4.7.2 below.

Cannot be overruled by others

This rule is kept to even if the Act of Parliament may have been passed because of incorrect information. This was shown by *British Railways Board* v *Pickin* (1974). A private Act of Parliament, the British Railways Act 1968, was enacted by Parliament. *Pickin* challenged the Act on the basis that that the British Railways Board had fraudulently concealed certain matters from Parliament. This alleged fraud had led to Parliament passing the Act which had the effect of

depriving *Pickin* of his land or proprietary rights. The action was struck out because no court is entitled to go behind an Act once it has been passed. A challenge cannot be made to an Act of Parliament even if there was fraud.

4.7.2 Limitations on parliamentary sovereignty

There are now some limitations on Parliament's sovereignty, but all these limits have been self-imposed by previous Parliaments. The main limitations are through:

- membership of the European Union
- the effect of the Human Rights Act 1998.

Membership of the European Union

The United Kingdom joined the European Union in 1973. In order to become a member, Parliament passed the European Communities Act 1972. Although, as Parliament passed that Act, it is theoretically possible for a later Parliament to pass an Act withdrawing from the European Union, political reality means that this is very unlikely. Membership of the EU affects so much of our law and political system.

Membership of the EU means that EU laws take priority over English law even where the English law was passed after the relevant EU law. This was shown by the Merchant Shipping Act 1988, which set down rules for who could own or manage fishing boats registered in Britain. The Act stated that 75 per cent of directors and shareholders had to be British. The European Court of Justice ruled that this was contrary to European Union law, under which citizens of all member states can work in other member states. The Merchant Shipping Act 1988 could not be effective so far as other EU citizens were concerned.

Human Rights Act 1998

This states that all Acts of Parliament have to be compatible with the European Convention on Human Rights. It is possible to challenge an Act on the ground that it does not comply with the Convention. Under s 4 of the Human Rights Act, the courts have the power to declare an Act incompatible with the Convention.

This happened in *H* v *Mental Health Review Tribunal* (2001). When a patient was making an application to be released, the Mental Health Act 1983 placed the burden of proof on the patient to show that he should be released. Human rights meant that it should be up to the state to justify the continuing detention of such a patient. The court made a declaration that the law was not compatible with human rights. Following this declaration of incompatibility, the Government changed the law.

However, a declaration of incompatibility does not mean that the Government has to change the law. Also, if Parliament wishes it can pass a new Act which contravenes the European Convention on Human Rights.

Chapter 5

Delegated legislation

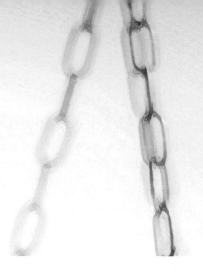

Delegated legislation is law made by some person or body other than Parliament, but with the authority of Parliament. That authority is usually laid down in a 'parent' Act of Parliament known as an enabling Act which creates the framework of the law and then delegates power to others to make more detailed law in the area. An example of enabling Acts include the Access to Justice Act 1999 which gave the Lord Chancellor wide powers to alter various aspects of the legal funding schemes. Another example is the Criminal Justice Act 2003 which gives the Secretary of State the power to make delegated legislation in several areas. One of these powers enables a code of practice to be created for the use of conditional cautions. A conditional caution is used instead of taking an offender to court.

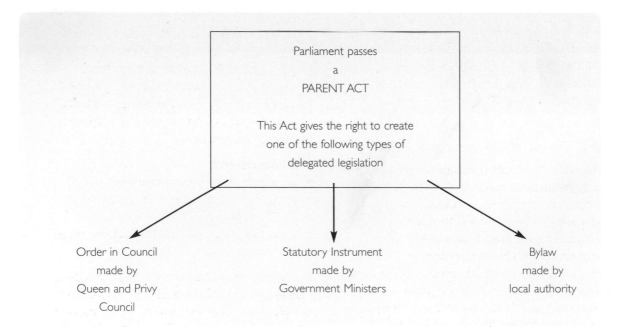

Figure 5.1 *Different types of delegated legislation*

5.1 Types of delegated legislation

There are three different types of delegated legislation. These are:

- Orders in Council
- statutory instruments
- bylaws.

5.1.1 Orders in Council

The Queen and the Privy Council have the authority to make Orders in Council. The Privy Council is made up of the Prime Minister and other leading members of the Government. So this type of delegated legislation effectively allows the Government to make legislation without going through Parliament. Its main use today is to give legal effect to European Directives (see Chapter 6). However, the Privy Council has power to make law in emergency situations under the Emergency Powers Act 1920 and the Civil Contingencies Act 2004. Occasionally, Orders in Council will be used to make other types of law. For example, in 2004 an Order in Council was used to alter the Misuse of Drugs Act 1971 so as to make cannabis a Class C drug (see Figure 5.2).

5.1.2 Statutory instruments

The term 'statutory instruments' refers to rules and regulations made by Government Ministers. Ministers and Government departments are given authority to make regulations for areas under their particular responsibility. This means that, for example, the Lord Chancellor has power regarding the legal aid schemes, while the Minister for Transport is able to deal with necessary road traffic regulations. The use of statutory instruments is a major method of law-making as there are about 3,000 statutory instruments brought into force each year.

There are many Acts which give a Minister of State the power to make delegated legislation. Some examples are:

- **Constitutional Reform Act 2005**
  Section 65 gives the Lord Chancellor the power to issue guidance on the procedures for the Judicial Appointments Commission which recommends who should be appointed as a judge (see section 16.3).
- **Serious Organised Crime and Police Act 2005**
  Section 27 gives the Secretary of State the power to make regulations requiring equipment used by the Serious Crime Agency to satisfy certain levels of design and performance.

These examples show that very different powers can be given to Ministers.

The Legislative and Regulatory Reform Act 2006

In addition to specific Acts giving Ministers powers to make statutory instruments, the Legislative and Regulatory Reform Act 2006 gives Ministers power to make *any* provision by order if it will remove or reduce a 'burden' resulting from legislation. For this purpose a burden is defined as:

- a financial cost
- an administrative inconvenience
- an obstacle to efficiency, productivity or profitability
- a sanction which affects the carrying on of any lawful activity.

This means that Ministers can change Acts of Parliament, even though the original Act did not give them the power to do this. However, when the Legislative and Regulatory Reform

2003 No. 3201

DANGEROUS DRUGS

The Misuse of Drugs Act 1971 (Modification) (No. 2) Order 2003

Made   *10th December 2003*

Coming into force   *29th January 2004*

At the Court at Buckingham Palace, the 10th day of December 2003

Present,

The Queen's Most Excellent Majesty in Council

Whereas a draft of this Order has been laid before Parliament on the recommendation of the Advisory Council on the Misuse of Drugs and has been approved by a resolution of each House of Parliament;

Now, therefore, Her Majesty, in pursuance of section 2(2) of the Misuse of Drugs Act 1971[1], is pleased, by and with the advice of Her Privy Council, to order, and it is hereby ordered, as follows: –

1. This Order may be cited as the Misuse of Drugs Act 1971 (Modification) (No. 2) Order 2003 and shall come into force on 29th January 2004.

2. – (1) Schedule 2 to the Misuse of Drugs Act 1971[2] (which specifies the drugs which are subject to control under that Act) shall be amended as follows.

(2) In paragraph 1(a) of Part I of that Schedule, "Cannabinol, except where contained in cannabis or cannabis resin" and "Cannabinol derivatives" shall be deleted.

(3) In paragraph 1(a) of Part II of that Schedule, "Cannabis and cannabis resin" shall be deleted.

(4) In paragraph 1(a) of Part III of that Schedule, there shall be inserted after "Camazepam", "Cannabinol", "Cannabinol derivatives" and "Cannabis and cannabis resin".

(5) In paragraph 1(d) of Part III of that Schedule, there shall be inserted after "above", "or of cannabinol or a cannabinol derivative".

A. K. Galloway
Clerk of the Privy Council

Figure 5.2 Example of an Order in Council

Act was being discussed, the Government gave a clear undertaking that orders made under the Act would 'not be used to implement highly controversial reforms'.

5.1.3 Bylaws

These can be made by local authorities to cover matters within their own area, for example, Norfolk County Council can pass laws affecting the whole county, while a District or Town council can only make bylaws for its district or town. Many local bylaws will involve traffic control, such as parking restrictions.

Bylaws can also be made by public corporations and certain companies for matters within their jurisdiction which involve the public. This means that bodies such as the British Airports Authority and the railways can enforce rules about public behaviour on their premises. An example of such a bylaw is the smoking ban on the London Underground system.

5.2 The need for delegated legislation

1. Parliament does not have time to consider and debate every small detail of complex regulations.

2. In addition Parliament may not have the necessary technical expertise or knowledge required; for example, health and safety regulations in different industries need expert knowledge, while local parking regulations need local knowledge. Modern society has become very complicated and technical, so that it is impossible for members of Parliament to have all the knowledge needed to draw up laws on controlling technology, ensuring environmental safety, dealing with a vast array of different industrial problems or operating complex taxation schemes. It is thought that it is better for Parliament to debate the main principles thoroughly, but leave the detail to be filled in by those who have expert knowledge of it.

3. Ministers can have the benefit of further consultation before regulations are drawn up. Consultation is particularly important for rules on technical matters, where it is necessary to make sure that the regulations are technically accurate and workable. In fact, some Acts giving the power to make delegated legislation set out that there must be consultation before the regulations are created. For example, before any new or revised police Code of Practice under the Police and Criminal Evidence Act 1984 is issued, there must be consultation with a wide range of people including:

   - persons representing the interests of police authorities
   - the General Council of the Bar
   - the Law Society.

4. As already seen, the process of passing an Act of Parliament can take a considerable time and in an emergency, Parliament may not be able pass law quickly enough. This is another reason why delegated legislation is sometimes preferred. It can also be amended or revoked easily when necessary, so that the law can be kept up to date, and Ministers can respond to new or unforeseen situations by amending or amplifying statutory instruments.

5.3 Control of delegated legislation

As delegated legislation in many instances is made by non-elected bodies and, since there are so many people with the power to make delegated legislation, it is important that there should be some control over this. Control is exercised by Parliament and by the courts. In addition there may sometimes be a Public Inquiry before a law is passed on an especially sensitive matter, such as planning laws which may affect the environment.

5.3.1 Control by Parliament

This is fairly limited, though obviously Parliament has the initial control with the enabling Act which sets the boundaries within which the delegated legislation is to be made. In addition, a Delegated Powers Scrutiny Committee was established in 1993 in the House of Lords to consider whether the provisions of any Bills delegated legislative power inappropriately. It reports its findings to the House of Lords before the Committee stage of the Bill, but has no power to amend Bills. The main problem is that there is no general provision that the regulations made under the enabling Act have to be laid before Parliament for the MPs to consider them. However a few enabling Acts will say that this has to happen.

Affirmative resolutions

A small number of statutory instruments will be subject to an affirmative resolution. This means that the statutory instrument will not become law unless specifically approved by Parliament. The need for an affirmative resolution will be included in the enabling Act. For example an affirmative resolution is required before new or revised police Codes of Practice under the Police and Criminal Evidence Act 1984 can come into force. One of the disadvantages of this procedure is that Parliament cannot amend the statutory instrument; it can only be approved, annulled or withdrawn.

Negative resolutions

Most other statutory instruments will be subject to a negative resolution, which means that the relevant statutory instrument will be law unless rejected by Parliament within 40 days. Individual Ministers may also be questioned by MPs in Parliament on the work of their departments, and this can include questions about proposed regulations.

Scrutiny Committee

A more effective check is the existence of a Joint Select Committee on Statutory Instruments (formed in 1973), usually called the Scrutiny Committee. This committee reviews all statutory instruments and, where necessary, will draw the attention of both Houses of Parliament to points that need further consideration. However, the review is a technical one and not based on policy. The main grounds for referring a statutory instrument back to the Houses of Parliament are that:

- It imposes a tax or charge – this is because only an elected body has such a right
- It appears to have retrospective effect which was not provided for by the enabling Act
- It appears to have gone beyond the powers given under the enabling legislation or it makes some unusual or unexpected use of those powers
- It is unclear or defective in some way.

The Scrutiny Committee can only report back its findings; it has no power to alter any statutory instrument. The Hansard Society in their 1992 report found that some of the critical findings of the Committee were ignored by Ministers.

5.3.2 The Legislative and Regulatory Reform Act 2006

This Act sets out procedure for the making of statutory instruments which are aimed at repealing an existing law in order to remove a 'burden' (see section 5.1.2). Under s 13 of the Act, the Minister making the statutory instrument must consult various people and organisations. These include:

- organisations which are representative of interests substantially affected by the proposals
- the Welsh Assembly in relation to matters upon which the Assembly exercises functions
- the Law Commission, where appropriate

Orders made under this power of this Act must be laid before Parliament. There are three possible procedures:

1. **Negative resolution procedure**:
   where the Minister recommends that this procedure should be used, it will be used unless within 30 days one of the Houses of Parliament objects to this.

2. **Affirmative resolution procedure**:
   this requires both Houses of Parliament to approve the order: even though the Minister has recommended this procedure, Parliament can still require the super-affirmative resolution procedure to be used.

3. **Super-affirmative resolution procedure**:
   under this the Minister must have regard to:

- any representations
- any resolution of either House of Parliament
- any recommendations by a committee of either House of Parliament who are asked to report on the draft order.

This super-affirmative resolution procedure gives Parliament more control over delegated legislation made under the Legislative and Regulatory Reform Act 2006. It is important that this is the position, as the Act gives Ministers very wide powers to amend Acts of Parliament.

5.3.3 Control by the courts

Delegated legislation can be challenged in the courts on the ground that it is *ultra vires*, i.e. it goes beyond the powers that Parliament granted in the enabling Act. This questioning of the validity of delegated legislation may be made through the judicial review procedure (see Chapter 16), or it may arise in a civil claim between two parties, or on appeal (especially case-stated appeals).

Any delegated legislation which is ruled to be *ultra vires* is void and not effective. This was illustrated by R v *Home Secretary, ex parte Fire Brigades Union* (1995) where changes made by the Home Secretary to the Criminal Injuries Compensation scheme were held to have gone beyond the power given to him in the Criminal Justice Act 1988.

The courts will presume that unless an enabling act expressly allows it, there is no power to do any of the following:

- Make unreasonable regulations – in *Strictland* v *Hayes Borough Council* (1896) a bylaw prohibiting the singing or reciting of any obscene song or ballad and the use of obscene language generally, was held to be unreasonable and so *ultra vires*, because it was too widely drawn in that it covered acts done in private as well as those in public
- Levy taxes
- Allow sub-delegation.

It is also possible for the courts to hold that delegated legislation is *ultra vires* because the correct procedure has not been followed. For example in the *Aylesbury Mushroom* case

Definition
- Law made by bodies other than Parliament, but with the authority of Parliament

Types of delegated legislation
- Orders in Council
  - Made by Crown and Privy Council
- Statutory instruments
  - Made by Government Ministers
- Bylaws
  - Made by local authorities and public corporations

Reasons for delegated legislation
- Knowledge and expertise
- Saving of Parliamentary time
- More flexible than Acts of Parliament

Control over delegated legislation
- By Parliament
  - Affirmative/negative resolutions
  - Scrutiny Committee
- By the courts
  - Judicial review
  - Doctrine of *ultra vires*

Disadvantages of delegated legislation
- Undemocratic
- Risk of sub-delegation
- Large volume
- Lack of publicity

Figure 5.2 Key fact chart for delegated legislation

(1972) the Minister of Labour had to consult 'any organisation . . . appearing to him to be representative of substantial numbers of employers engaging in the activity concerned'. His failure to consult the Mushroom Growers' Association, which represented about 85 per cent of all mushroom growers meant that his order establishing a training board was invalid as against mushroom growers, though it was valid in relation to others affected by the order, such as farmers, as the minister had consulted with the National Farmers' Union.

In *R* v *Secretary of State for Education and Employment, ex parte National Union of Teachers* (2000) a High Court judge ruled that a statutory instrument setting conditions for appraisal and access to higher rates of pay for teachers was beyond the powers given under the Education Act 1996. In addition, the procedure used was unfair as only four days had been allowed for consultation.

Statutory instruments can also be declared void if they conflict with European Union legislation.

5.4 Criticisms of the use of delegated legislation

1. The main criticism is that it takes law-making away from the democratically elected House of Commons and allows non-elected people to make law. This is acceptable provided there is sufficient control, but, as already seen, Parliament's control is fairly limited. This criticism cannot be made of bylaws made by local authorities since these are elected by local citizens.

2. Another problem is that of sub-delegation, which means that the law-making authority is handed down another level. This causes comments that much of our law is made by civil servants and merely 'rubber-stamped' by the Minister of that department.

3. The large volume of delegated legislation also gives rise to criticism since it makes it difficult to discover what the present law is. This problem is aggravated by a lack of publicity, as much delegated legislation is made in private in contrast to the public debates of Parliament.

4. Finally, delegated legislation shares with Acts of Parliament the same problem of obscure wording that can lead to difficulty in understanding the law. This difficulty of how to understand or interpret the law is dealt with in Chapter 7.

Examination Questions

1. Read the source material below and answer parts (a), (b) and (c) which follow.

SOURCE A

In many ways the most important type of legislation is delegated legislation. This describes legislation made by a subordinate body (a body other than Parliament) authorised to make law by an Act of Parliament. The Health and Safety at Work Act 1974, for example, authorised a government minister to make new safety laws by issuing regulations (see Source B below). Safety laws are complex and may need frequent updating. It would be impractical to put every complex change in the law through the full stages of parliamentary procedure. Technically, regulations of this kind are known as statutory instruments.

Adapted from: *A Level Law*, AM Dugdale, MP Furmston, SP Jones, CH Sherrin: Butterworths

SOURCE B

(This statutory instrument was introduced to implement an EU directive. In Marshall v Southampton and South West Hampshire Area Health Authority (1986) it was stated that Directives only have vertical direct effect, not horizontal direct effect. If Mrs Marshall had been employed by a private company she would have had no remedy.)

The Health and Safety (Display Screen Equipment) Regulations 1992 (a Statutory Instrument)

Some Important Definitions

• Display Screen Equipment used at workstations includes computer monitors. Screens showing mainly TV or film pictures are *not* covered.

• Users: Uses the display screen equipment more or less *daily* and for *continuous* spells of an hour or more at a time.

The Regulations:

Regulation 1: requires every employer to perform a suitable and sufficient assessment of workstations to assess any health and safety risks and to take action to reduce those risks to the lowest extent possible.

Regulation 2: requires employers to plan the activities of those using workstations so that daily work is periodically interrupted by breaks or activity changes. These could be informal breaks away from the screen for a short period each hour.

Regulation 3: gives users the opportunity to have an appropriate eye and eyesight test as soon as practicable after requesting one and at regular intervals thereafter. The costs will be met by the employer.

Adapted from the Regulations

(a) With reference to Source B, briefly explain, with example, the terms 'vertical direct effect' and 'horizontal direct effect'. *[12 marks]*

(b) Apply the content of the Health and Safety (Display Screen Equipment) Regulations 1992, in Source B, to each of the situations below.

(i) Mario is about to start a new job as a librarian in a small school. The job will require occasional use of a computer monitor. The Deputy Head is also the school Health and Safety Officer and is anxious to comply with all relevant legislation.

(ii) Amir works as a telephone-sales representative. His regular daily work requires long periods of sustained concentration as he transfers information from customers onto a computer system. He is finding it increasingly difficult to sustain his concentration.

(iii) Julie works as a receptionist in a busy office. Her daily work involves monitoring a TV screen (fed from security cameras) and constant use of a computer monitor to perform a variety of functions. She has started to suffer with blurred vision.

[15 marks]

(c) (i) Source A refers to 'statutory instruments'. Describe with examples the nature of statutory instruments and the process of bringing them into force. *[15 marks]*

(ii) Using Source A and other examples, discuss the advantages and disadvantages of delegated legislation. *[12 marks]*

QWC marks 6

Total marks 60

OCR specimen paper

NB You will not be able to answer part (a) until you have studied European Law (see Chapter 6).

2. (a) Explain the reason for the growth of delegated legislation. *[10 marks]*

and

(b) What are the methods used to produce delegated legislation? *[15 marks]*

LW2 WJEC, January 2005

Chapter 6

European law

On 1 January 1973 the United Kingdom joined what was then the European Economic Community, and another source of law came into being: European law. Since then it has had increasing significance as a source of law. The European Economic Community was originally set up by Germany, France, Italy, Belgium, the Netherlands and Luxembourg in 1957 by the Treaty of Rome. The name 'European Union' was introduced by the Treaty of European Union in 1993. Denmark and Ireland joined at the same time as the United Kingdom. In the 1980s and 1990s Greece, Spain, Portugal, Austria, Finland and Sweden joined. Then on 1 May 2004 another ten countries joined the EU. These were Cyprus, Czech Republic, Estonia, Hungary, Latvia, Lithuania, Malta, Poland, Slovak Republic and Slovenia. The most recent members are Bulgaria and Romania who joined on 1 January 2007. There are now 27 Member States (see Figure 6.1).

6.1 The institutions of the European Union

In order to implement the aims of the Treaty of Rome, the European Union has a vast and complex organisation with institutions established by the Treaty of Rome. The main institutions which exercise the functions of the Union are:

- The Council of the European Union
- The Commission
- The European Parliament
- The European Court of Justice.

In addition there are a number of ancillary bodies, the most important of which is the Economic and Social Committee.

6.1.1 The Council of Ministers

The government of each nation in the Union sends a representative to the Council. The Foreign Minister is usually a country's main representative, but a government is free to send any of its Ministers to Council meetings. This means that usually the Minister responsible for the topic under consideration will attend the meetings of the Council, so that the precise membership will vary with the subject being discussed. For example, the Minister for Agriculture will attend when the issue to be discussed involves agriculture. Twice a year government heads meet in the European Council or 'Summit' to discuss broad matters of policy. The Member States take it in turn to provide the President of the Council,

DATE	COUNTRIES JOINING	COMMENT
1957	Belgium France Germany Italy Luxembourg The Netherlands	These are the founder members Treaty of Rome signed
1973	Denmark Ireland United Kingdom	UK passes the European Communities Act 1972 on joining
1981	Greece	
1986	Portugal Spain	
1995	Austria Finland Sweden	
2004	Cyprus, Czech Republic, Estonia, Hungary, Latvia, Lithuania, Malta, Poland, Slovak Republic and Slovenia	
2007	Bulgaria Romania	

Figure 6.1 *Chart showing the Member States of the European Union*

each for a six-month period. To assist with the day-to-day work of the Council there is a committee of permanent representatives known as Coreper.

The Council is the principal decision-making body of the Union. Voting in the Council is on a weighted basis with each country having a number of votes roughly in proportion to the size of its population.

6.1.2 The Commission

This consists of 27 Commissioners who are supposed to act independently of their national origin. Each Member State has one Commissioner.

The Commissioners are appointed for a five-year term and can only be removed during this term of office by a vote of censure by the European Parliament. Each Commissioner heads a department with special responsibility for one area of Union policy, such as economic affairs, agriculture or the environment.

The Commission as a whole has several functions as follows:

- It is the motive power behind Union policy as it proposes policies and presents drafts of legislation to the Council for the Council's consideration. In its own booklet on Union law, the European Union says the relationship between the Commission and the Council can be briefly summarised by saying 'the Commission proposes and the Council disposes'

Figure 6.2 *Map showing countries of the European Union*

- The Commission is also the 'guardian' of the treaties. It ensures that treaty provisions and other measures adopted by the Union are properly implemented. If a Member State has failed to implement Union law within its own country, or has infringed a Provision in some way, the Commission has a duty to intervene and, if necessary, refer the matter to the European Court of Justice. The Commission has performed this duty very effectively, and as a result there have been judgments given by the Court against Britain and other Member States

Activity

Use the Internet to find out more about the European Commission. Find out who is the Commissioner for the United Kingdom. Try *http://europa.eu*

- It is responsible for the administration of the Union and has executive powers to implement the Union's budget.

6.1.3 The Assembly

Parliament's main function is to discuss proposals put forward by the Commission, but it has no direct law-making authority. The members of the European Parliament are directly elected by the people of the Member States in elections which take place once every five years. Within the Parliament the Members do not operate in national groups, but form political groups with those of the same political allegiance. The Assembly meets on average about once a month for sessions that can last up to a week. It has standing committees which discuss proposals made by the Commission and then report to the full Parliament for debate. Decisions made by the Parliament are not binding, though they will influence the Council of Ministers.

The main criticism is that the Parliament has no real power. However, the assent of Parliament is required to any international agreements the Union wishes to enter into. This allows it an important role in deciding whether new members should be admitted to the Union. It also has some power over the Union budget, especially in non-compulsory expenditure, where it has the final decision on whether to approve the budget or not.

6.1.4 Economic and Social Committee

This advises the Council and the Commission on economic matters. It is made up of representatives of influential interest groups such as manufacturers, farmers, employees and businesses. It must be consulted on proposed Union measures and although its role is purely consultative, it does exert strong influence on the Union's decision-making process.

6.2 The European Court of Justice

Its function is set out in Article 220 of the Treaty of Rome. This states that the Court must 'ensure that in the interpretation and application of the Treaty the law is observed'. The court sits in Luxembourg and has 27 judges, one from each Member State. For a full court 11 judges will sit, but it also sits in chambers of five judges or three judges. Judges are appointed under Article 222 of the Treaty of Rome from those who are eligible for appointment to the highest judicial posts in their own country or who are leading academic lawyers. Each judge is appointed for a term of six years, and can be re-appointed for a further term of six years. The judges select one of themselves to be President of the Court.

The Court is assisted by nine Advocates General who also hold office for six years. Each case is assigned to an Advocate General whose task under Article 223 is to research all the legal points involved and 'to present publicly, with complete impartiality and independence, reasoned conclusions on cases submitted to the Court of Justice with a view to assisting the latter in the performance of its duties'.

6.2.1 Key functions

The court's task is to ensure that the law is applied uniformly in all Member States (see Figure 6.3) and it does this by performing two key functions.

The first is that it hears cases to decide whether Member States have failed to fulfil obligations under the Treaties. Such actions are usually initiated by the European Commission, although they can also be started by another Member State. An early example of such a case was *Re Tachographs: The Commission* v *United Kingdom* (1979) in which the court held that the United Kingdom had to implement a Council Regulation on the use of mechanical recording equipment (tachographs) in road vehicles used for the carriage of goods (see section 6.2.2 for further information on the effect of Regulations).

6.2.2 Preliminary rulings

The second key function is that it hears references from national courts for preliminary rulings on points of European law. This function is a very important one since rulings made by the European Court of Justice are then binding on courts in all Member States. This ensures that the law is indeed uniform throughout the European Union.

Article 234

A request for a preliminary ruling is made under Article 234 of the Treaty of Rome. This says that:

'the Court of Justice shall have jurisdiction to give preliminary rulings concerning:
(a) the interpretation of treaties;
(b) the validity and interpretation of acts of the institutions of the Union;
(c) the interpretation of the statutes of bodies established by an act of the Council, where those statutes so provide.'

Article 234 goes on to state that where there is no appeal from the national court within the national system, then such a court *must* refer points of European Law to the European Court of Justice. Other national courts are allowed to make an Article 234 reference, but as there is still an appeal available within their own system, such courts do not have to do so. They have a discretion (ie they can choose whether or not to refer the case).

Applied to the court structure in England and Wales, this means that the House of Lords must refer questions of European law, since it is the highest appeal court in our system. However, the Court of Appeal does not have to refer questions. It has a choice, it may refer if it wishes or it may decide the case without any referral. The same is true of all the lower courts in the English court hierarchy.

However, even courts at the bottom of the hierarchy can refer questions of law under Article 234, if they feel that a preliminary ruling is necessary to enable a judgment to be given. An example of this was in *Torfaen Borough Council* v *B & Q* (1990) when Cwmbran Magistrates' Court made a reference on whether the restrictions which then existed on Sunday were in breach of the Treaty of Rome.

Whenever a reference is made the European Court of Justice only makes a preliminary ruling on the point of law; it does not actually decide the case. The case then returns to the original court for it to apply the ruling to the facts in the case.

6.2.3 Discretionary referrals

In *Bulmer* v *Bollinger* (1974) the Court of Appeal set out the approach to be used when deciding whether a discretionary referral should be made to the European Court of Justice. The guidelines are as follows:

- Guidance on the point of law must be necessary to come to a decision in the case
- There is no need to refer a question which has already been decided by the European Court of Justice in a previous case
- There is no need to refer a point which is reasonably clear and free from doubt; this is known as the '*acte clair*' doctrine
- The court must consider all the circumstances of the case
- The English court retains the discretion on whether to refer or not.

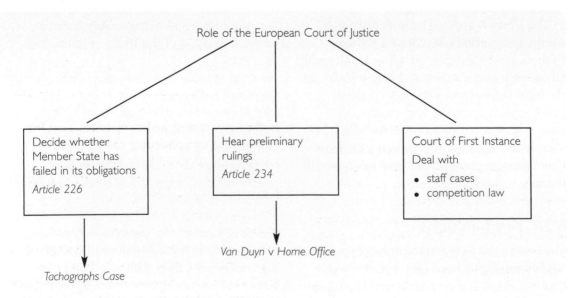

Figure 6.3 *Role of the European Court of Justice*

Key Facts

Council of Ministers	• Consists of ministers from each Member State • Responsible for broad policy decisions • Under Article 249 can issue regulations, directives and decisions
Commission	• 27 Commissioners whose duty it is to act in Union's interest • Proposes legislation • Tries to ensure the implementation of the Treaties and can bring court action against Member States who do not comply with EU law
Economic and Social Committee	• Non-elected consultative body to represent such groups as employers, employees, consumer associations, etc
Assembly or European Parliament	• Members voted for by electorate in each of the Member States • Consultative body, has limited powers
European Court of Justice	• Judges from each Member State, assisted by Advocates-General • Rules on European law when cases are referred under Article 234

Figure 6.4 *Key fact chart on the institutions of the European Union*

The first case to be referred to the European Court of Justice by an English court was *Van Duyn* v *Home Office* (1974).

6.2.4 Court of First Instance

Since 1988 there has also existed a Court of First Instance which was created to relieve the European Court of Justice of some of its heavy workload. This court hears staff cases, i.e. disputes between the European Institutions and their employees. It also hears complex economic cases in the field of competition law, 'anti-dumping' law and under the European Coal and Steel Community Treaty. The Court of First Instance has 12 judges and operates with panels of six, four or three judges.

6.2.5 The operation of the European Court of Justice

When compared with English courts there are several major differences in the way the European Court of Justice operates. First the emphasis is on presenting cases 'on paper'. Lawyers are required to present their arguments in a written form and there is far less reliance on oral presentation of a case. This requirement is, of course, partly because of the wide range of languages involved, though French is the traditional language of the Court. It also represents the traditional method of case presentation in other European countries. An interesting point to note is that the English system in some areas is now beginning to use this 'paper' submission.

A second major difference is the use of the Advocate General. This independent lawyer is not used in the English system. However in the European Court of Justice the Advocate General who was assigned to the case will present his findings on the law after the parties have made their submissions. The court, therefore, has the advantage of having all aspects of the law presented to them.

The deliberations of the judges are secret and where necessary the decision will be made by a majority vote. However, when the judgment is delivered, again in a written form, it is signed by all the judges who formed part of the panel, so that it is not known if any judges disagreed with the majority. This contrasts strongly with the English system, whereby a dissenting judge not only makes it known that he disagrees with the majority, but also usually delivers a judgment explaining his reasoning.

The other points to be noted are that the European Court of Justice is not bound by its own previous decisions and that it prefers the purposive approach to interpretation (see section 7.9 for an explanation of the purposive approach).

The court has wide rights to study extrinsic material when deciding the meaning of provisions and may study preparatory documents. The European Court of Justice is important, not only because its decisions are binding on English courts, but also because its attitude to interpretation is increasingly being followed by English courts. The European Court of Justice pointed this out in *von Colson* v *Land Nordrhein-Westfalen* (1984) when it said:

'national courts are required to interpret their national law in the light of the wording and the purpose of the directive.'

6.3 European sources of law

These are classed as primary and secondary sources of law. Primary sources are mainly the Treaties, the most important of which is the Treaty of Rome itself. Secondary sources are legislation passed by the Institutions of the Union under Article 249 of the Treaty of Rome. This secondary legislation is of three types: regulations, directives and decisions, all of which are considered below.

6.3.1 Treaties

So far as our law is concerned all treaties signed by our head of government become part of English law automatically. This is as a result of the European Communities Act 1972, section 2(1) which states that:

'All such rights, powers, liabilities, obligations and restrictions from time to time created or arising by or under the Treaties and all such remedies and procedures from time to time provided for by or under the Treaties, as in accordance with the Treaties <u>are without further enactment to be given legal effect</u> or used in the United Kingdom, shall be recognised and available in law and be enforced, allowed and followed accordingly.'

This not only makes Community law part of our law but also allows individuals to rely on it. In the case of *Van Duyn* v *Home Office* (1974) the European Court of Justice held that an individual was entitled to rely on Article 39 giving the right of freedom of movement. The Article had direct effect and conferred rights on individuals which could be enforced not only in the European Court of Justice, but also in national courts.

This means that citizens of the United Kingdom are entitled to rely on the rights in the Treaty of Rome and other treaties, even

Type of law	Effect	Source
Treaties	Directly applicable	Section 2(1) of the European Communities Act 1972
	Have direct effect (both vertically and horizontally) if give individual rights and are clear	*Macarthys* v *Smith* (1979)
Regulations	Directly applicable	Article 249 of the Treaty of Rome
	Have direct effect (both vertically and horizontally) if give individual rights and are clear	
Directives	NOT directly applicable	Article 249 of the Treaty of Rome
	Have vertical direct effect if give individual rights and are clear	*Marshall* case
	NO horizontal direct effect	*Duke* v *GEC Reliance*
	But individual can claim against state for loss caused by failure to implement	*Francovich* v *Italian Republic*

Figure 6.5 *Key fact chart showing effect of EU laws*

though those rights may not have been specifically enacted in English law. This is clearly illustrated by the case of *Macarthys Ltd* v *Smith* (1980). In this case Wendy Smith's employers paid her less than her male predecessor for exactly the same job. As the two people were not employed at the same time by the employer there was no breach of English domestic law. However, Wendy Smith was able to claim that the company which employed her was in breach of Article 141 of the Treaty of Rome over equal pay for men and women and this claim was confirmed by the European Court of Justice.

The growing influence of European law is shown in that British courts are now prepared to apply European Treaty law directly rather than wait for the European Court of Justice to make a ruling on the point. This is illustrated in *Diocese of Hallam Trustee* v *Connaughton* (1996). In this case the Employment Appeal Tribunal had to consider facts which had some similarity to the Wendy Smith case; Josephine Connaughton was employed as director of music by the Diocese of Hallam from 1990 to September 1994, at which time her salary was £11,138. When she left the position, the post was advertised at a salary of £13,434, but the successful applicant, a man, was actually appointed at a salary of £20,000. In other words, where in Wendy Smith's case she had discovered that her male predecessor was paid

With decisions such as the two above it is not surprising that Professor Michael Zander has denounced the literal rule as being mechanical and divorced from the realities of the use of language.

7.4 The golden rule

This rule is a modification of the literal rule. The golden rule starts by looking at the literal meaning but the court is then allowed to avoid an interpretation which would lead to an absurd result. There are two views on how far the golden rule should be used. The first is very narrow and is shown by Lord Reid's comments in *Jones* v *DPP* (1962) when he said:

'It is a cardinal principle applicable to all kinds of statutes that you may not for any reason attach to a statutory provision a meaning which the words of that provision cannot reasonably bear. If they are capable of more than one meaning, then you can choose between those meanings, but beyond this you cannot go.'

So under the narrow application of the golden rule the court may only choose between the possible meanings of a word or phrase. If there is only one meaning then that must be taken. This narrow view can be seen in practice in *R* v *Allen* (1872) where section 57 of the Offences against the Person Act 1861 made it an offence to 'marry' whilst one's original spouse was still alive (and there had been no divorce). The word 'marry' can mean to become legally married to the other person or in a more general way it can mean that the person takes part or 'goes through' a ceremony of marriage. The court decided that in the Offences against the Person Act 1861 the word had this second meaning of go through a ceremony of marriage. This was because a person who is still married to another person cannot legally marry anyone else, so if the first meaning of being legally married was applied then there would be the absurd situation that no one could ever be guilty of bigamy.

The second and wider application of the golden rule is where the words have only one clear meaning, but that meaning would lead to a repugnant situation. In such a case the court will invoke the golden rule to modify the words of the statute in order to avoid this problem. A very clear example of this was the case of *Re Sigsworth* (1935), where a son had murdered his mother. The mother had not made a will, so normally her estate would have been inherited by her next of kin according to the rules set out in the Administration of Estates Act 1925. This meant that the murderer son would have inherited as her 'issue'. There was no ambiguity in the words of the Act, but the court was not prepared to let a murderer benefit from his crime, so it was held that the literal rule should not apply, the golden rule would be used to prevent the repugnant situation of the son inheriting. Effectively the court was writing into the Act that the 'issue' would not be entitled to inherit where they had killed the deceased.

7.5 The mischief rule

This rule gives a judge more discretion than the other two rules. The definition of the rule comes from *Heydon's case* (1584), where it was said that there were four points the court should consider. These, in the original language of that old case, were:

1. 'What was the common law before the making of the Act?
2. What was the mischief and defect for which the common law did not provide?
3. What was the remedy the Parliament hath resolved and appointed to cure the disease of the commonwealth?

No, Romeo, I am not a prostitute!

not been 'in a street'; one had been on a balcony and the others had been at the windows of ground floor rooms, with the window either half open or closed. In each case the women were attracting the attention of men by calling to them or tapping on the window, but they argued that they were not guilty under this section since they were not literally 'in a street or public place'. The court decided that they were guilty, with Lord Parker saying:

'For my part I approach the matter by considering what is the mischief aimed at by this Act. Everybody knows that this was an Act to clean up the streets, to enable people to walk along the streets without being molested or solicited by common prostitutes. Viewed in this way it can matter little whether the prostitute is soliciting while in the street or is standing in the doorway or on a balcony, or at a window, or whether the window is shut or open or half open.'

4. The true reason of the remedy.
   Then the office of all the judges is always to make such construction as shall suppress the mischief and advance the remedy.'

Under this rule therefore, the court should look to see what the law was before the Act was passed in order to discover what gap or 'mischief' the Act was intended to cover. The court should then interpret the Act in such a way that the gap is covered. This is clearly a quite different approach to the literal rule.

7.5.1 Cases using the mischief rule

The mischief rule was used in *Smith* v *Hughes* (1960) to interpret section 1(1) of the Street Offences Act 1959 which said 'it shall be an offence for a common prostitute to loiter or solicit in a street or public place for the purpose of prostitution'. The court considered appeals against conviction under this section by six different women. In each case the women had

A similar point arose in *Eastbourne Borough Council* v *Stirling* (2000) where a taxi driver was charged with 'plying for hire in any street' without a licence to do so. His vehicle was parked on a taxi rank on the station forecourt. He was found guilty as, although he was on private land, he was likely to get customers from the street. The court referred to *Smith* v *Hughes* and said that it was the same point. A driver would be plying for hire in the street when his vehicle was positioned so that the offer of services was aimed at people in the street.

Another case in which the House of Lords used the mischief rule was *Royal College of Nursing* v *DHSS* (1981). In this case the wording of the Abortion Act 1967 which provided that a pregnancy should be 'terminated by a registered medical practitioner', was in issue. When the Act was passed in 1967 the procedure to carry out an abortion was such that only a doctor (a registered medical practitioner) could do it.

Activity

Read the facts of the case set out below then apply the different rules of interpretation.

CASE: *Fisher* v *Bell* [1960] 1 QB 394

The Restriction of Offensive Weapons Act 1959 s1(1)

'Any person who manufactures, sells or hires or offers for sale or hire or lends or gives to any other person – (a) any knife which has a blade which opens automatically by hand pressure applied to a button, spring or other device in or attached to the handle of the knife, sometimes known as a "flick knife" . . . shall be guilty of an offence.'

FACTS: The defendant was a shop keeper, who had displayed a flick knife marked with a price in his shop window; he had not actually sold any. He was charged under s1 (1) and the court had to decide whether he was guilty of offering the knife for sale. There is a technical legal meaning of 'offers for sale', under which putting an article in a shop window is not an offer to sell. (Students of contract law should know this rule!)

Questions

Consider the phrase 'offers for sale' and explain how you think the case would have been decided using:

(a) The literal rule

(b) The golden rule

(c) The mischief rule

Note: The court's decision on the case is given in Appendix 1.

From 1972 onwards improvements in medical technique meant that the normal method of terminating a pregnancy was to induce premature labour with drugs. The first part of the procedure was carried out by a doctor, but the second part was performed by nurses without a doctor present. The court had to decide if this procedure was lawful under the Abortion Act. The case went to the House of Lords where the majority (three) of the judges held that it was lawful, whilst the other two said that it was not lawful.

The three judges in the majority based their decision on the mischief rule, pointing out that the mischief Parliament was trying to remedy was the unsatisfactory state of the law before 1967 and the number of illegal abortions. They also said that the policy of the Act was to broaden the grounds for abortion and ensure that they were carried out with proper skill in hospital. The other two judges took the literal view and said that the words of the Act were clear and that terminations could only be carried out by a registered medical practitioner. They said that the other judges were not interpreting the Act but 'redrafting it with a vengeance'.

It is clear that these three rules can lead to different decisions on the meanings of words and phrases. Below is an activity based on a real case in which the different rules could result in different decisions.

7.6 Rules of language

Even the literal rule does not take words in complete isolation. It is common sense that the other words in the Act must be looked at to see if they affect the word or phrase which is in dispute. In looking at the other words in the Act the courts have developed a number of minor rules which can help to make the meaning of words and phrases clear where a particular sentence construction has been used. These rules, which also have Latin names, are:

- the *ejusdem generis* rule
- the express mention of one thing excludes others
- a word is known by the company it keeps.

7.6.1 The *ejusdem generis* rule

This states that where there is a list of words followed by general words, then the general words are limited to the same kind of items as the specific words. This is easier to understand by looking at cases. In *Powell* v *Kempton Park Racecourse* (1899) the defendant was charged with keeping a 'house, office, room or other place for betting'. He had been operating betting at what is known as Tattersall's Ring, which is outdoors. The court decided that the

general words 'other place' had to refer to indoor places since all the words in the list were indoor places and so the defendant was not guilty.

There must be at least two specific words in a list before the general word or phrase for this rule to operate. In *Allen* v *Emmerson* (1944) the court had to interpret the phrase 'theatres and other places of amusement' and decide if it applied to a funfair. As there was only one specific word, 'theatres', it was decided that a funfair did come under the general term 'other places of amusement' even though it was not of the same kind as theatres.

7.6.2 *Expressio unius exclusio alterius* (the mention of one thing excludes others)

Where there is a list of words which is not followed by general words, then the Act applies only to the items in the list. In *Tempest* v *Kilner* (1846) the court had to considered whether the Statute of Frauds 1677 (which required a contract for the sale of 'goods, wares and merchandise' of more than £10 to be evidenced in writing) applied to a contract for the sale of stocks and shares. The list 'goods, wares and merchandise' was not followed by any general words, so the court held that only contracts for those three types of things were affected by the statute; because stocks and shares were not mentioned they were not caught by the statute.

7.6.3 *Noscitur a sociis* (a word is known by the company it keeps)

This means that the words must be looked at in context and interpreted accordingly; it involves looking at other words in the same section or at other sections in the Act. Words in the same section were important in *Inland Revenue Commissioners* v *Frere* (1965), where the section set out rules for 'interest, annuities or other annual interest'. The first use of the word 'interest' on its own could have meant any interest paid, whether daily, monthly or annually. Because of the words 'other annual interest' in the section, the court decided that 'interest' only meant annual interest.

Other sections of the Act were considered by the House of Lords in *Bromley London Borough Council* v *Greater London Council* (1982). The issue in this case was whether the GLC could operate a cheap fare scheme on their transport systems, where the amounts being charged meant that the transport system would run at a loss. The decision in the case revolved around the meaning of the word 'economic'. The House of Lords looked at the whole Act and, in particular, at another section which imposed a duty to make up any deficit as far as possible. As a result they decided that 'economic' meant being run on business lines and ruled that the cheap fares policy was not legal since it involved deliberately running the transport system at a loss and this was not running it on business lines.

7.7 Presumptions

The courts will also make certain presumptions or assumptions about the law, but these are only a starting point. If the statute clearly states the opposite, then the presumption will not apply and it is said that the presumption is rebutted. The most important presumptions are:

1. **A presumption against a change in the common law**
   In other words it is assumed that the common law will apply unless Parliament has made it plain in the Act that the common law has been altered. An example of this occurred in *Leach* v *R* (1912), where the question was whether a wife could be made to give

evidence against her husband under the Criminal Evidence Act 1898. Since the Act did not expressly say that this should happen, it was held that the common law rule that a wife could not be compelled to give evidence still applied. If there had been explicit words saying that a wife was compellable then the old common law would not apply. This is now the position under s 80 of the Police and Criminal Evidence Act 1984, which expressly states that in a crime of violence one spouse can be made to give evidence against the other spouse.

2. **A presumption that *mens rea* is required in criminal cases**
   The basic common law rule is that no-one can be convicted of a crime unless it is shown that they had the required intention to commit it. In *Sweet* v *Parsley* (1970) the defendant was charged with being concerned with the management of premises which were used for the purposes of smoking cannabis. The facts were that the defendant was the owner of premises which she had leased out and the tenants had smoked cannabis there without her knowledge. She was clearly 'concerned in the management' of the premises and cannabis had been smoked there, but because she had no knowledge of the events she had no *mens rea*. The key issue was whether *mens rea* was required; the Act did not say there was any need for knowledge of the events. The House of Lords held that she was not guilty as the presumption that *mens rea* was required had not been rebutted.

3. **A presumption that the Crown is not bound** by any statute unless the statute expressly says so.

4. **A presumption that legislation does not apply retrospectively**
   This means that no Act of Parliament will apply to past happenings; each Act will

normally only apply from the date it comes into effect.

7.8 Unified approach

So how do all these rules fit together? Sir Rupert Cross wrote that there was a unified approach to interpretation, so that:

1. A judge should start by using the grammatical and ordinary or, where appropriate, technical meaning of the words in the general context of the statute.

2. If the judge considers that this would produce an absurd result, then he may apply any secondary meaning which the words are capable of bearing.

3. The judge may read in words which he considers to be necessarily implied by the words which are in the statute, and he has a limited power to add to, alter or ignore words in order to prevent a provision from being unintelligible, unworkable or absurd.

4. In applying these rules the judge may resort to the various aids and presumptions (see sections 7.7 and 7.10).

However, this unified approach is based on the literal approach and does not allow for the purposive approach. Today there is a move towards the purposive approach, although not all judges agree that it should be used.

Comment

Should there be one preferred rule?

It would be helpful if there was one specific method of statutory interpretation which was always used in cases. At the moment it is entirely up to the individual judge who is hearing the case to use whichever rule or approach he wants. Some judges may use the literal rule; other judges may use the mischief rule or the modern purposive approach. This makes it difficult for lawyers to advise on what meaning a court may put on a disputed phrase in an Act of Parliament.

In some instances, a judge may decide to use the literal rule in one case and the mischief rule in another case. This happened with Lord Parker, who used the mischief rule in *Smith* v *Hughes* (see section 3.3.4) but in the case of *Fisher* v *Bell* he used the literal rule. It could be said that this means that a judge decides what result he wants in the case and then finds the rule which brings about that result.

In 1969 the Law Commission proposed that Parliament should pass an Act of Parliament which would mean that the mischief rule was to be used in order 'to promote the general legislative purpose'. However, this proposal has been ignored, although Lord Scarman in both 1980 and 1981 introduced a Bill on the matter into the House of Lords. The first time he was forced to drop the proposal; the second time the House of Lords voted for it, but the matter was never taken to the House of Commons.

There is an argument that, even if there were an Act of Parliament, there would still be variations in which rule judges would use. This has been shown in New Zealand, which has a law that encourages interpretation 'as will best ensure the attainment of the object of the Act'. Even though this should mean that this is done in every case, one writer points out that it is sometimes difficult to discover which approach has been used and 'the most that can be said is that some judges at some periods have been fairly consistent in using the approach that they prefer'.

Comment

The Law Commission was set up by Parliament; many of its law reform projects have been referred to it by the Government. Yet, despite this, Parliament is slow to implement the reforms recommended by the Law Commission and make them into law.

It is true that the Law Commission has had a major impact, with more than two-thirds of its reports becoming law, but a number of reports still await Government action. This is partly due to limited parliamentary time, but also partly due to lack of commitment to reform of 'lawyers'

law'. Perhaps delegated legislation could be used in some areas of technical law. But this raises the problem that law should only be made by our democratically elected Parliament. Using delegated legislation is undesirable in politically sensitive areas of law-making.

Another way in which more might be achieved is if a separate Ministry of Justice were to be created as new Government department. This would then provide more support for law reform and create more pressure on Governments to act on proposals of the Law Commission.

Key Facts

Originated	By the Law Commissions Act 1965
Personnel	Chairman and four other Commissioners
	Support staff including Parliamentary Draftsmen
Function	Under s 3 Law Commissions Act 1965 to 'keep the law under review'
Success rate	First 10 years – 85 per cent of proposals enacted
	Second 10 years – 50 per cent of proposals enacted
	1990 – no enactments
	1994-95 – use of special procedure leads to greater action
	In 2006 the Law Commission stated that 26 reports were awaiting implementation. Fourteen of them, the oldest dating back to 1991, had been accepted by the Government to be implemented 'when parliamentary time becomes available'.
Recent reforms	Contract (Rights of Third Parties) Act 1999 which allows third parties to claim under a contract made for their benefit
	Land Registration Act 2002 modernised the law on registration of land making it easier to transfer land (houses etc)

Figure 8.1 Key fact chart on the Law Commission

8.5 Royal Commissions

Apart from the full-time bodies there are also temporary committees or Royal Commissions set up to investigate and report on one specific area of law. These are dissolved after they have completed their task. Such Royal Commissions were used frequently from 1945 to 1979, but from 1979 to 1990 when Margaret Thatcher was Prime Minister, none was set up. In the 1990s there was a return to the use of such commissions.

Some Royal Commissions have led to important changes in the law; the Royal Commission on Police Procedure (the Phillips Commission) reported in 1981 and many of its recommendations were given effect by the Police and Criminal Evidence Act 1984. However the Government does not always act on recommendations as was seen with the Pearson Commission on Personal Injury cases which reported in 1978.

With the Runciman Commission (the Royal Commission on Criminal Justice) which reported in 1993, the Government implemented many of the proposals but not all.

In 1999 a Royal Commission (the Wakeham Commission) considered how the House of Lords could be reformed. In December 2001, the Government issued a White Paper showing that it was only partly accepting the proposals of the Commission.

8.5.1 Reviews by judges

Apart from actual Royal Commissions, judges may be asked to lead an investigation into technical areas of law. Recent examples of this have been the Woolf Committee on civil justice which led to major reforms of the civil court system in 1999 (see Chapter 9) and the review of the criminal justice system carried out by Sir Robin Auld in 2001 (see Chapters 12 and 13).

8.5.2 Other reviews

As well as using judges to carry out reviews, the Government has in recent times asked business people to review the workings of the some areas of the English Legal System. For example, Sir David Clementi was asked to report on the legal profession. His report was published in 2004 (see section 15.3).

Examination Questions

(a) Identify and discuss the agencies promoting reform of the Law in England and Wales.

[11 marks]

and

(b) How successful has the Law Commission been in promoting law reform in England and Wales?

[14 marks]

LW2 January 2004, WJEC

the main County Court viewed it as 'an inappropriate and disproportionately expensive way of resolving' their dispute.

Cases are heard by Circuit Judges, though in rare cases it is possible for a jury of eight to sit with the judge. (For further information on the use of juries in civil cases see Chapter 18.)

9.4.1 Fast track cases

Claims between £5,000 and £15,000 needed a faster and cheaper method of dealing with them. In 1998, before the Woolf reforms, the statistics for the year show that the average wait for cases in the County Court was 85 weeks from the issue of the claim to the actual hearing in court. As well as delay, cases were too expensive. Indeed, the Woolf Report found that the costs of cases were often higher than the amount claimed.

As a result of this the new fast track idea was brought in. Once a case is defended, the District Judge at the County Court will send out the allocation questionnaire and then make the decision of whether the case is suitable for the fast track. Personal injury cases and housing cases over £1,000 and up to £15,000 are also dealt with as fast track cases.

Fast track means that the court will set down a very strict timetable for the pre-trial matters. This is aimed at preventing one or both sides from wasting time and running up unnecessary costs. Once a case is set down for hearing, the aim is to have the case heard within 30 weeks. The new timetables have lessened the delays a little. In 2005 the wait from issue of claim to hearing was 58 weeks. This is a six-month improvement on the pre-Woolf era. However, the total time of 58 weeks is still a long time to wait for a trial of what is meant to be a fast track case. The actual trial will usually be heard by a Circuit Judge and take place in open court with a more formal procedure than for small claims. In order to

speed up the trial itself, the hearing will be limited to a maximum of one day and the number of expert witnesses restricted, with usually only one expert being allowed.

9.4.2 Multi-track cases

Claims for more than £15,000 are usually allocated to the multi-track. If the case was started in a County Court then it is likely to be tried there, though it can be sent to the High Court, especially for claims of over £50,000. The case will be heard by a Circuit Judge who will also be expected to 'manage' the case from the moment it is allocated to the multi-track route. The judge can set timetables. It is even possible to ask the parties to try an alternative method of dispute resolution in an effort to prevent waste of costs.

9.5 High Court

The High Court is based in London but also has judges sitting at 26 towns and cities throughout England and Wales. It has the power to hear any civil case and has three divisions each of which specialises in hearing certain types of case. These divisions are the Queen's Bench Division, the Chancery Division and the Family Division.

9.5.1 Queen's Bench Division

The President of the Queen's Bench Division is the Lord Chief Justice and there are nearly 70 judges sitting in the division. It deals with contract and tort cases where the amount claimed is over £50,000, though, as seen earlier in this chapter, a claimant can start an action for any amount of £15,000 and above. The intention is that only multi-track cases should be dealt with in the High Court. Also, certain types of action are thought to be more suitable

Figure 9.5 *Outside of the Royal Courts of Justice*

for the High Court than the County Court.

Usually cases are tried by a single judge but there is a right to jury trial for fraud, libel, slander, malicious prosecution and false imprisonment cases. When a jury is used there will be 12 members.

Cases in the High Court are expensive and can take a long time. The average time between issuing a claim and the trial is about three years. Cases are expensive because of the need to use lawyers and also because of court fees. As well as fees for issuing the claim and other preliminary stages, hourly trial fees were brought in for High Court cases from April 2005.

Commercial Court

This is a special court which is part of the Queen's Bench Division. This court has specialist judges to deal with insurance, banking and other commercial matters, for example the problems of the Lloyd's 'names' for the losses caused by large insurance claims. In this court a simplified speedier procedure is used and the case may be decided on documentary evidence.

Admiralty Court

There is also an Admiralty Court dealing with shipping and deciding such matters as claims for damage caused by collision at sea. It also decides disputes over salvage rights when a ship has sunk or been stranded. The judge in the Admiralty Court sits with two lay assessors, who are chosen from Masters of Trinity House, and who are there to advise the judge on questions of seamanship and navigation.

Also, in 1998 the Technology and Construction Court was set up to take over from what had been called the Official Referee's Court. This court deals with any cases in the Chancery or the Queen's Bench Division which involve technically complex issues, such as building and engineering disputes or litigation over computers.

Judicial review

The Queen's Bench Division also has important supervisory functions over inferior courts and other bodies with decision-making powers, such as Government ministers or local councils. Judicial review is concerned with whether a decision-making process has been carried out legally, as distinct from the merits of the decision in question.

9.5.2 Chancery Division

The Lord Chancellor is technically the head of the division, but for practical purposes the Vice-Chancellor is the head. There are about 17 High Court judges assisting in the division. The main business of this division involves disputes concerned with such matters as insolvency, for both companies and individuals, the enforcement of mortgages, disputes relating to trust property, copyright and patents, intellectual property matters and contested probate actions. There is also a special Companies Court in the division which deals mainly with winding up companies.

Juries are never used in the Chancery

Activity

Advise the people in the following situations:

1. Sarah has bought a DVD player costing £70 from a local electrical superstore. The DVD player has never worked properly, but the store has refused to replace it or to refund the purchase price to Sarah. She wishes to claim against the store. Advise her as to which court to start the case in and how she should go about this. Also explain to her the way in which the case will be dealt with if the store defends it and there is a court hearing.
2. Thomas has been badly injured at work and alleges that the injuries were the result of his employer's failure to take proper safety precautions. He has been advised that his claim is likely to be worth £200,000. Advise him as to which court or courts could hear his case.
3. Imran wishes to start an action for defamation against a national newspaper. Advise him as to which court he should use and explain to him who tries defamation cases.

Division and cases are heard by a single judge. The criticisms of cost and delay which apply to the Queen's Bench Division apply equally to the Chancery Division.

9.5.3 Family Division

The head of this division is the President and 17 High Court judges are assigned to the division. It has jurisdiction to hear wardship cases and all cases relating to children under the Children Act 1989. It also deals with other matters regarding the family, such as declarations of nullity of marriage, and grants probate in non-contentious probate cases.

Cases are heard by a single judge and, although juries were once used to decide defended divorce cases, juries are not now used in this division.

9.6 The Woolf reforms

The present system of civil justice is based on the reforms recommended by Lord Woolf in his report *Access to Justice* (1996).

In 1995 Lord Woolf stated that a civil justice system should:

- Be just in the results it delivers
- Be fair in the way it treats litigants
- Offer appropriate procedures at a reasonable cost
- Deal with cases at a reasonable speed
- Be understandable to those who use it
- Provide as much certainty as the nature of particular cases allows
- Be effective, adequately resourced and organised.

The Report found that virtually none of these points was being achieved in the civil courts, and criticised the system for being unequal, expensive, slow, uncertain and complicated. The report contained 303 recommendations.

The most important ones proposed:

- Extending small claims up to £3,000
- A fast track for straightforward cases up to £10,000
- A multi-track for cases over £10,000, with capping of costs
- Encouraging the use of alternative dispute resolution
- Giving judges more responsibility for managing cases
- More use of information technology
- Simplifying documents and procedures and having a single set of rules governing proceedings in both the High Court and the County Court
- Shorter timetables for cases to reach court and for lengths of trials.

The proposal to increase the small claims limit to £3,000 was implemented before the full report was issued. Before committing itself to the remainder of the reforms, the Labour Government, which came to power in 1997, commissioned the Middleton Report as a 'second opinion'. This supported most of the Woolf proposals, but suggested that the small claims limit should be raised to £5,000 and the fast track route to £15,000. As a result of the Woolf and Middleton Reports, the civil justice system was radically reformed in April 1999.

9.6.1 The Civil Procedure Rules

From 26 April 1999, new Civil Procedure Rules were brought into effect. These use much simpler language than previous rules. They also changed the vocabulary used in court cases. For example, anyone starting a civil case is now called 'the claimant'; previously the term used in most cases was 'the plaintiff'. The document used to start cases is a claim form, rather than a writ or a summons. The new terms are used in this book, but the old terms

still appear in reports of cases decided before April 1999.

Overriding objective

Rule 1.1 of the Civil Procedure Rules states that the overriding objective is to enable the court to deal with cases justly. This means that courts should try to:

- Ensure that the parties in any case are on an equal footing
- Save expense
- Deal with cases in a way which is proportionate to:
  – the amount involved (that is avoid the costs of the case being more than the amount claimed)
  – the importance of the case (for example, is there a major point of law involved?)
  – the complexity of the issues in the case
- Ensure that the case is dealt with quickly and fairly
- Allocate an appropriate share of the court's resources (so smaller claims do not take up more time than they justify).

Judges have more control over proceedings than previously. They can set timetables and make sure that the parties do not drag out a case unnecessarily. Rule 1.4 of the Civil Procedure Rules explains that as well as fixing timetables, 'active case management' by judges includes:

- Identifying the issues at an early stage
- Deciding which issues need investigation and trial
- Encouraging the parties to use alternative dispute resolution if this is appropriate
- Dealing with any procedural steps without the need for the parties to attend court
- Giving directions to ensure that the trial of a case proceeds quickly and efficiently.

9.6.2 Applying the rules in court

Case management has led to the issues in cases being identified more quickly, so that more cases are settling without the need for a trial. Judges are also staying cases so that mediation can be tried. The Centre for Dispute Resolution reported that, in 2000, 27 per cent of the disputes it dealt with were cases which had been stayed by a judge. This compared with 19 per cent of cases in 1999 and only 8 per cent in 1998.

The judges are also applying the timetables strictly. This is illustrated by *Vinos* v *Marks and Spencer plc* (2000). In this case the claimant's solicitors had issued the claim just within the time limit and had told the defendant's insurers that they had done so. However, they were then nine days late in serving that claim on the defendant. The claim was struck out by the court because of this.

Comment

It is now seven years since the Woolf Reforms came into effect. What effect have the reforms had? Suzanne Burn in an article in *Legal Action*, July 2003, considered all the available evidence and research and pointed out that it is difficult to isolate 'the Woolf factor' because there were a number of other factors that came into effect either at the same time as the Woolf reforms or shortly afterwards.
These included:

- the withdrawal of legal aid from certain types of civil claim, in particular personal injury cases
- the widening of the scope of conditional fee agreement together with the ability to recover success fees and insurance premiums (see Chapter 19 for detailed information)
- the introduction of tougher standards and controls by both the Law Society and the Legal Services Commission
- the implementation of the Human Rights Act 1998 in October 2000

With the overlapping effects of these other changes and also the fact that there has been only limited research, Burn pointed out that measuring the success or otherwise of the Woolf Reforms is difficult. However, she found there had been some positive effects:

- the total volume of litigation has fallen since April 1999 (although it had also been decreasing before the Woolf reforms)
- the number of fast track trials, in particular, has dropped sharply in many courts
- the rate of settlement of cases has increased

However, there are still problems. These include:

- the time taken for cases to get to trial has, surprisingly, improved very little post-April 1999
- the fact that the new Civil Procedure Rules are very lengthy and too many amendments have been issued
- small claims listings seem to have suffered, as priority has been given to fast track and multi-track conferences and trials
- increases in court fees and problems in the enforcement of judgments may also have played a part in reducing the number of small claims cases
- there are claims that case management 'takes extra time and cost, but adds little value'.

Another problem is that many County Courts are under-resourced. This leads to delays in issuing, allocation, listing and production of court orders.

9.7 Appellate courts

These are courts which hear appeals from lower courts. The main appellate courts are the Divisional Courts, the Court of Appeal and the House of Lords.

9.7.1 Divisional Courts

Each division of the High Court has what is called a Divisional Court which has the power to hear appeals from inferior courts and tribunals. For most appeals two or three of the judges from the particular division will sit together to hear the case.

Queen's Bench Divisional Court

The most important of the Divisional Courts is the Queen's Bench Divisional Court. This has two main functions:

1. It hears appeals by way of case stated from criminal cases decided in the Magistrates' Court. This is dealt with more fully in Chapter 13.

2. It has supervisory powers over inferior courts and tribunals and also over the actions and decisions of public bodies and Government Ministers. This process is known as 'judicial review' and for this purpose the court has the power to make what are called 'prerogative orders'. These orders are *mandamus*, which is a command to perform a duty; prohibition, which is an order to prevent an inferior court from hearing a case which it has no power to deal with; and *certiorari*, which removes the decision to the Queen's Bench Division so that its legality can be enquired into and the decision quashed if it is found to be invalid.

Key Facts

Courts dealing with civil cases	• County Court • High Court
Different tracks for claims	• Small claims • Fast track • Multi-track
Problems of civil cases	• Cost • Delay • Complexity
1999 reforms	• Encourage use of ADR • Simpler forms and language • Increase small claims limit to £5,000 • Fast track for claims between £5,000 and £15,000 • Judges responsible for case management • Strict timetables
Effect of 1999 reforms	• Cases settle earlier • Initial costs are high • Delays are getting shorter • Courts strict on timetables

Figure 9.4 Key fact chart on civil justice

matter is best dealt with by a technical expert or by a lawyer or by a professional arbitrator

- If there is a question of quality this can be decided by an expert in the particular field, saving the expense of calling expert witnesses and the time that would be used in explaining all the technicalities to a judge
- The hearing time and place can be arranged to suit parties
- The actual procedure used is flexible and the parties can choose that which is most suited to the situation; this will usually result in a more informal and relaxed hearing than in court
- The matter is dealt with in private and there will be no publicity
- The dispute will be resolved more quickly than through a court hearing
- Arbitration proceedings are usually much cheaper than going to court
- The award is normally final and can be enforced through the courts.

10.4.6 Disadvantages of arbitration

However, there are some disadvantages of arbitration, especially where the parties are not on an equal footing as regards their ability to present their case. This is because legal aid is not available for arbitration and this may disadvantage an individual in a case against a business; if the case had gone to court, a person on a low income would have qualified for legal aid and so had the benefit of a lawyer to present their case. The other main disadvantages are that:

- An unexpected legal point may arise in the case which is not suitable for decision by a non-lawyer arbitrator
- If a professional arbitrator is used, his fees may be expensive

- It will also be expensive if the parties opt for a formal hearing, with witnesses giving evidence and lawyers representing both sides
- The rights of appeal are limited
- The delays for commercial and international arbitration may be nearly as great as those in the courts if a professional arbitrator and lawyers are used.

This problem of delay and expense has meant that arbitration has, to some extent, lost its popularity with companies as a method of dispute resolution. More and more businesses are turning to the alternatives offered by centres such as the Centre for Dispute Resolution or, in the case of international disputes, are choosing to have the matter resolved in another country,

D Complaints

3. Disputes arising out of, or in connection with, this contract which cannot be amicably settled may (if you so wish) be referred to arbitration under a special scheme devised by arrangement with the Association of British Travel Agents (ABTA) but administered independently by the Chartered Institute of Arbitrators. The scheme provides for a simple and inexpensive method of Arbitration on documents alone, with restricted liability on you in respect of costs. The scheme does not apply to claims greater than £1,500 per person or £7,500 per booking form or to claims which are solely or mainly in respect of physical injury or illness or the consequences of such injury or illness. If you elect to use the scheme, written notice requesting arbitration must be made within 9 months after the scheduled date of return from holiday.

Figure 10.3 Optional arbitration clause in a consumer contract

One of the problems was that the law on arbitration had become complex and the Arbitration Act 1996 is an attempt to improve the process. In general it can be said that certain types of dispute are suitable for arbitration. This especially includes commercial disagreements between two businesses where the parties have little hope of finding sufficient common ground to make mediation a realistic prospect, and provided there is no major point of law involved.

Activity

Find an arbitration clause in a consumer contract, for example for a package holiday or insurance or for a mobile phone.

10.5 Tribunals

Tribunals operate alongside the court system and have become an important and integral part of the legal system. Most tribunals have been created in the second half of the twentieth century, with the development of the welfare state, in order to give people a method of enforcing their entitlement to certain social rights. However, unlike alternative dispute resolution where the parties decide not to use the courts, the parties in tribunal cases cannot go to court to resolve their dispute. The tribunal must be used instead of court proceedings.

10.5.1 Administrative tribunals

These are tribunals which have been created by statute to enforce rights which have been granted through social and welfare legislation. There are many different rights, such as: the right to a mobility allowance for those who are too disabled to walk more than a very short distance; the right to a payment if one is made redundant from work; the right not to be discriminated against because of one's sex or race and the right of immigrants to have a claim for political asylum heard. As tribunals have been set up as the welfare state has developed, new developments will often result in the creation of a new tribunal. For example following the Child Support Act 1993, the Child Support Appeals Tribunal was created. There are now 70 different types of tribunal, and many of these will have panels sitting at several places around the country so that there are over 2,000 tribunals in total.

The main types of tribunal are:

- Social security tribunals which deal with appeals against the refusal of various benefit rights
- Rent tribunals which are involved with fixing fair rents
- Immigration tribunals to hear appeals on the right of immigrants to enter and stay in this country
- The Mental Health Review Tribunal which decides if a mental patient should continue to be detained in hospital
- Employment tribunals which deal with disputes arising from employment.

10.5.2 Employment tribunals

These were originally called industrial tribunals. They were first set up in 1964 under the Industrial Training Act 1964 with only a limited role, but they have become increasingly important. The role of employment tribunals covers all aspects of work-related disputes. This includes key matters of disputed deductions from wages, unfair dismissal, redundancy and discrimination on the grounds of sex, race or disability.

10.5.3 Composition and procedure

Since the different tribunals have been set up at different times over a number of years, they do not all operate in the same way. In fact Lord Woolf in the Council on Tribunals Annual Report for 1991–92 said:

'The development of the tribunal system has been quite haphazard. It has been left very much to the inclination of particular departments of government as to whether or not a tribunal system should be created, and if so, what should be the form of that system.'

However, the majority of tribunals sit with a panel of three: a legally-qualified chairman and two lay members who have expertise in the particular field of the tribunal. For example, the lay members of an industrial injuries tribunal would be medically qualified, while those on a tribunal hearing an unfair dismissal claim would be representatives of organisations for employers and employees respectively.

The procedure for each type of tribunal also tends to vary, but there are common elements in that the system is designed to encourage individuals to bring their own cases and not use lawyers. Generally there are no formal rules of evidence and procedure but the rules of natural justice apply. This means that both parties must be given an equal chance to state their side. Employment tribunals are the most formal and their procedure is similar to that of a court.

As the use of lawyers is not encouraged at tribunals, legal funding is not available for most tribunal hearings. Exceptions to this include the Mental Health Review Tribunal, the Protection of Children Tribunal, the Lands Tribunal and the Employment Appeal Tribunal, where those who come within the legal aid criteria can obtain help.

10.5.4 Reform of tribunals

In 2001 a report about the workings of tribunals was prepared under the chairmanship of Sir Andrew Leggatt. This Report on tribunals was the first since the Franks inquiry in 1957. Some of the main recommendations included:

- The administration of tribunals should become the responsibility of the Lord Chancellor
- There should be a single system which is divided by subject matter into Divisions; this will prevent the current problem of the isolation of individual tribunals which leads to duplication of effort and each tribunal inventing its own processes and standards
- There should also be a single route of appeal with a right of appeal by permission on a point of law or on the basis that the decision of the tribunal was unlawful; the appeal route should be from first-tier tribunals to second-tier tribunals and from these to the Court of Appeal.

It was also recommended that there should be a Tribunals Board directing the system whose functions should include:

- advising the Lord Chancellor's Department on qualifications for chairmen
- overseeing the appointment of members
- co-ordinating their training
- investigating complaints against them and
- recommending changes to the rules of procedure governing all Divisions.

Most of these recommendations have been included in the Tribunals, Courts and Enforcement Bill 2006. This creates a new simplified statutory framework for tribunals. The new system is aimed at providing coherence and also enabling future reform. It creates a two-tier system of tribunals:

- First-tier tribunal – first instance
- Upper tribunal – mostly appellate.

The Lord Chancellor will be given power to transfer the jurisdiction of existing tribunals to these.

The Bill places the Lord Chancellor under a general duty to provide administrative support to the new tribunals, and the employment tribunals, Employment Appeal Tribunal and Asylum and Immigration Tribunal.

The Bill also creates a new judicial office – Senior President of Tribunals – to oversee the tribunal system.

10.5.5 Control of tribunals

Since tribunals work outside the court system and are so varied in their procedures, it is important that there is some supervisory body. This was emphasised following what is called the Crichel Down Affair in which civil servants did not follow the correct procedure for offering land requisitioned during the Second World War for military purposes back to the family of the former owner. This matter was investigated by the Franks Committee which reported in 1957 and made several recommendations about decisions by civil servants and tribunals. One recommendation was that there should be an 'ombudsman' appointed to deal with complaints of maladministration, and eventually the post of Parliamentary Ombudsman was set up on 1967. The other recommendations more directly concerned with tribunals were that all tribunal chairmen should be legally qualified, and that reasons should be given for decisions. The Franks Committee also recommended that a Council on Tribunals should be set up to oversee the whole vast array of tribunals.

Following this the Tribunals and Inquiries Act 1958 set up the Council on Tribunals to supervise and keep under review the working

of tribunals. The Council has up to 15 members who visit tribunals and observe their work at first hand. It also receives complaints about tribunals and issues an annual report. The main problem is that the Council has very little power; it can only make recommendations.

The Tribunals, Courts and Enforcement Bill 2006 will replace the Council on Tribunals with the Administrative Justice and Tribunals Council. This new Council will have a broader role in the administrative justice system.

It will also have more power than the present Council on Tribunals.

Control by the courts

This can occur in two ways. First there is an appeal system against the decisions of some tribunals. In particular there is a right of appeal from employment tribunals to the Employment Appeals Tribunal, which is headed by a High Court judge, and from there to the Court of Appeal. Similarly, in immigration cases, there is the Immigration Appeal Tribunal which hears appeals from decisions of Immigration Adjudicators; since 1993 there has been the right to appeal from the Immigration Appeal Tribunal to the Court of Appeal on a point of law. There is also a Social Security Appeals Tribunal to hear appeals in this area, with the possibility of a further appeal to the Social Security Commissioners – again an appeal can go from here to the Court of Appeal if there is a point of law at issue.

A formal route of appeal is in itself a safeguard as well as allowing the Court of Appeal to develop the law on the basis of judicial precedent, so that the law becomes more stable and predictable.

Second, the Queen's Bench Divisional Court has the power to hear applications for judicial review against tribunal decisions, and can use its prerogative powers to quash a decision. This could occur, for example, where there has been a breach of natural justice.

10.5.6 Advantages and disadvantages of tribunals

Tribunals were set up to prevent the overloading of the courts with the extra cases that social and welfare rights claims generate. In 1979 the Benson Commission on legal services pointed out the importance of the role of tribunals in this respect, as they heard six times the number of cases dealt with by the courts.

For the applicant in tribunal cases, the advantages are that such cases are dealt with more cheaply, more quickly and more informally than they would be if there was a court hearing. There is also the fact that the panel is composed of a mix of legal expertise and lay expertise in the field concerned. However, all these claims need to be evaluated.

Cost-effectiveness

As applicants are encouraged to represent themselves and not use lawyers, it is true to say that tribunal hearings do not normally involve the costs associated with court hearings. It is also rare for an order for costs to be made by a tribunal, so that an applicant need not fear a large bill if they lose the case. However, applicants who are not represented have a lower chance of winning their case than those who are represented, so the saving on cost of a lawyer may not be that cost-effective. Statistics in the early 1990s showed that the success rate for those with lawyers was 49 per cent, while for those without lawyers it was 28 per cent.

Speedy hearings

This was one of the advantages of tribunal hearings, but it is no longer true to say that cases will be dealt with speedily. Reports by the Council on Tribunals have highlighted delays, due to the vast volume of work that tribunals now face, together with the fact that the lay members only sit part-time. This creates a particular problem if the case is complex and likely to last several days. An extreme example of this was seen in the case of Allison Halford who brought proceedings for sex discrimination against the Police Authorities. The case lasted 39 days, which were spread over a period of several months, and it was more than two years from the date of her original application to the conclusion of the case. Even then the case only finished because the parties settled the matter; if the case had continued in front of the tribunal with its part-time hearings it could have taken several months more to come to a conclusion.

However, this is nothing compared with the case of *Darnell* v *United Kingdom* (1993) in which a doctor who was dismissed in 1984 started proceedings for unfair dismissal. The final decision in those proceedings was made in 1993 by the Employment Appeal Tribunal. In the meantime the doctor had complained to the European Court of Human Rights over the delay and this complaint was upheld.

Simple procedure

It is true that there is a more informal hearing than in court; in addition, most cases are heard in private. These comments do not apply to industrial tribunals which are open to the public and tend to be more formal. The procedure is also relatively flexible and the tribunals are not bound by strict rules of evidence. However, for individuals presenting their own cases the venue is unfamiliar and the procedure can be confusing. Where applicants are not represented, the chairman is expected to take an inquisitorial role and help to establish the points that the applicant

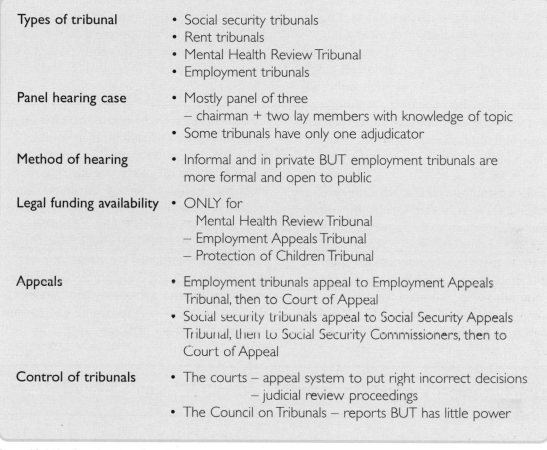

Key Facts

Types of tribunal	• Social security tribunals • Rent tribunals • Mental Health Review Tribunal • Employment tribunals
Panel hearing case	• Mostly panel of three – chairman + two lay members with knowledge of topic • Some tribunals have only one adjudicator
Method of hearing	• Informal and in private BUT employment tribunals are more formal and open to public

Legal funding availability	• ONLY for
	  Mental Health Review Tribunal
	  – Employment Appeals Tribunal
	  – Protection of Children Tribunal

Appeals	• Employment tribunals appeal to Employment Appeals Tribunal, then to Court of Appeal • Social security tribunals appeal to Social Security Appeals Tribunal, then to Social Security Commissioners, then to Court of Appeal
Control of tribunals	• The courts – appeal system to put right incorrect decisions – judicial review proceedings • The Council on Tribunals – reports BUT has little power

Figure 10.4 *Key fact chart on tribunals*

wishes to make. This is not always achieved, as shown by research into social security cases carried out by Baldwin, Wikeley and Young in their study *Judging Social Security*, published in 1992. They found that out of the hearings they attended, the chairman's handling of the case could be described as good or excellent in 57 per cent of cases and adequate in a further quarter of cases. However, in one-sixth of cases the chairman's conduct was open to serious criticism.

This type of criticism has also been levelled at employment tribunals. In these cases an applicant in person may often find themselves opposed by a lawyer representing the

employer, and so it is even more important that the proceedings should be kept simple and that the chairman should act inquisitorially to redress the balance.

The problem of the unrepresented applicant comes about because public funding is not available for most tribunals, which may put an applicant at a disadvantage if the other side (often an employer or Government department) uses a lawyer.

Other problems

Other problems can arise because a few tribunals still do not have to give reasons for their decisions. Nor do some tribunals follow a system of precedent, which makes it difficult to predict the outcome of cases (these criticisms do not apply to employment tribunals). In addition, there is no right of appeal from some tribunals (although an application for judicial review may be made) – this problem has lessened as a final appeal on a point of law has been brought in for both the social security cases, and immigration cases.

Impartiality

There used to be a criticism that the chairmen of tribunals were not sufficiently impartial, as they were in many cases appointed by the Minister of the Government department against whom the case was being brought. This problem was highlighted by the Franks Committee who recommended that all appointments should be impartial. Now the system is that the Independent Tribunal Service recommends potential chairmen to the Lord Chancellor. The Lord Chancellor then decides which of these people will be placed on a panel of chairmen for tribunal hearings.

10.5.7 Domestic tribunals

These are effectively 'in-house' tribunals set up by private bodies, usually for their own internal disciplinary control. They must keep to the rules of natural justice and their decisions are subject to judicial review. In addition, for many professional disciplinary tribunals there is an appeal route to the Judicial Committee of the Privy Council, in cases where the tribunal has decided to strike off a member from the professional register. For example, this applies to decisions of the disciplinary committee of the General Medical Council, and also to other medical disciplinary tribunals.

Examination Questions

1. (a) What are the advantages and disadvantages of Alternative Dispute
        Resolution (ADR)?   *[10 marks]*
    and
    (b) Explain the development, role and control of tribunals.   *[15 marks]*

                                                                LW2 WJEC, June 2005

2. (a) Describe the different methods of Alternative Dispute Resolution available to deal
        with civil disputes.   *[18 marks]*
    (b) Discuss the advantages and disadvantages of using Alternative Dispute
        Resolution.   *[9 marks]*

                                                        Quality of language mark 3

                                                            OCR Specimen paper

Chapter 11

Crime and police investigations

11.1 Crime statistics

Criminal cases are frequently headline news in the papers; society as a whole is concerned about the crime rate. The statistics for recorded crime show that there has been a massive increase over the last 50 years: in 1950 there were only half a million recorded crimes, but by the 1990s the figure had reached five million. Then for each of the years 1993 to 1997 the number of recorded crimes fell. However, in 1998–99 the number showed an increase from 4.5 million to a total of 5.4 million crimes. This increase was because of a new way of recording crime which used the number of victims whereas before this might have been classified as one incident. From 1998–99 to 2001–02 there was a small increase in recorded crime most years (except for 2000–01).

In 2002 the National Crime Recording Standard was introduced to try to make sure that all police forces kept to the same guidelines for recording crime. Following this the recorded crime rate increased for two years, before decreasing again. The figures for 2005–06 show a decrease of 1 per cent on the previous year. The number of recorded crimes in this year was 5.6 million.

Even these crime figures are not believed to give a true picture of the amount of criminal activity in England and Wales. It is thought that a large amount of crime is not recorded –

this is shown by surveys such as the British Crime Survey which is conducted every two years.

11.1.1 The British Crime Survey

The British Crime Survey showed a gradual decrease in crime over the period 1995–2005. According to the Survey, the highest year for crime was 1995, when there were over 19 million crimes. There was, however, a small increase of 1 per cent from 2004–05 to 2005–06.

For 2005–06 the British Crime Survey interviewed nearly 48,000 people about their experience of crime. The Survey then used the figures to estimate the full extent of crime. The fact that the Survey relied on people's experience of crime meant that crimes where there was no victim would not be reported in this survey. For 2005–06 the Survey estimated that there were 10.9 million crimes.

11.1.2 Annual variations

Within the figures for any one year, there will be a variation in different crimes, with some showing large increases, others small increases or even a decrease. These variations can be caused by police policy in targeting certain types of crime. Full statistics for recorded crime are published by the Home Office each year, Figure 11.1 shows the change in recorded crime between 2004–05 and 2005–06.

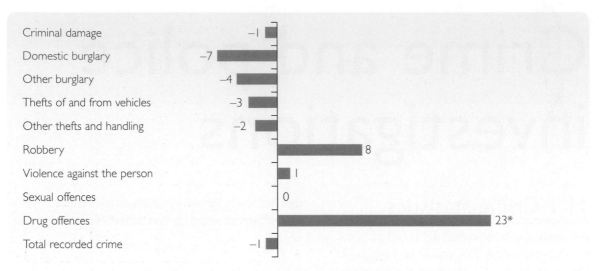

Source: Crime in England and Wales, Home Office Statistical Bulletin 12/06

Figure 11.1 *Percentage changes in recorded crime, 2004–05 to 2005–06*

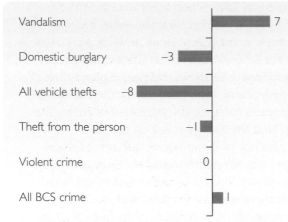

Source: Crime in England and Wales, Home Office Statistical Bulletin 12/06

Figure 11.2 *Percentage changes in the main crime types according to BCS interviews in 2005–06 compared with 2004–05*

Figure 11.2 shows the change in different offences for the same period according to the British Crime Survey.

Activity

Look at Figures 11.1 and 11.2.

Questions

1. Which offence do the recorded crime figures show as having the biggest increase for 2004–05 to 2005–06?

2. Which offence do the BCS figures show as having the biggest increase for the same period?

3. What factors might explain why the two charts show different offences for the biggest increase?

4. Compare what the two charts show as happening for domestic burglary.

11.1.3 Investigating crime

It is still clear that the crime rates are worryingly high. It is obviously necessary to have an authority who has sufficient power to investigate possible crimes by being able to stop suspects, search them, arrest people and interview them about suspected criminal activity. In this country the police are given this authority.

About one in four recorded crimes is detected (see Figure 11.3).

However, while it is necessary that the police should have appropriate power to investigate crimes, it is also necessary to keep a balance between protecting individual liberty by preventing people from being unnecessarily harassed and/or detained, and giving the police adequate powers to prevent or detect crime.

During the 1970s and 1980s there were several serious miscarriages of justice in individual cases. Many of these miscarriages stemmed from questionable police procedures and as a result Parliament has tried to regulate this area of the law. The main police powers are set out in the Police and Criminal Evidence Act 1984 (PACE), with some additions and amendments made by the Criminal Justice and Public Order Act 1994, the Criminal Justice Act 2003 and the Serious Organised Crime and Police Act 2005. PACE also provides for Codes of Practice giving extra detail on the procedures for searching, detaining, questioning and identifying suspects. These Codes of Practice are issued by the Home Secretary.

11.2 Legislative history

11.2.1 Royal Commission on Criminal Procedure

The Royal Commission on Criminal Procedure (the Phillips Commission) was set up in 1978

Source: Adapted from Criminal Statistics: England and Wales 2005

Figure 11.3 *Levels of crimes – detection and outcome*

as a result of concern over police procedures. One of the main concerns was the over-use (or abuse) of what used to be called the 'sus' law under which police officers could stop people if they felt there was anything suspicious. This usually meant young men, and particularly members of ethnic minorities, were likely to be stopped, often for no real cause.

The Royal Commission found that the law on police powers that existed before 1984 was piecemeal and haphazard. There were provisions in the common law, local bylaws and over 70 different Acts of Parliament giving the right to stop, search or arrest in a variety of different circumstances. This obviously made the law confusing, both for suspects and the police. The Commission also stressed the need to find a balance between 'the interests of the community in bringing offenders to justice and the rights and liberties of persons suspected or accused of crime'.

The findings of this Commission led to Parliament enacting the Police and Criminal Evidence Act 1984. This Act tried to both rationalise and modernise the law on many aspects of police procedure. Some of the most significant changes were in the requirement that police should keep records of such matters as stops and searches, and custody records relating to those in police detention and that the police should tape-record the questioning of suspects.

11.2.2 Miscarriages of justice

When the miscarriages of justice of the 1970s and 1980s came to light, these placed doubt on police methods and interviewing techniques. However, most of the original investigations involved had been prior to the implementation of the Police and Criminal Evidence Act 1984. They also cast doubt on some of the methods used in obtaining scientific evidence. In some cases, miscarriages had arisen where the prosecution had evidence which would have helped establish the defendant's innocence, but had not disclosed that evidence to the defence.

Four of the cases involved separate allegations of terrorist activities on behalf of the IRA. These were the Guildford Four, the Birmingham Six, the Maguires and Judith Ward. The Guildford Four were convicted in 1975 of bombing a pub in Guildford and the evidence against them consisted almost entirely of confessions which were supposed to have been made to police during interviews. The original police evidence claimed that police officers had made a contemporaneous handwritten note of what was said during the interview with Armstrong, one of the four accused. Eventually a set of typed police notes with amendments, both typed and written, and rearrangement of material was discovered. This cast considerable doubt on the police version of the interview and, when the case was finally referred back to the Criminal Division of the Court of Appeal in 1989, the Court quashed the convictions.

In the Birmingham Six case, the accused claimed that they had been beaten up by the police and forced into making untrue confessions and, as with the Guildford Four case, later evidence cast doubt on police notes and the credibility of the police evidence. Later evidence also supported the men's claim that they had been beaten up by the police while in custody, being questioned about the bomb attack. There was also a problem with scientific evidence as to whether the men had handled nitroglycerine (an explosive substance). Scientific knowledge showed that such tests could be faulty and give a positive reading from quite innocent substances such as paint, or even from the washing-up liquid used to clean the dishes in which the samples were then tested. When it was first discovered that the men had tested 'positive' this had been put down to them touching adhesive tape. However, Dr Skuse, a forensic scientist, said 'categorically' in evidence that the only possible explanation of the 'positive' tests was that they had been handling explosives. Their convictions were finally quashed by the Court of Appeal.

The case of Stefan Kiszko was different in that scientific evidence, which supported his innocence had been available to the prosecution defence (see article).

These various cases also cast doubts on the appeal system as the defendants had appealed against conviction in all the cases, but the original appeal had not been allowed. At the same time, there was concern over the number of acquittals in criminal trials and a belief that the rules of PACE under which the police worked were too restrictive and led to many guilty people going free. It was clear that a full review of the criminal justice system was necessary.

Evidence could have prevented prosecution: Court's quashing of murder conviction reopens questions over judicial system

The latest in the litany of miscarriages of justice is arguably the most shocking.

For even before Stefan Kiszko stood trial, there was unequivocal evidence of his innocence.

Scientists had shown that Mr Kiszko was infertile and that Lesley Molseeds's attacker was not. Mr Kiszko has a condition known as hypogonadism, making it impossible for him to secrete sperm. Spermheads were found on the dead girl's clothing.

The evidence lay buried for 16 years, until yesterday when it was used to prove his innocence.

The Lancashire police investigation into the affair will seek to discover who was involved in that suppression and whether it was deliberate, negligent or accidental.

Certainly Dr Edward Tierney, the police surgeon who ordered the tests, said he knew of the evidence's potential to clear Mr Kiszko. He said he had informed senior investigating officers in the West Yorkshire murder squad, headed by Detective Chief Supt Jack Dibb, who has since died, of its importance.

It is not known whether this information was passed to the prosecution authorities and lawyers. However, its suppression meant that Mr Kiszko served those years at first in prison and then, when his mental health deteriorated in jail, in a secure psychiatric hospital, and that the real attacker escaped justice.

An extract from an article by Heather Mills in
The Independent, 19 February 1992

11.2.3 The Runciman Commission

The terms of reference of this Commission on Criminal Justice were to:
'examine the effectiveness of the criminal justice system in England and Wales in securing the conviction of those guilty of criminal offences and the acquittal of those who are innocent, having regard to the efficient use of resources.'

This was neatly put by Michael Zander, one of the Commission, as a remit with three distinct component elements:

• the need to convict the guilty

• the need not to convict the innocent, and
• due economy.

The Commission had 22 research studies carried out into how the criminal justice system worked in practice; it also heard evidence from over 600 organisations and its report was published in 1993, containing 352 recommendations.

These recommendations ranged from police investigations, for example, suggesting continuous videoing of police custody suites to pre-trial procedures such as the suggestion for abolishing the defendant's right to choose trial

Rights of a detained person

Detainees must be told their rights by the custody officer. These rights include:

- having someone informed of the arrest
- being told that independent legal advice is available free and being allowed to consult privately with a solicitor
- being allowed to consult the code of practice.

The right to have someone informed of the arrest

The right to have someone informed of the arrest is given by s 56 of PACE. The arrested person can nominate any friend, relative or any other person who they think is likely to take an interest in their welfare. The person nominated by the detainee must be told of the arrest and where the person is being held. This should normally be done as soon as practicable, but, in the case of an indictable offence a senior police officer may authorise that there be a delay of up to 36 hours. This can only be done if there are reasonable grounds for believing that telling the named person will lead to: interference; harm to evidence or to other persons; the alerting of others involved in the offence or hinder the recovery of property obtained through the offence. Code C states that, in addition to the right to have someone informed of the arrest, a detained person should be allowed to speak on the telephone 'for a reasonable time to one person'. If the suspect is under the age of 17

	Right	Source	Comment
Key Facts	To have someone informed of detention	s 56 PACE	Can be delayed for up to 36 hours if an indictable offence
	To speak to someone on the telephone	Code of Practice C	Not compulsory – police can refuse
	To be told of their right to legal advice	Code of Practice C	Notices displayed in police stations Duty of custody officer to bring this to the suspect's attention
	To legal advice	s 58 PACE	Can be delayed for up to 36 hours if an indictable offence BUT only in exceptional circumstances: R v Samuel
	To have appropriate adult present at interview	Code of Practice C	Applies to those under 17 and also to mentally ill or handicapped: R v Aspinall
	To consult the Codes of Practice	The Codes of Practice	

Figure 11.8 Key fact chart on rights of suspects in police detention

the police must also contact a person 'responsible for his welfare' and inform them of the arrest.

The right to legal advice

A detained person may either contact their own solicitor, or they can use the system of duty solicitors which is provided free for anyone under arrest. In fact the code of practice tries to make sure that detained people are aware of their right to legal advice. Under the code the custody officer, when authorising the detention of someone at the police station, must get the suspect to sign the custody record at that time saying whether he/she wishes to have legal advice. Police stations must have posters 'prominently displayed' advertising the right to free legal advice, and an arrested suspect must not only be told orally of this right, but also given a written notice of it.

It is possible for a senior police officer to authorise a delay to a suspect's right to see a solicitor in the case of an indictable offence for up to 36 hours. However, this can only occur if there are reasonable grounds for believing that giving access to a solicitor will lead to: interference with, or harm to, evidence or to other persons; the alerting of others involved in the offence, or hinder the recovery of property obtained through the offence. The case of *R v Samuel* (1988) stressed that it would only be on rare occasions that such a delay was justified, and that it must be based on specific aspects of the case, not a general assumption that access to a solicitor might lead to the alerting of accomplices. In *Samuel*'s case, the defendant was a 24-year-old man, whose mother had already been informed of her son's arrest some hours before he was refused access to a solicitor. The Court of Appeal felt that if anyone was likely to be alerted then it would already have happened, and that there was no reason to deny Samuel

his 'fundamental freedom' of consulting a solicitor. As his final interview with the police had taken place after his solicitor had been refused access, the evidence of what was said at that interview was inadmissible in court and so Samuel's conviction for robbery was quashed.

In *R v Grant* (2005) the Court of Appeal held that the court would not tolerate illegal conduct by the police. In this case there had been deliberate interference by the police with the detained suspect's right to the confidence of privileged communication with his solicitor. This was such a serious abuse of process that it justified his conviction for murder being quashed.

11.3.6 Police interviews of suspects

Any detained person may be questioned by the police. All interviews at a police station must be tape-recorded and trials are being conducted on the feasibility of videoing rather than just audio-taping. A problem in many cases is that questioning of the suspect starts before they arrive at the police station (possibly in the police car on the way to the station) and these informal interviews are not recorded. In many cases, the defendant challenges the truth of police evidence about an alleged informal interview. In order to protect suspects from the possibility of police fabricating evidence of a confession made outside the police station, the Runciman Commission recommended that if a confession was allegedly made outside the police station, then that confession should be put to the suspect at the beginning of any tape-recorded interview that subsequently takes place. This allows a suspect a chance to make comments about it in the taped interview.

Suspects have the right to have a solicitor present at any interview, unless it is one of the rare occasions referred to in *Samuel* above. However, if the suspect does not ask for a solicitor, the police may conduct the interview without one being present. In addition, if the matter is urgent or the solicitor likely to be delayed for some time, the police have the right to start questioning a suspect before a solicitor arrives.

Appropriate adult

If the suspect is under the age of 17 or is mentally handicapped then there must be an 'appropriate adult' present during all interviews. This right is in addition to the right to legal advice. Research suggests that many mentally vulnerable individuals are not being given this protection; the Runciman Commission recommended that the police should be given clearer guidelines on identifying suspects who need an appropriate adult. The Commission also suggested there should be trials of the use of 'duty psychiatrist schemes' to see whether a permanent scheme would be appropriate in busy city centre police stations.

In *R* v *Aspinall* (1999) the Court of Appeal ruled that a defendant who suffered from schizophrenia should have had an appropriate adult present when interviewed by police. This was so even though the defendant appeared able to understand the police questions. The interview was, therefore, not admissible as evidence.

Treatment of suspects and exclusion of evidence

The law gives some protection to suspects as to the way they should be treated whilst being detained and questioned. Section 76 of PACE states that the court shall not allow statements which have been obtained through oppression to be used as evidence. Oppression is defined as including torture, inhuman or degrading treatment and the use or threat of violence. Code C also gives protection to suspects who

are being questioned in regard to the physical conditions of the interview. For example, the code states that interview rooms must be adequately lit, heated and ventilated and that suspects must be given adequate breaks for meals, refreshments and sleep.

In theory the treatment of a suspect is monitored by the custody officer who is supposed to keep accurate records of all happenings during the detention period. This should include the length and timing of interviews and other matters, such as visits of police officers to the defendant's cell, so that any breaches of the rules will be obvious. However, research by Sanders and Bridge suggests that a substantial minority of custody records (about 10 per cent) are falsified.

The right to silence

Until the Criminal Justice and Public Order Act 1994 was enacted, defendants could refuse to answer any questions without any adverse conclusion being drawn on their silence if the case came to trial. In fact, the previously used caution given before a police interview commenced, contained the phrase 'you do not have to say anything'. This right to remain silent was considered by the Runciman Commission, which recommended that it should be retained in essence. However, the Government decided that this rule was allowing guilty people to go free and that the right to silence should be curbed. This was done by ss 34–39 of the Criminal Justice and Public Order Act 1994.

These sections allow inferences to be made from the fact that a defendant has refused to answer questions. As a result the wording of the caution given to a suspect before interviewing commences now states:

'You do not have to say anything. But it may harm your defence if you do not mention when questioned something which you later rely on in court. Anything you do say may be given in evidence.'

Key Facts

Power	Sections in PACE or other Act	Code of Practice	Comments
Stop and search	ss 1–7 of PACE, also other Acts, eg Misuse of Drugs Act 1971	A	• Must be in a public place and must have reasonable grounds for suspecting person
Enter premises	With search warrant (s 8 PACE) OR to arrest person (s 17 PACE) OR to prevent breach of the peace	B	• Magistrates issue warrant • Even applies to private homes
Arrest	With a warrant OR under sections 24 or 25 of PACE		• Magistrates issue warrant • Must have reasonable grounds
Detention	ss 34–46 PACE Limits 24 hours OR 36 (extendible to 96) for serious arrestable offence	C	• Detainee has rights to: – have someone told – to be told of availability of legal advice – to see Code of Practice
Searches	ss 54, 55 PACE	C	• Intimate search must be by person of same sex
Fingerprinting	ss 61 PACE		
Samples	ss 62, 63 PACE		• Intimate samples must be taken by qualified person
Police interviews	s 53 PACE Also ss 34–39 Criminal Justice and Public Order Act 1994 re 'silence'	E	• Police must caution • Should tape-record • Appropriate adult present for those under 17

Figure 11.9 *Key fact chart on police powers*

This change in the law does not mean that the defendant can be forced to speak; he can still remain silent. At any trial which follows however, the judge may comment on the defendant's failure to mention a crucial matter, and this failure can form part of the evidence

Activity

Read these two extracts and then answer the questions which follow each

1. Some common public interest factors in the favour of prosecution

Para 5.9 The more serious the offence, the more likely it is that a prosecution will be needed in the public interest. A prosecution is likely to be needed if:

a a conviction is likely to result in a significant sentence;

b a conviction is likely to result in a confiscation or any other order;

c a weapon was used or violence was threatened during the commission of the offence;

d the offence was committed against a person serving the public (for example, a police or prison officer, or a nurse);

e the defendant was in a position of authority or trust;

f the evidence shows that the defendant was a ringleader or an organiser of the offence;

g there is evidence that the offence was premeditated;

h there is evidence that the offence was carried out by a group;

i the victim of the offence was vulnerable or has been put in considerable fear or suffered personal attack, damage or disturbance;

j the offence was committed in the presence of, or in close proximity to, a child;

k the offence was motivated by any form of discrimination against the victim's ethnic or national origin, disability, sex, religious beliefs, ... political views or sexual orientation;

l there is a marked difference between the actual or mental ages of the defendant and the victim, or if there is any element of corruption;

m the defendant's previous convictions or cautions are relevant to the present offence;

n the defendant is alleged to have committed the offence whilst under an order of the court;

o there are grounds for believing that the offence is likely to be continued or repeated, for example, by a history of recurring conduct; or

p the offence, although not serious in itself, is widespread in the area where it was committed;

q a prosecution would have a significant positive impact on maintaining community confidence.

Questions

1. Look at the list of factors in favour of prosecution and decide if you think any of the factors should be more important than others.

2. Are there any factors in this list which you do not think should be considered when deciding whether to prosecute a defendant?

3. What, if any, other factors would you like to see considered?

Activity

2. Some common public interest factors against prosecution

Para 5.10 A prosecution is less likely to be needed if:

a the court is likely to impose a nominal penalty;

b the defendant has already been made the subject of a sentence and any further conviction would be unlikely to result in the imposition of an additional sentence or order, unless the nature of the particular offence requires a prosecution...

c the offence was committed as a result of a genuine mistake or misunderstanding (these factors must be balanced against the seriousness of the offence);

d the loss or harm can be described as minor and was the result of a single incident, particularly if it was caused by misjudgment;

e there has been a long delay between the offence taking place and the date of the trial, unless:

- the offence is serious;
- the delay has been caused in part by the defendant;
- the offence has only recently come to light; or
- the complexity of the offence has meant that there has been a long investigation;

f a prosecution is likely to have a bad effect on the victim's physical or mental health, always bearing in mind the seriousness of the offence;

g the defendant is elderly or is, or was at the time of the offence, suffering from significant mental or physical ill health, unless the offence is serious or there is a real possibility that it may be repeated...

h the defendant has put right the loss or harm that was caused (but defendants must not avoid prosecution simply because they pay compensation); or

i details may be made public that could harm sources of information, international relations or national security.

Source: The Code for Crown Prosecutors

Questions

1. Do you think any of the factors in this list are more important than others? Give reasons for your answer.

2. Which, if any, of the above factors do you think should not be considered when deciding whether or not to prosecute a defendant?

3. Compare the two lists. Are they well balanced? Do they provide a good framework for deciding when it is in the public interest to prosecute? Give reasons for your answer.

In 2005–06 the CPS prosecuted over one million people in the Magistrates' Courts. The conviction rate has steadily increased over the past few years, so that in 2005–06, 82.8 per cent of all cases in the Magistrates' Courts resulted in a conviction. In the same period in the Crown Court the CPS prosecuted nearly 100,000 defendants. Of these, 77.2 per cent of cases resulted in a conviction.

However, there are still cases in which the CPS have been heavily criticised for discontinuation; as a result of the CPS discontinuing cases, there have been instances where private prosecutions have been brought for serious crimes. For example in 1995, there was a successful prosecution in a rape case which the CPS had refused to prosecute – a press report of this case is shown on this page.

There are also criticisms that the CPS often reduces the charge against the defendant to a less serious crime than is revealed by the evidence. This makes it more likely that the defendant will plead guilty, but, as the sentence will probably be less serious as well, it can leave the victim of a crime feeling that justice has not been done.

To improve matters since 2000 the code of practice stresses that victims must be told about any decision made by the CPS which makes significant difference to the case (such as reducing the charge).

In 2005 a Code of Practice for Victims was issued. This Code sets out the services that victims can expect to receive from the criminal justice system. This includes notifying vulnerable victims within one working day, and all other victims within five working days, if there is insufficient evidence to charge a suspect.

Rapist is jailed after private court case

A man was jailed for 14 years yesterday in the first successful private prosecution for rape in England and Wales.

The sentence imposed on Christopher Davies, 44, a chef, is expected to prompt a spate of actions.

The case against Davies was brought by two prostitutes, who cannot be named, after the Crown Prosecution Service decided not to proceed. Both counsel and the solicitors acted free of charge. Davies was convicted earlier this year and sentence was deferred until yesterday.

Afterwards, one of the women said: 'This case has proved all women have the right to say "no".' Yesterday Women Against Rape said: 'This is especially a victory, given that the Crown Prosecution Service dismissed the case as having insufficient evidence'.

Taken from an article by Frances Gibb in
The Times, 20 September 1995

Civil actions

There have also been cases in which a civil case has been taken because the Crown Prosecution Service refuses to prosecute. The standard of proof in civil cases is not as high as in criminal cases, but even so some of these cases have then spurred the Crown Prosecution Service to prosecute. In particular in 1998 the family of a murdered black woman doctor, Joan Francisco, took a civil case for trespass to the person against her ex-boyfriend. The family alleged that the boyfriend had murdered her. They were successful in this civil case: The police and the Crown Prosecution Service then reviewed the evidence and discovered that there was a test for discovering very small amounts of blood which they had not used in the first investigation. When this test was used, it revealed that there were spots of the boyfriend's blood on the woman's T-shirt. The CPS then prosecuted the man for murder and in 1999, six years after the murder, he was convicted.

12.3.4 The Glidewell Report

Because of the problems and criticism of the CPS, Sir Iain Glidewell was asked to conduct an inquiry into the service. The Glidewell Report was published in 1998. A main criticism in the Report was the number of judge-ordered acquittals, which made up over 20 per cent of all acquittals. The report stated that in one in five of these cases something appeared to have been wrong with the preparation of the case.

The report also criticised the organisation of the CPS, finding that it was too bureaucratic and over-centralised. As a result the CPS was reorganised in 1999 into 42 areas (instead of 13). New Chief Crown Prosecutors were appointed for each area and the DPP, David Calvert-Smith, stated that these Chief Crown Prosecutors would have the power to act on their own initiative. It is intended that they can place a priority on prosecution work which will benefit the local communities they serve.

The re-organisation was also intended to create better working relationships with other local agencies in the criminal justice system, including the police and the courts.

Criminal Justice Units

The Narey Report into delay in the criminal justice system suggested that CPS staff should work in police stations in order to prevent delay in cases being passed to the CPS. During 1998 and 1999 pilot schemes were run in six areas of the country. As it was impractical to have a CPS lawyer in every police station, they were assigned to Criminal Justice Units or Administrative Support Units. The evaluation of the pilot schemes found that not only did this help to prevent delay, but it also created better working practices between the police and the CPS with greater continuity in cases.

It was also found that fewer cases were discontinued by the CPS: 7 per cent in the pilot areas as against 12 per cent nationally. This was thought to be due to the fact that CPS staff were available to advise police at an early stage in a case.

Criminal Justice Units now operate in all areas of the country. There is also CPS Direct, which is an out-of-hours telephone service. This allows experienced prosecutors to work from home to provide police with charging advice throughout the night.

Criticism of the CPS

The Public Accounts Committee reported on the CPS in October 2006 in *Crown Prosecution Service: Effective Use of Magistrates' Courts Hearings* for 2004–05. It pointed out that there were a large number of cases, both trial and pre-trial which did not proceed on the day.

In 2004–05 there were 190,466 trials in Magistrates' Courts and over 2.8 million pre-trial hearings. Just under two-thirds of trials and over a quarter of pre-trial hearings did not go ahead as planned.

Where the trial did not go ahead, the defence was most often to blame. However, the CPS was responsible in 38 per cent of cases. It was either not ready to proceed, or dropped charges on the day of the trial. The Committee identified that delays cost the taxpayer over £173 million. Of this it identified £24 million as being attributable to the CPS.

The CPS's response was to point out that the ineffective trial rate has dropped sharply over the past few years, from 31 per cent in July to September 2002 to 23 per cent in January to March 2005. It also pointed out that more progress has been made since the period considered by the Committee. For June–August 2006 the rate was 19 per cent.

Examination Questions

1. (a) What are the factors taken into account in the decision to grant or refuse bail?   *[10 marks]*

   (b) How far would you agree that the law relating to bail provides the police and courts with an effective alternative to remand in custody as a means of exercising supervision and control over suspected offenders?   *[15 marks]*

   LW2 WJEC, January 2006

2. Steve has been charged with the murder of his mother, who was dying of cancer. Phil has been charged with the theft of £5,000 worth of parts from a car accessories dealer.
   Explain how it will be decided whether bail is likely to be granted to Steve and Phil.

   Part of a question, OCR 2568, January 2003

3. What factors are taken into account by the Crown Prosecution Service (CPS) in deciding whether to prosecute?   *[11 marks]*

   WJEC LW2, June 2003

Chapter 13

Criminal courts

The two courts which hear criminal trials are the Magistrates' Court and the Crown Court. As already explained in Chapter 12, the actual court for the trial is decided by the category of crime involved in the charge. Summary offences can only be tried at the Magistrates' Court, indictable offences can only be tried at the Crown Court, while triable either way offences may be tried at either court.

In both the Magistrates' Court and the Crown Court the majority of defendants plead guilty to the charge against them. In these cases the role of the court is to decide what sentence should be imposed on the defendant. Where the accused pleads not guilty, the role of the court is to try the case and decide if the accused is guilty or not guilty; the burden of proof is on the prosecution who must prove the case beyond reasonable doubt. The form of the trial is an adversarial one, with prosecution and defence presenting their cases and cross-examining each other's witnesses, while the role of the judge is effectively that of referee, overseeing the trial and making sure that legal rules are followed correctly. The judge cannot investigate the case, nor ask to see additional witnesses.

13.1 Magistrates' Courts

There are about 430 Magistrates' Courts in England and Wales. They are local courts so there will be a Magistrates' Court in almost every town, while big cities will have several courts. Each court deals with cases that have a connection with its geographical area and they have jurisdiction over a variety of matters involving criminal cases. Cases are heard by magistrates, who may be either qualified District judges or unqualified lay justices (see Chapter 17 for further details on magistrates). There is also a legally qualified clerk attached to each court to assist the magistrates.

13.1.1 Jurisdiction of the Magistrates' Courts

So far as criminal cases are concerned the courts have jurisdiction in a variety of matters. They have a very large workload and they do the following:

1. Try all summary cases.
2. Try any triable either way offences which it is decided should be dealt with in the Magistrates' Court (see section 13.1.3).

   These first two categories account for about 97 per cent of all criminal cases.

3. Deal with the first hearing of all indictable offences. These cases are then sent to the Crown Court.

4. Deal with all the side matters connected to criminal cases, such as issuing warrants for arrest and deciding bail applications.

5. Try cases in the Youth Court where the defendants are aged 10–17 inclusive.

Civil jurisdiction

The Magistrates' Courts also have some civil jurisdiction. Strictly speaking, this side of their work belongs in Chapter 9 – however, for completeness, and to illustrate the wide variety of work carried out by Magistrates' Court, this side of their work is listed below. It includes:

- Enforcing council tax demands and issuing warrants of entry and investigation to gas and electricity authorities
- Family cases including orders for protection against violence and maintenance orders (NB Magistrates' Courts cannot grant divorces)
- Proceedings concerning the welfare of children under the Children Act 1989
- Hearing appeals against the refusal of a licence to sell alcohol.

13.1.2 Summary trials

These are the least serious criminal offences and are sub-divided into offences of different 'levels' – level one being the lowest level and level five the highest. The use of levels allows a maximum fine to be set for each level which is increased in line with inflation from time to time. The current maximum fines date from the Criminal Justice Act 1991 and are level one: maximum £200, level two: £500, level three: £1,000, level four: £2,500 and level five: £5,000. However, for certain breaches of environmental law and health and safety legislation, business can be fined up to £20,000 by the magistrates. The maximum prison sentence that can be given on summary trial is six months, but the Criminal Justice Act 2003 gives power for this to be increased to 15 months in future.

At the start of any case, the clerk of the court will check the defendant's name and address and then ask whether he pleads guilty or not guilty. Over 90 per cent of defendants in the Magistrates' Court plead guilty and the process is then concerned with establishing an appropriate penalty for the case.

Guilty plea

The usual sequence of events where the defendant pleads guilty to a summary offence is as follows:

1. The Crown Prosecutor or lay presenter from the CPS will give the court a resume of the facts of the case.

2. The defendant is asked if he agrees with those facts (if he does not the magistrates may have to hold an inquiry, called a Newton hearing, to establish the facts).

3. The defendant's past record of convictions, if any, is given to the court.

4. Other information about the defendant's background, especially his financial position, is given to the court.

5. Any relevant reports are considered by the magistrates; these may include a pre-sentence report prepared by a probation officer and/or a medical report on the defendant's mental health.

6. The defendant or his lawyer can then explain any matter which might persuade the magistrates to give a lenient sentence. This is called making a speech in mitigation.

7. The magistrates decide the sentence.

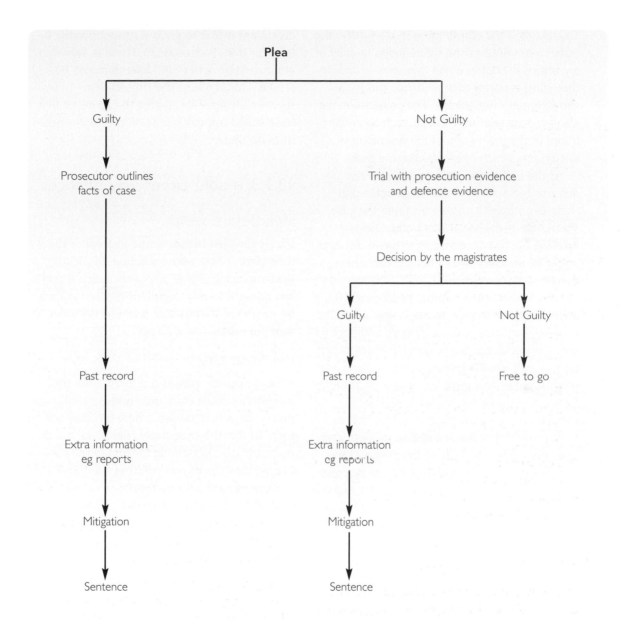

Figure 13.1 *Flow chart of proceedings for a summary offence in the Magistrates' Court*

This is shown in a flow chart form in Figure 13.1.

Not guilty plea

When a defendant pleads not guilty the procedure is longer and more complicated, as both sides produce evidence to the court. Since the burden of proof is on the prosecution, it will begin the case – usually by making a short speech outlining what the case is about and what they hope to prove. The prosecution witnesses will then be called one at a time to give evidence, and the prosecutor will question each to establish what he or she saw and heard.

This is called the examination in chief. After the prosecution finishes the examination in chief of a witness, the defence will then cross-examine that witness to test their evidence and try to show that it is not reliable. The prosecution may also produce relevant exhibits, such as property found in the possession of the defendant or documents which help establish the case.

At the end of the prosecution case the defence can submit to the magistrates that there is no case to answer and that the case should be dismissed at this point. This is because the prosecution has to prove the case and if its evidence does not establish a case, then it must be dismissed.

Only a very small number of cases will be dismissed at this stage. In the vast majority the case will continue and the defence will have to give their evidence to the court. The defendant himself will usually give evidence, though he does not have to. However, since the Criminal Justice and Public Order Act 1994, the magistrates can draw their own conclusions from the fact that the accused stays silent and does not explain his side of the matter. If the defendant does give evidence, he can be cross-examined by the prosecutor, as can any defence witnesses. The defence can call any witnesses and produce any evidence that it believes will help to disprove the prosecution's case.

Once all the evidence has been given, the defence has the right to make a speech pointing out the weaknesses of the case to the magistrates and try to persuade them to acquit the defendant. Further speeches are not usually allowed unless there is a point of law to be argued. The magistrates then decide if the defendant is guilty or not guilty. If they convict, they will then hear about his past record and may also look at reports and hear a speech in mitigation from the defence. They will then pass sentence.

If the magistrates dismiss the case, the defendant is free to go and cannot usually be tried for that offence again. There is, however, one exception when the defendant can be retried. This is where the prosecution successfully appeals against the acquittal in a 'case stated' appeal (see section 13.3.2 for the rules on these).

13.1.3 Triable either way offences

Plea before venue

Under the plea before venue procedure the defendant is first asked whether he pleads guilty or not guilty. If he pleads guilty, then he has no right to ask to go to the Crown Court although the magistrates may still decide to send him there for sentence.

Mode of trial

If the defendant pleads not guilty then the magistrates must carry out 'mode of trial' proceedings to establish where the case will be tried. In this the magistrates first decide if they think the case is suitable for trial in the Magistrates' Court and whether they are prepared to accept jurisdiction.

Under s 19 of the Magistrates' Court Act 1980 they must consider the nature and seriousness of the case, their own powers of punishment and any representations of the prosecution and defence.

Cases involving complex questions of fact or law should be sent to the Crown Court. Other relevant factors which may make a case more suitable for trial at the Crown Court include:

- where there was breach of trust by a person
- where the crime was committed by an organised gang
- where the amount involved was more than twice the amount the magistrates can fine the defendant.

In rare cases where the Attorney-General, Solicitor-General or the Director of Public Prosecutions is the prosecutor, the magistrates, under s 19(4) of the Magistrates' Court Act 1980, must send the case to the Crown Court if that is what the prosecution wants. In other cases the prosecution's wishes are just part of the matters to be considered by the magistrates before they decide whether they are prepared to hear the case or whether it should be tried at the Crown Court.

Defendant's election

If the magistrates are prepared to accept jurisdiction, the defendant is then told he has the right to choose trial by jury, but may be tried by the magistrates if he agrees to this course. However, he is also warned that if the case is tried by the magistrates and at the end of the case he is found guilty, the magistrates can send him to the Crown Court for sentence if they feel their powers of punishment are insufficient.

The procedure for triable either way offences is shown in flow chart form in Figure 13.2.

13.1.4 Choosing trial by jury

Since 1997 defendants pleading guilty to a triable either way offence at the Magistrates' Court in the plea before venue procedure have not been able to choose to go to the Crown Court. This is sensible since there will be no trial of the case, so the defendants are not losing a right to trial by jury. Defendants who are pleading not guilty have had the right to

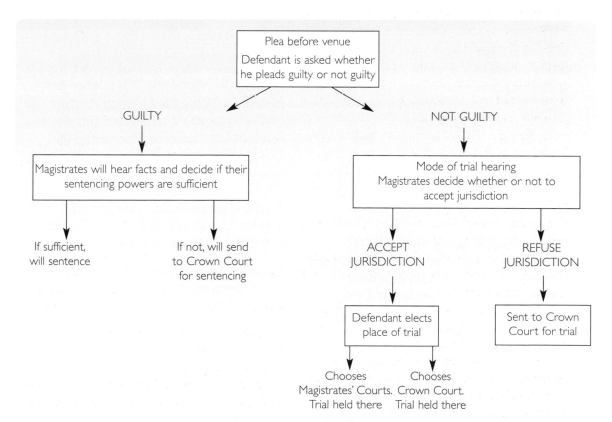

Figure 13.2 *Flow chart of procedure for triable either way offences*

Inside of a Magistrates' Court

choose where they want the case to be dealt with. This has been seen as an important part of civil liberties, as trial by jury is viewed as a protection of individual rights.

However, not many defendants elect to go to the Crown Court. It was noticeable that when all defendants could choose to go to the Crown Court less than one out of 20 elected to do so.

Implications of choosing jury trial

There are several factors involved in a defendant's choice of the Crown Court as the venue for his trial. The main reason for choosing the Crown Court is that the decision on guilt or innocence is made by a jury and this gives a better chance of an acquittal. Only 20 per cent of defendants who plead not guilty at the Magistrates' Court will be found not guilty by the magistrates, whereas 60 per cent of those who plead not guilty at the Crown Court are acquitted. This does not mean the jury acquit a large number as this figure

includes cases where the case is discharged by the judge without a trial. This is when the prosecution at the Crown Court does not offer evidence against the defendant. This may be because by the time the case reaches the Crown Court, the prosecution accept that the defendant is not guilty, or it may be because witnesses have failed or refused to come to court and the prosecution are left with insufficient evidence for the case to proceed.

Other points to be considered are that:

- There will be a longer wait before the trial and there will also be committal proceedings in the Magistrates' Court before the case goes to the Crown Court
- Cases at the Crown Court are more expensive, but the defendant is also more likely to get legal representation through the Criminal Defence Service
- If the defendant is represented this must be by a barrister or solicitor with a certificate of

advocacy giving rights of audience at the Crown Court

- There is a risk of a higher sentence if the defendant is found guilty in the Crown Court.

A study by Hedderman and Moxon showed that most defendants who chose the Crown Court did so on the advice of their lawyers and the main factor was the higher chance of an acquittal. There were many factors, however, which influenced the choice, including (where defendants were in custody) a wish to serve part of the sentence in a remand prison!

Should the right to choose trial by jury be kept?

It is very much more expensive to hold trials at the Crown Court than at the Magistrates' Court. In addition, statistics show that many of the defendants who choose jury trial then go on to plead guilty at the Crown Court. This has led to the questioning of whether defendants should have the right to elect trial by jury in cases where they are charged with a triable either way offence. In fact this right to jury trial has already been cut down by the fact that many offences which used to be triable either way have been reclassified as summary offences. These include the offences of assaulting a police officer in the execution of his duty, and driving whilst disqualified and drink driving.

In the past few years the Government has attempted to limit the defendant's right to jury trial. In 1999 and 2000 the Labour Government tried to pass laws abolishing the defendant's right to elect trial by jury in triable either way cases. On both occasions the House of Lords voted against the change in the law.

Then, in 2003, the Criminal Justice Bill contained two measures aimed at limiting jury trials. One proposal would have allowed a defendant to apply for a trial to be conducted without a jury. This was defeated by the House of Lords and withdrawn by the Government. The other proposal allowed the prosecution to apply for trial without a jury in lengthy or complex cases or where there was danger of the jury being interfered with.

This was defeated by the House of Lords, but the Government reinstated it. The House of Lords voted against it again. Finally, a compromise was reached and the final Criminal Justice Act 2003 has provision for the prosecution to apply for trial by a judge alone in:

- complex fraud cases, or
- where there has already been an effort to tamper with a jury in the case.

However, this provision is subject to an affirmative resolution which means that it cannot be brought into effect without both Houses voting for it.

Because of the difficulty of getting the House of Lords' agreement to abolish jury trial, the Government introduced a new Bill in Parliament in 2006. This was the Fraud (Trials without a Jury) Bill 2006. It is intended to repeal the need for an affirmative resolution. If this Bill is passed it would allow the Lord Chancellor to issue a statutory instrument allowing fraud cases to be tried without a jury. There would be no need for the House of Lords to agree to it.

The strong opposition to abolishing the right to trial by jury is because this right is seen as a safeguard of people's liberty.

Activity

Find out whether the Fraud (Trials without a Jury) Bill 2006 is now an Act. Try looking on the Internet at *www.opsi.gov.uk*. If it is not there, look at *www.parliament.uk* to see if the Bill is still going through Parliament.

13.1.5 Sending cases to the Crown Court

Where the trial is going to be held at the Crown Court, the magistrates must officially send the case to the Crown Court.

For indictable offences the case is transferred to the Crown Court immediately from the first hearing at the Magistrates' Court. This is under s 51 of the Crime and Disorder Act 1998. For triable either way offences, magistrates will hold a plea before venue and, if the defendant pleads not guilty, a mode of trial hearing. If, at this hearing it is decided that the case is to be tried in the Crown Court, the magistrates will then transfer the case to the Crown Court.

13.1.6 Committal proceedings

Magistrates can commit a defendant charged with a triable either way offence for sentence to the Crown Court. However this will only happen when, at the end of a case, having heard the defendant's past record, they feel that their powers of punishment are insufficient.

The magistrates must be of the opinion that the offence, or the combination of offences, is so serious that a greater punishment than they have power to inflict should be imposed. In cases of violent or sexual offences, the magistrates may commit for sentence if they think that a long sentence of imprisonment is necessary to protect the public from serious harm.

After the introduction of plea before venue (see section 13.1.3) the number of committals for sentence more than doubled. About 28,000 defendants each year are sent by the magistrates to the Crown Court for sentencing. There are criticisms that magistrates commit too many defendants for sentence, since a significant percentage of those committed for sentence do not receive more than the magistrate could have imposed on them.

The number of defendants who need to be committed to the Crown Court for sentence will reduce when the magistrates' sentencing power is increased to 15 months.

13.1.7 The role of the clerk

Every bench of magistrates is assisted by a clerk who is also known as legal adviser. The senior clerk in each court has to be a barrister or solicitor of at least five years' standing. The role of the clerk is to guide the magistrates on questions of law, practice and procedure. The clerk makes sure that the correct procedure is followed in court. For example, at the start of a case it is the clerk who will ask the defendant if he pleads guilty or not guilty. The clerk is not meant to take part in the decision-making process; that is the magistrates' role. This means that the clerk should not retire with the justices when they leave the court at the end of a case to consider their verdict.

The senior clerk has been granted greater powers to deal with routine matters which previously had to be done by magistrates. For example clerks can now issue warrants for arrest, extend police bail, adjourn criminal proceedings (where the defendant is on bail and the terms on the bail are not being changed), and conduct early administrative hearings.

13.2 Youth Courts

Young offenders aged from 10 to 17 are dealt with in the Youth Court which is a branch of the Magistrates' Court. Children under the age of 10 cannot be charged with a criminal offence.

There are some exceptional cases in which young offenders can be tried in the Crown Court. These are cases where the defendant is charged with murder or manslaughter, rape, and causing death by dangerous driving. In addition it is possible for those aged 14 and over, to be sent to the Crown Court for trial in any case where they are charged with a serious offence (usually one which for an adult carries a maximum prison sentence of at least 14 years).

The Youth Court sits in private, with only those who are involved in the case allowed into the court room. Members of the press may be present, but they cannot publish the name of any young offender or other information which could identify him, such as address or school.

The magistrates who sit on the bench in these courts must be under 65 and have had special training to deal with young offenders. There must be at least one female magistrate and one male magistrate on the bench. The procedure in the court is less formal than in the adult courts and the parents or guardian any child under 16 are required to be present for the proceedings. The court can also ask parents of those aged 16 or 17 to attend.

13.3 Appeals from the Magistrates' Court

There is a system of appeal routes available from a decision by the Magistrates' Court. The route used will depend on whether the appeal is only on a point of law, or whether it is for other reasons. The two appeal routes are to the Crown Court, or to the Queen's Bench Divisional Court.

13.3.1 Appeals to the Crown Court

This is the normal route of appeal and is only available to the defence. If the defendant pleaded guilty at the Magistrates' Court, then he can only appeal against sentence. If the defendant pleaded not guilty and was convicted, then the appeal can be against conviction and/or sentence. In both cases the defendant has an automatic right to appeal and does not need to get leave (permission) to appeal.

At the Crown Court the case is completely re-heard by a judge and two magistrates. They can come to the same decision as the magistrates and confirm the conviction, or they can decide that the case is not proved and reverse the decision. In some cases it is possible for them to vary the decision and find the defendant guilty of a lesser offence.

Where the appeal is against sentence, the Crown Court can confirm the sentence or they can increase or decrease it. However, any increase can only be up to the magistrates' maximum powers for the case.

Over the last few years there have been about 12,000 appeals to the Crown Court each year, and judicial statistics published by the Lord Chancellor Department show that the appeal is allowed in approximately one quarter of cases, while the magistrates' order is varied in about another quarter. This means that about half of those who appeal have some success.

If it becomes apparent that there is a point of law to be decided, then the Crown Court can decide that point of law, but there is the possibility of a further appeal by way of a case stated appeal being made to the Queen's Bench Divisional Court (see section 13.3.2). A diagram setting out the appeal routes from the Magistrates' Court is shown in Figure 13.3.

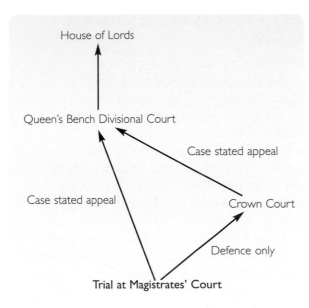

Figure 13.3 *Appeal routes from the Magistrates' Court*

13.3.2 Case stated appeals

These are appeals on a point of law which go to the Queen's Bench Divisional Court. Both the prosecution and the defence can use this appeal route and it can be direct from the Magistrates' Court, or following an appeal to the Crown Court. The magistrates (or the Crown Court) are asked to state the case by setting out their findings of fact and their decision. The appeal is then argued on the basis of what the law is on those facts; no witnesses are called. The appeal is heard by a panel of two or three High Court judges from the Queen's Bench Division, though in some cases a judge from the Court of Appeal may form part of the panel.

This route is only used by the defendant against a conviction, or by the prosecution against an acquittal. It cannot be used to challenge the sentence. The appeal is because they claim the magistrates came to the wrong decision because they made a mistake about the law. The Divisional Court may confirm,

vary or reverse the decision or remit (send back) the case to the Magistrates' Court for the magistrates to implement the decision on the law.

There are only a small number of appeals by way of case stated made each year. In 2003 there were 116 appeals to the Queen's Bench Divisional Court.

Further appeal to the House of Lords

From the decision of the Queen's Bench Divisional Court there is a possibility of a further appeal to the House of Lords. Such an appeal can only be made if:

1. The Divisional Court certifies that a point of law of general public importance is involved.

2. The Divisional Court or the House of Lords gives leave (permission) to appeal because the point is one which ought to be considered by the House of Lords.

An example of a case which followed this appeal route was *C v DPP* (1994). This case concerned the legal point about the presumption of criminal responsibility of children from the age of 10 up to their fourteenth birthday. Until this case, it had been accepted that a child of this age could only be convicted if the prosecution proved that the child knew he was doing wrong. The Divisional Court held that times had changed and that children were more mature and the rule was not needed. They decided that children of this age were presumed to know the difference between right and wrong, and that the prosecution, did not need to prove 'mischievous discretion'.

The case was then appealed to the House of Lords who overruled the Divisional Court, holding that the law was still that a child of this age was presumed not to know he or she was doing wrong, and therefore not to have the necessary intention for any criminal offence. A child of this age could only be convicted if the prosecution disproved this presumption by bringing evidence to show that the child was aware that what he or she was doing was seriously wrong. The House of Lords ruling was on the basis that it was for Parliament to make such a major change to the law, not the courts. The courts were bound by precedent.

13.4 The Crown Court

Until 1971 very serious criminal cases were dealt with by High Court judges when they toured the country holding Assize Courts. Other indictable offences were heard at Quarter Sessions, which were intended to sit four times a year. This system was out of date and unable to cope with the growing number of criminal cases – following the Beeching Commission Report 1969, both Assizes and Quarter Sessions were abolished. In their place, the Courts Act 1971 set up the Crown Court to deal with all cases which were not tried at the Magistrates' Court.

The Crown Court currently sits in 90 different centres throughout England and Wales. There are three kinds of centre:

1. **First tier**
   These exist in main centres throughout the country, for example there are first tier Crown Courts in Bristol, Birmingham, Leeds and Manchester. At each court there is a High Court and a Crown Court with separate judges for civil and criminal work. The Crown Court is permanently staffed by High Court judges as well as Circuit judges and Recorders, and the court can deal with all categories of crime triable on indictment.

2. **Second tier**
   This is a Crown Court only, but High Court judges sit there on a regular basis to hear criminal cases, as well as Circuit judges and Recorders. All categories of crime triable on indictment can be tried here.

3. **Third tier**
   This is staffed only by Circuit judges and Recorders. The most serious cases, such as murder, manslaughter and rape are not usually tried here as there is no High Court judge to deal with them.

13.4.1 Preliminary matters

The indictment

This is a document which formally sets out the charges against the defendant. Although the defendant will have been sent for trial charged with specific crimes, the indictment can be drawn up for any offence that the witness statements reveal. In more complicated cases the indictment may be for several counts. Figure 13.4 shows a sample indictment.

Criminal Procedure Rules

Criminal Procedure Rules to deal with all aspects of criminal cases came into force in April 2005. The overriding objective of the Rules is that 'criminal cases be dealt with justly'.

Disclosure by prosecution and defence

The Criminal Procedure and Investigations Act 1996 places a duty on both sides to make certain points known to the other. The prosecution, who have already given the defence statements of all the evidence they propose to use at the trial, must also disclose previously undisclosed material 'which in the prosecutor's opinion might reasonably be considered capable of undermining the case for the prosecution against the accused'. This is designed to prevent the sort of miscarriage of justice which occurred in Stefan Kiszko's case (see Chapter 8) through the prosecution 'hiding' something which could help prove the innocence of the defendant.

DONBRIDGE CROWN COURT

The Queen v John Wilkie
charged as follows:

STATEMENT OF OFFENCE
Murder contrary to the common law

PARTICULARS OF OFFENCE
John Wilkie on the 4th day of April 1997 murdered
Abraham Lincoln

Figure 13.4 Sample indictment

The 1996 Act also imposes a duty on the defence in cases which are to be tried on indictment. In these, after the prosecution's primary disclosure, the defence must give a written statement to the prosecution setting out:

- the nature of the accused's defence, including any particular defences on which he intends to rely
- the matters of fact on which he takes issue with the prosecution and why he takes issue
- any point of law which he wishes to take, and the case authority on which he will be relying.

The defendant also has to give details about any alibi and the witnesses he intends calling to support that alibi. This information allows the prosecution to run police checks on the alibi witnesses.

Plea and case management hearing

Under the Criminal Procedure Rules, most cases sent to the Crown Court are dealt with first at a plea and case management hearing (PCMH). The first purpose of a PCMH is to find out whether the defendant is pleading guilty or not guilty. All the charges on the indictment are read out to the defendant in open court, and he is asked how he pleads to each charge. This process is called the 'arraignment'.

If the defendant pleads guilty, the judge will, if possible, sentence the defendant immediately. This means that defendants who plead guilty will not have an unnecessarily long wait for their case to come to court.

Where a defendant pleads not guilty the judge will require the prosecution and defence to identify the key issues, both of fact and law, that are involved in the case. He will then give any directions that are necessary to organise the actual trial, for instance the prosecution and defence may agree that certain witnesses need not attend court as their evidence is not in dispute. Other points such as whether it will be necessary to use a video link for any witnesses are also agreed on. The aim of the PCMH is to speed up the actual trial process and to ensure that time will not be wasted on unnecessary points. It also allows the court to plan its lists.

The Criminal Procedure Rules encourage active case management. Case management in the Crown Court includes:

- the early identification of the real issues
- the early identification of the needs of witnesses
- achieving a certainty as to what must be done, by whom, and when, in particular by the early setting of a timetable for the progress of a case
- monitoring the progress of the case and compliance with directions

- ensuring that the evidence, whether disputed or not, is presented in the shortest and clearest way
- discouraging delay, dealing with as many aspects of the case as possible on the same occasion, and avoiding unnecessary hearings
- encouraging the participants to co-operate in the progression of the case and
- making use of technology.

The full Criminal Procedure Rules are available online on the DCA website, *www.dca.gov.uk*.

13.4.2 The trial

It is normal for a defendant appearing at the Crown Court to be represented, usually by a barrister, although solicitors who have a certificate of advocacy can also appear at the Crown Court. Defendants can represent themselves, but there was concern over the effect this could have on witnesses who were cross-examined at length by a defendant in person. As a result the Youth Justice and Criminal Evidence Act 1999 forbids cross-examination in person by defendants who are charged with sexual offences, or where there is a child witness.

At the trial where the defendant pleads not guilty, the order of events will normally be:

1. The jury is sworn in to try the case (for further information on juries see Chapter 18).
2. The prosecution will make an opening speech to the jury explaining what the case is about and what they intend to prove.
3. The prosecution witnesses give evidence and can be cross-examined by the defence; the prosecution will also produce any other evidence such as documents or video recordings.
4. At the end of the prosecution case the defence may submit that there is no case to go to the jury; if the judge decides there is

no case he will direct the jury to acquit the defendant.

5. The defence may make an opening speech provided they intend calling evidence other than the defendant.
6. The defence witnesses give evidence and are cross-examined by the prosecution; the defendant does not have to give evidence personally but the judge may comment on the failure to do in his summing up to the jury.
7. The prosecutor makes a closing speech to the jury pointing out the strengths of the prosecution case.
8. The defence makes a closing speech to the jury pointing out the weaknesses of the prosecution.
9. The judge sums up the case to the jury and directs them on any relevant law.
10. The jury retire to consider their verdict in private.
11. The jury's verdict is given in open court.
12. If the verdict is guilty the judge then sentences the accused; if the verdict is not guilty the accused is discharged. Normally, once a defendant is found not guilty he can never be tried for that offence again. However, the Criminal Justice Act 2003 removes this 'double jeopardy' rule for serious cases if 'new and compelling evidence' comes to light, so that a defendant can be tried a second time.

13.5 Appeals from the Crown Court

It is important that there should be adequate routes of appeal. The functions of an appeal process serve not only to protect the defendant from a miscarriage of justice, but also to allow uniform development of the law. Figure 13.5 shows appeal routes from the Crown Court.

13.5.1 Appeals by the defendant

The defendant has the possibility of appealing against conviction and/or sentence to the Court of Appeal (Criminal Division). So, at the end of any trial in which a defendant has been found guilty, his lawyer should advise him on the possibility of an appeal. This must be done verbally at the court, or in writing within 14 days of the trial. It is intended to make sure that each defendant has advice within the time limits for making an appeal. In order to appeal, a notice of appeal must be filed at the Court of Appeal (Criminal Division) within 28 days of conviction.

Leave to appeal

The rules on appeals are set out in the Criminal Appeal Act 1995 and in all cases the defendant must get leave to appeal from the Court of Appeal, or a certificate that the case is fit for appeal from the trial judge. The idea of having to get leave is that cases which are without merit are filtered out and the court's time saved.

The application for leave to appeal is considered by a single judge of the Court of Appeal in private, although if he refuses it is possible to apply to a full Court of Appeal for leave. It is difficult to get leave to appeal – in 2003, 7,451 applications were considered by a single judge, but leave to appeal was granted in only 2,218 cases (about 30 per cent). Even when a defendent gets leave to appeal that does not mean that the actual appeal will be successful.

The Criminal Appeal Act 1995

The Criminal Appeal Act 1995 simplified the grounds under which the court can allow an appeal. The Act states that the Court of Appeal:

'(a) shall allow an appeal against conviction if they think that the conviction is unsafe; and

(b) shall dismiss such an appeal in any other case.'

Since the European Convention on Human Rights has been incorporated into our law by the Human Rights Act 1998, the Court of Appeal has taken a broad approach to the meaning of 'unsafe'. In particular, a conviction has been held to be 'unsafe' where the defendant has been denied a fair trial.

New evidence

Any new evidence must appear to be capable of belief and would afford a ground for an appeal. This has to be considered together with whether it would have been admissible at the trial and why it was not produced at that trial.

Court of Appeal's powers

The Court of Appeal can allow a defendant's appeal and quash the conviction. Alternatively it can vary the conviction to that of a lesser offence of which the jury could have convicted the defendant. As far as sentencing is concerned the court can decrease, but not increase it on the defendant's appeal. Where the appeal is not successful, the court can decide to dismiss the appeal.

The Court of Appeal also has the power to order that there should be a re-trial of the case in front of a new jury. The power was given to it in 1988, but initially was not often used, for example, in 1989 only one re-trial was ordered. However, its use has increased with between 50 and 70 re-trials being ordered each year.

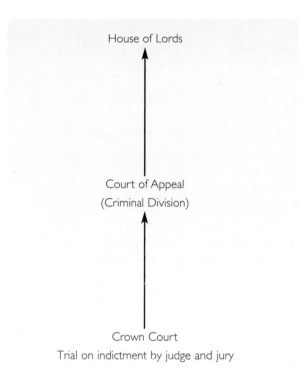

House of Lords

Court of Appeal
(Criminal Division)

Crown Court
Trial on indictment by judge and jury

Figure 13.5 *Appeal routes from the Crown Court*

13.5.2 Appeals by the prosecution

Originally the prosecution had no right to appeal against either the verdict or sentence passed in the Crown Court. Gradually, however, some limited rights of appeal have been given to them by Parliament.

Against an acquittal

With one small exception, the prosecution cannot appeal against a finding of not guilty by a jury. The exception is for cases where the acquittal was the result of the jury or witnesses being 'nobbled', i.e. where some jurors are bribed or threatened by associates of the defendant. In these circumstances, provided there has been an actual conviction for jury nobbling, the Criminal Procedure and Investigations Act 1996 allows an application to be made to the High Court for an order quashing the acquittal. Once the acquittal is quashed, the prosecution could then start new proceedings for the same offence. As yet this power has never been used.

Referring a point of law

However, the prosecution have a special referral right in cases where the defendant is acquitted. This is under s 36 of the Criminal Justice Act 1972 which allows the Attorney-General to refer a point of law to the Court of Appeal, in order to get a ruling on the law. The decision by the Court of Appeal on that point of law does not affect the acquittal but it creates a precedent for any future case involving the same point of law.

Against sentence

Under s 36 of the Criminal Justice Act 1988 the Attorney-General can apply for leave to refer an unduly lenient sentence to the Court of Appeal for re-sentencing. This power was initially available for indictable cases only, but was extended in 1994 to many triable either way offences, provided that the trial of the case took place at a Crown Court. This power is used successfully in a number of cases each year. There has recently been an increase in the number of such referrals.

One case which was referred in 2004 was that of Luan Plakici, who had been found guilty of kidnapping, procuring girls for sex and living off prostitution. He had brought young girls into Britain from Eastern Europe and then forced them to work as prostitutes. At his trial he was sentenced to ten years' imprisonment. On the Attorney-General's reference, the Court of Appeal increased this to 23 years' imprisonment.

The main difficulty is: how does the Attorney-General learn of cases which ought to be referred to the Court of Appeal? In fact, about 300 cases are brought to the Attorney-General's attention each year, with most of

Party	Court which hears appeal	Reason for appealing	Relevant Act of Parliament
Defence	Court of Appeal	against sentence and/or conviction need leave to appeal	Criminal Appeal Act 1995 conviction 'unsafe'
Defence	Further appeal to House of Lords	on point of law of general public importance need leave to appeal	
Prosecution	High Court	asking for order to quash acquittal because of interference with witness or jury	Criminal Procedure and Investigations Act 1996
Prosecution	Court of Appeal	Attorney-General's reference on a point of law: does not affect acquittal	Criminal Justice Act 1972
Prosecution	Court of Appeal	Attorney-General against lenient sentence	Criminal Justice Act 1988
Prosecution	Further appeal to House of Lords	on point of law of general public importance need leave to appeal	

Figure 13.6 *Key fact chart on appeal rights from the Crown Court*

these being sent to him by the Crown Prosecution Service. However, it is possible for the public to write to the Attorney-General's office and a small number of cases a year are reported in this way, usually by distressed relatives of the victim of the crime, who feel that the original sentence was inadequate. Members of Parliament will also sometimes refer cases to the Attorney-General on behalf of aggrieved constituents.

Whenever a case is sent to the Attorney-General he will look through the papers on the trial and decide whether to refer the case to the Court of Appeal.

13.5.3 Appeals to the House of Lords

Both the prosecution and the defence may appeal from the Court of Appeal to the House of Lords, but it is necessary to have the case certified as involving a point of law of general public importance, and to get leave to appeal, either from the House of Lords or from the

Court of Appeal. There are very few criminal appeals heard by the House of Lords. In 2003 there were 22 petitions for leave to appeal considered, but leave was granted in only seven of these.

References to the European Court of Justice

Where a point of European law is involved in a case it is possible for any court to make a reference to the European Court of Justice under Article 177 of the Treaty of Rome (see Chapter 6). However, this is a fairly rare occurrence in criminal cases, as most of the criminal law is purely 'domestic' and not affected by European Union law.

13.6 The Criminal Cases Review Commission

The large number of miscarriages of justice (see section 11.1.2) which had not been corrected through the normal appeal system led to demands for a review body. It was true that the Home Secretary had power to review cases and refer them to the Court of Appeal, but cases such as the Birmingham Six and Judith Ward left people feeling that the Home Secretary was not sufficiently independent of the Government. The Runciman Commission, when considering the question, recommended that an independent review body should be set up to consider possible miscarriages of justice. This recommendation was implemented by the Criminal Appeal Act 1995 which set up the Criminal Cases Review Commission.

The Commission has the power to investigate possible miscarriages of justice (including summary offences) and to refer cases back to the courts. In addition the Court of Appeal may direct the Commission to investigate and report to the court on any matter which comes before it in an appeal if it feels an investigation is likely to help the court resolve the appeal.

The members of the Commission are appointed by the Queen – at least one third are legally qualified and at least two thirds have relevant experience of the criminal justice system. They have about 60 support staff, treble the number previously used in the Home Office for such work. However, most of the re-investigation work is done by the police. This is felt to be unsatisfactory as it does not really make such a re-investigation independent, although it is true to say that many of the past miscarriages of justice have come to light as the result of investigation by other police forces.

Work

The Criminal Cases Review Commission took over the investigation of miscarriages of justice at the beginning of April 1997.

The main bulk of cases it investigates are brought to its attention by defendants themselves or by defendants' families, though some cases have been referred by the Court of Appeal and others have been identified by the Commission itself. Some of the first cases it investigated were alleged miscarriages of justice from over 40 years ago, such as the case of Derek Bentley. Bentley was hanged for murder in 1953, while his co-defendant, Craig, who actually fired the fatal shot, was not hanged due to his youth. Over the years there have been many attempts to have the case re-opened but it was not until the Criminal Cases Review Commission took over the investigation that the case was referred back to the Court of Appeal. In July 1998 the Court of Appeal held that the summing-up of the judge at the trial had not been fair and it quashed the conviction.

Other cases are more recent, such as the case of Ryan James who was convicted in 1995 of murdering his wife. A year after his trial an apparent suicide note written by his wife was found. This was investigated by the Commission and the decision made to refer the case back to the Court of Appeal. Mr James' conviction was then quashed by the Court of Appeal in 1998.

Referrals to the Court of Appeal

By September 2006 the Criminal Cases Review Commission had received over 9,000 applications and had dealt with about 8,300 of these. The Commission had referred 341 cases to the Court of Appeal – 291 of these had been heard and the convictions quashed in 199 cases.

Recent cases included that of Sally Clark who, in 2003, had her conviction for murdering her two babies quashed after the scientific evidence was shown to be flawed. In 2004, Sion Jenkins' conviction for the murder of his foster daughter was quashed, also because of flawed scientific evidence.

Activity

Check the website for the Criminal Cases Review Commission *(www.ccrc.gov.uk)* and find out:

1. How many cases has the Commission now dealt with?

2. How many cases has it referred to the Court of Appeal?

3. In how many cases has the defendant had his or her conviction quashed?

Examination Questions

Baldrick has been charged with the theft of a large quantity of turnips.

Theft is a triable either way offence.

(i) Describe how the decision is made as to which court the case is tried in.

(ii) Discuss the advantages and disadvantages to Baldrick of being tried in either court.

Part of a question, OCR 2568, January 2002

Chapter 14

Sentencing

14.1 The role of the courts

Whenever a person pleads guilty, or is found guilty of an offence, the role of the court is to decide what sentence should be imposed on the offender. Judges and magistrates have a fairly wide discretion as to the sentence they select in each case, although they are subject to certain restrictions. Magistrates can only impose a maximum of six months' imprisonment for one offence (12 months' for two) and a maximum fine of £5,000. The Criminal Justice Act 2003 has provision for these sentencing powers to increase to 12 months for one offence and 15 months for two or more offences. Judges in the Crown Court have no such limits; they can impose up to life imprisonment for some crimes and there is no

maximum figure for fines. Figure 14.1 shows the percentages of different sentences imposed in Magistrates' Courts and at the Crown Court in 2005. The differing percentages of offenders given an immediate custodial sentence stresses that the Crown Court is dealing with more serious offences.

14.1.1 Restrictions on the courts' powers

However, there are other restrictions, both in the Magistrates' Court and the Crown Court. Each crime has a maximum penalty for that type of offence set by Parliament – for example, the crime of theft has a fixed maximum of seven years' imprisonment, so that no matter how much has been stolen, the

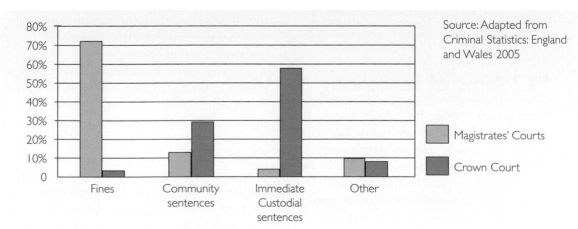

Source: Adapted from Criminal Statistics: England and Wales 2005

Figure 14.1 Sentencing in the Magistrates' Courts and Crown Court

judge can never send an offender to prison for longer that this. Some offences have a maximum sentence of life imprisonment: these include manslaughter and rape. In such cases the judge has complete discretion when sentencing; the offender may be sent to prison for life or given a shorter prison sentence, or a non-custodial sentence may even be thought appropriate. Murder is the exception as it carries a mandatory life sentence; in other words, the judge has to pass life imprisonment: there is no other sentence available.

14.1.2 Minimum sentences

Although Parliament has set down various maximum sentences for offences, there are no minimum sentences for first time offenders. However, Parliament in the Crime (Sentences) Act 1997 set down minimum sentences for some persistent offenders. This idea followed American laws which impose minimum sentences for those who offend repeatedly. As well as minimum sentences for drug dealers and burglars, the Crime (Sentences) Act 1997 brought in an automatic life sentence for those who commit a second serious or violent offence. These provisions were very controversial and are considered further in section 14.4.1.

14.2 Aims of sentencing

When judges or magistrates have to pass a sentence they will not only look at the sentences available, they will also have to decide what they are trying to achieve by the punishment they give. Section 142 of the Criminal Justice Act 2003 sets out the purposes of sentencing for those aged 18 and over saying that a court must have regard to:

- the punishment of offenders
- the reduction of crime (including its reduction by deterrence)
- the reform and rehabilitation of offenders)
- the protection of the public, and
- the making of reparation by offenders to persons affected by their offences.

Punishment is often referred to retribution. In addition to the purposes of sentencing given in the 2003 Act, denunciation of crime is also recognised as an aim of sentencing. Each of the aims will now be examined in turn.

14.2.1 Retribution

This is based on the idea of punishment because the offender deserves punishment for his or her acts. It does not seek to reduce crime or alter the offender's future behaviour. This idea was expressed in the nineteenth century by Kant in *The Metaphysical Elements of Justice* when he wrote:

'Judicial punishment can never be used merely as a means to promote some other good for the criminal himself or for civil society, but instead it must in all cases be imposed on him only on the ground that he has committed a crime.'

Retribution is therefore concerned only with the offence that was committed and making sure that the punishment inflicted is in proportion to that offence.

The crudest form of retribution can be seen in the old saying 'an eye for an eye and a tooth for a tooth and a life for a life'. This was one of the factors used to justify the death penalty for the offence of murder. In America, at least one judge has been known to put this theory into practice in other offences, by giving victims of burglary the right to go, with a law officer, to the home of the burglar and take items up to the approximate value of those stolen from them. In other crimes it is not so easy to see how this principle can operate to produce an exact match between crime and punishment.

Tariff sentences

Retribution, today, is based more on the idea that each offence should have a set tariff.

Some states in the USA operate a very rigid system in which each crime has a set tariff with the judge being allowed only to impose a penalty within the tariff range. This removes almost all the element of discretion in sentencing from the judges and ensures that sentences for offences are uniform. The objections to this are that it does not allow sufficient consideration of mitigating factors, and may produce a sentence which is unjust in the particular circumstances. The concept of retribution and giving the offender his 'just deserts' should not be so rigid as to ignore special needs of the offender.

There is also a problem in applying this principle to fines. A tariff system of fines involves having a fixed sum as the correct fine for particular offences, however, this takes no account of the financial situation of the offender. So a fine of £500 might be a very severe penalty for an offender who is unemployed, while the same amount would be negligible to a millionaire.

Revenge

Retribution contains an element of revenge: society (and the victim) is being avenged for the wrong done. It is on the basis of revenge that long prison sentences for causing death by dangerous or drink driving can be justified. In 1993 the Government, in response to public opinion, increased the maximum penalties available these offences from five years' to 10 years' imprisonment.

14.2.2 Denunciation

This is society expressing its disapproval of criminal activity. A sentence should indicate both to the offender and to other people that society condemns certain types of behaviour. It shows people that justice is being done. Lord Denning when giving written evidence to the Royal Commission on Capital Punishment put it in this way:

'Punishment is the way in which society expresses its denunciation of wrong doing: and in order to maintain respect for the law it is essential that the punishment inflicted for grave crimes should adequately reflect the revulsion felt by the great majority of citizens for them.'

Denunciation also reinforces the moral boundaries of acceptable conduct and can mould society's views on the criminality of particular conduct – for example, drink driving is now viewed by the majority of people as unacceptable behaviour. This is largely because of the changes in the law and the increasingly severe sentences that are imposed. By sending offenders to prison, banning them from driving and imposing heavy fines, society's opinion of drink driving has been changed.

The ideas of retribution and denunciation were foremost in the concepts behind the Criminal Justice Act 1991. That Act was based on the Government White Paper on Crime and Punishment (1990) which stated that: 'The first objective for all sentences is the denunciation of and retribution for crime.'

However, as already seen, this aim of sentencing is not included in the purposes of sentencing set out in the Criminal Justice Act 2003. This demonstrates how different purposes may be considered more at one time than at another.

14.2.3 Incapacitation or protection of the public

The concept behind this and the next three principles of sentencing is that the punishment must serve a useful purpose. Useful in this context can mean that it serves a purpose for society as a whole, or that it will help the offender in some way. Incapacitation means that in some way the offender is made incapable of re-offending. Of course, the ultimate method of incapacitation is the death penalty, and in some countries the hands of thieves are cut off to prevent them re-offending. Another controversial method of incapacitation is the use in some American states of medical means to incapacitate sex offenders, and thus ensure that they cannot re-offend.

The use of minimum sentences for persistent offenders is aimed at protecting the public from their repeated criminal activities. Electronic tagging of offenders is a method of protecting the public from the offender without having to send the offender to prison.

There are other penalties that can be viewed as incapacitating the offender – for example, in driving offences, the offender can be banned from driving. There is also a move to using community-based sentences that will incapacitate the offender in the short term and protect the public. These include exclusion orders under which an offender is banned from going to the place where he offends (usually a pub or a football ground), and curfew orders which order an offender to remain at a given address for certain times of the day or night.

14.2.4 Deterrence

This can be individual deterrence or general deterrence. Individual deterrence is intended to ensure that the offender does not re-offend, through fear of future punishment. General deterrence is aimed at preventing other potential offenders from committing crimes. Both are aimed at reducing future levels of crime.

Individual deterrence

There are several penalties that can be imposed with the aim of deterring the individual offender from committing similar crimes in the future. These include a prison sentence, a suspended sentence or a heavy fine. However, prison does not appear to deter as about 55 per cent of adult prisoners re-offend within two years of release. With young offenders, custodial sentences have even less of a deterrent effect. Over 70 per cent of young offenders given a custodial sentence re-offend within two years.

Critics of the theory of deterrence point out that it assumes that an offender will stop to consider what the consequences of his action will be. In fact most crimes are committed on the spur of the moment, and many are committed by offenders who are under the influence of drugs or alcohol. These offenders are unlikely to stop and consider the possible consequences of their actions.

It is also pointed out that fear of being caught is more of a deterrent and that while crime detection rates are low, the threat of an unpleasant penalty, if caught, seems too remote. Fear of detection has been shown to be a powerful deterrent by the success rate of closed circuit televisions used for surveying areas. In one scheme on London's District Line of the underground system there was an 83 per cent reduction in crime in the first full year that surveillance cameras were used.

General deterrence

The value of this is even more doubtful as potential offenders are rarely deterred by severe sentences passed on others. However,

Theory	Aim of theory	Suitable punishment
Retribution	Punishment imposed only on ground that an offence has been committed	• Tariff sentences • Sentence must be proportionate to the crime
Denunciation	Society expressing its disapproval Re-inforces moral boundaries	• Reflects blameworthiness of the offence
Incapacitation	Offender is made incapable of committing further crime Society is protected from crime	• Death penalty for murder • Long prison sentences • Tagging
Deterrence	Individual – the offender is deterred through fear of further punishment General – potential offenders warned as to likely punishment	• Prison sentence • Heavy fine • Long sentence as an example to others
Rehabilitation	Reform offender's behaviour	• Individualised sentence • Community sentence
Reparation	Repayment/reparation to victim or to community	• Compensation order • Unpaid work • Reparation schemes

Figure 14.2 *Key fact chart on aims of sentencing*

the courts do occasionally resort to making an example of an offender in order to warn other potential offenders of the type of punishment they face.

General deterrence also relies on publicity so that potential offenders are aware of the level of punishment they can expect. Deterrent sentences will, therefore, be even less effective in cases of drug smuggling by foreign nationals, yet this is one of the crimes in which the courts seem tempted to resort to the hope that a severe sentence passed on one (or more) offender, will somehow deter other potential offenders.

In 2002 crime statistics showed that in the previous year there had been about one million offences of street robbery involving taking a mobile phone. In an effort to deter offenders, the Lord Chief Justice said that stiffer sentences were needed and increased a sentence of six months to three and a half years. He also stated that offenders should be given a custodial sentence unless there were very exceptional circumstances.

General deterrence is in direct conflict with the principle of retribution, since it involves sentencing an offender to a longer term than is deserved for the specific offence. It is probably the least effective and least fair principle of sentencing.

14.2.5 Rehabilitation

Under this the main aim of the penalty is to reform the offender and rehabilitate him or her into society. It is a forward-looking aim, with the hope that the offender's behaviour will be altered by the penalty imposed, so that he or she will not offend in the future (it aims to reduce crime in this way). This principle of sentence came to the fore in the second half of the twentieth century with the development of community sentences.

As the abuse of drugs is the cause of many offences, there are also community sentences – drug testing and treatment orders and drug abstention orders – aimed at trying to rehabilitate drug abusers.

Reformation is a very important element in the sentencing philosophy for young offenders, but it is also used for some adult offenders. The court will be given information about the defendant's background, usually through a pre-sentence report prepared by the probation service. Where relevant, the court will consider other factors, such as school reports, job prospects, or medical problems.

Individualised sentences

Where the court considers rehabilitation, the sentence used is an individualised one aimed at the needs of the offender. This is in direct contrast to the concept of tariff-sentences seen in the aim of retribution. One of the criticisms of this approach is, therefore, that it leads to inconsistency in sentencing. Offenders who have committed exactly the same type of offence may be given different sentences because the emphasis is on the individual offender. Another criticism is that is tends to discriminate against the underprivileged. Offenders from poor home backgrounds are less likely to be seen as possible candidates for reform.

Activity

Read the following article and answer the questions below.

Unlocking the door to prison reform

The statutory purpose set out in the Prison Rules, first made under the Prisons Act 1898, is the rehabilitation of offenders. For years it has been accepted by those working in the prison service that this is an unattainable objective. But if rehabilitation is impracticable, what should be the object, or objects, of a prison sentence? So far there has been no answer. Is the purpose deterrence? Those with experience of the courts know that offenders with previous convictions are likely to reappear in the courts, whereas, for about 80 per cent of first offenders, appearing in court and being convicted – not the sentence imposed – is what deters.

No one knows whether prison sentences stop others from committing crime. Perhaps they do, but probably not among that section of society which seems to produce so many of the criminals.

By the Prisons Act 1865, Parliament approved a rigorous prison regime. Courts were empowered to impose sentences of imprisonment with hard labour. Some were put to work breaking stones in quarries, others excavating sites for new docks. The object was to make prisons terrifying places, but they did not stop recidivists.

The public conscience was disturbed by the brutality of the regime. In 1895, the Gladstone Committee was set up to report. It advised that the regime should be abandoned and that the object of prison administration should be rehabilitation. The Prisons Act 1898 was passed to implement the recommendations.

There is some value in imposing custodial sentences for the purpose of preventing crime. Persistent burglars cannot break into houses while in prison. Judges know that when they send a burglar with previous convictions to prison the probabilities are that he will take to crime again within weeks of being released. But if the prison sentences for this kind of offender are for the purpose of preventing crime, they should be longer, rather than shorter.

Twice this century, in 1908 and 1948, Parliament tackled this problem. In 1908 the offence of being a habitual offender was created. Juries did not like returning verdicts of guilty and the Act fell into disuse. The Criminal Justice Act 1948 gave judges power to pass extra long sentences on habitual offenders. Judges were reluctant to do so. By the 1960s few such sentences were being passed. The inference is that the public rejects the concept of a penal policy based on the prevention of crime by long sentences.

If rehabilitation is impractical, deterrence useless and sentencing for the prevention of crime unacceptable, what should be the purpose of a prison sentence? Of the four classical reasons for imposing prison sentences only retribution remains; but not in the sense of causing pain because of antecedent offences, but because society has to take action to show its disapproval of anti-social conduct. Since the 1820s, when most corporal punishments were abolished and the number of capital offences reduced from about 160 to four, the deprivation of liberty has become the only way of showing society's disapproval.

Taken from an article by Sir Frederick Lawton in
The Times, 27 August 1991

Questions

1. The article identifies four 'classical' reasons for imposing prison sentences; what are they?

2. Which one does the author give as the only valid reason for imposing a prison sentence?

3. Why does he reject the other three?

4. Do you agree with his arguments in rejecting these other three? Give reasons for your answer.

Persistent offenders are usually thought less likely to respond to a reformative sentence. The Powers of Criminal Courts (Sentencing) Act 2000 states that, in considering the seriousness of an offence, the court may take into consideration any previous failures to respond to previous sentences.

14.2.6 Reparation

This is aimed at compensating the victim of the crime usually by ordering the offender to pay a sum of money to the victim or to make restitution, for example, by returning stolen property to its rightful owner. The idea that criminals should pay compensation to the victims of their crimes is one that goes back to before the Norman Conquest to the Anglo-Saxon courts. In England today, the courts are required to consider ordering compensation to the victim of a crime, in addition to any other penalty they may think appropriate. Under s 130 of the Powers of Criminal Courts (Sentencing) Act 2000 courts are under a duty to give reasons if they do not make a compensation order. There are also projects to bring offenders and victims together, so that the offenders may make direct reparation.

The concept of restitution also includes making reparation to society as a whole. This can be seen mainly in the use of an unpaid work requirement where offenders are required to do so many hours work on a community project under the supervision of the probation service.

14.3 Sentencing practice in the courts

The court will usually consider both the offence and the background of the offender, as well as the aims of sentencing. In order to do this, the court must know details of the offence, so where the defendant pleads guilty the prosecution will outline the facts of the case. As seen in Chapter 13, the defendant is asked if he agrees with those facts and, if not, a Newton hearing will be held for the facts to be established. This is important as the details of the offence can affect the sentence. Where the defendant has pleaded not guilty and been convicted after a trial, the court will have heard full information about the case during the trial.

14.3.1 Factors surrounding the offence

In looking at the offence, the most important point to establish is how serious was it, of its type? This is now set out in s 143(1) of the Criminal Justice Act 2003 which states that:
'In considering the seriousness of the offence, the court must consider the offender's culpability in committing the offence and any harm which the offence caused, or was intended to cause or might reasonably forseeably have caused.'

The Act goes on to give certain factors which are considered as aggravating factors making an offence more serious. These are:

- previous convictions for offences of a similar nature or relevant to the present offence
- the fact that the defendant was on bail when he committed the offence
- racial or religious hostility being involved in the offence
- hostility to disability or sexual orientation being involved in the offence

Other points the courts will want to know may include, for example in a case of theft, how much was stolen, and was the defendant in a position of trust? In a case of assault the court will need to know what injuries were inflicted and whether the assault was premeditated;

was the victim particularly vulnerable (perhaps elderly).

Where the offender in a position of trust and abused that trust, then the offence will be considered as being more serious and meriting a longer than usual sentence.

Where several defendants are convicted of committing a crime jointly, the court will want to know if any of them played a greater part than the others, and who was involved in planning it. The sentences that each receive will reflect the part they played in the offence.

14.3.2 Reduction in sentence for a guilty plea

There can be a reduction in sentence for a guilty plea, particularly where made early in the proceedings. The Sentencing Guidelines Council has suggested that the reduction for a guilty plea at the first reasonable opportunity should attract a reduction of up to one-third, whereas a plea of guilty after the trial has started would only be given a one-tenth reduction. The amount of reduction is on a sliding scale as shown in Figure 14.3.

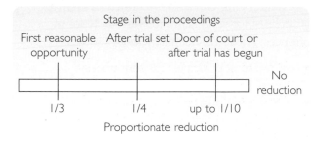

Figure 14.3 *Reduction in sentence for a guilty plea*

The concept of reducing the level of sentence imposed on a defendant just because he has pleaded guilty has caused controversy. Many people believe that if someone has 'done the crime, they should do the time'. However, in its draft guidelines, the Sentencing Guidelines

Council gave its reasons for allowing discounts in sentences for guilty pleas by stating:

'A reduction in sentence is appropriate because a guilty plea avoids the need for a trial, shortens the gap between charge and sentence, saves considerable cost, and, in the case of an early plea, saves victims and witnesses from the concern about having to give evidence.'

After publicity about cases where defendants had had their sentences reduced because they pleaded guilty, the Government decided to change the law. It felt that where there was abundant evidence that an offender was guilty, that offender should not be rewarded for pleading guilty. It is intended to give judges more discretion about the amount of 'time off' offenders should be given for a guilty plea. This should be in effect by late 2007.

14.3.3 The offender's background

Previous convictions

As far as the offender is concerned, the court will want to know whether he has any previous convictions. The court may also take into account the failure of an offender to respond to previous sentences, in deciding the seriousness of the current offence. The past record of the offender will also determine whether he has to receive a minimum sentence or an automatic life sentence for certain offences.

Another important factor is whether the offender was on bail when he committed the offence. If this is the case, the court must treat that fact as an aggravating factor.

Pre-sentence reports

These are prepared by the probation service. The court does not have to (but usually will) consider such a report before deciding to impose a custodial sentence, though for very serious offences such a report may not be relevant. Where the court is considering a community sentence, they are likely to have a report before they decide on the sentence. The report will give information about the defendant's background and suitability, or otherwise, for a community-based sentence. The defendant's background may be important in showing both why the offender committed a crime, and indicate if he is likely to respond to a community-based penalty.

Medical reports

Where the offender has medical or psychiatric problems, the court will usually ask for a report to be prepared by an appropriate doctor. Medical conditions may be important factors in deciding the appropriate way of dealing with the offender; the courts have special powers where the defendant is suffering from mental illness. The treatment of mentally ill defendants is considered further in section 14.6.

The financial situation of the offender

Where the court considers that a fine is a suitable penalty, it must inquire into the financial circumstances of the offender, and take this into account when setting the level of the fine.

14.3.4 Sentencing guidelines

Originally the Court of Appeal used to issue sentencing guidelines on the correct level of sentencing for certain types of offence. However, they could only do this when a suitable case came before them. For example, in *R* v *Billam* (1986) the court laid down tariffs for rape cases. In 1998 the Sentencing Advisory Panel was formed to give advice to the Court of Appeal on guidelines. But this is only an advisory body and has no power to issue its own guidelines.

Sentencing Guidelines Council

In 2003 the Sentencing Guidelines Council was set up under the Criminal Justice Act 2003. This Council can decide to issue guidelines on any aspect of sentencing. Also, if the Secretary of State or the Sentencing Advisory Panel makes a proposal to the Council that there should be guidelines for a particular offence or aspect of sentencing, then the Council must make guidelines on that point.

When the Sentencing Guidelines Council decides to make guidelines, it must have regard to:

- the need for consistency in sentencing
- the sentences imposed by courts for offences of the relevant category
- the cost of different sentences and their relative effectiveness in preventing re-offending
- the need to promote public confidence in the criminal justice system
- the views of the Sentencing Advisory Panel.

The Sentencing Guidelines Council has issued guidelines for sentencing for various types of offences. These guidelines include:

- overarching principles for seriousness factors in offences
- overarching principles on sentencing in domestic violence cases
- specific guidance on sentencing for robbery
- specific guidance for sentences in cases of manslaughter where there was provocation.

For this last category the Council stresses that:

- sentences for public protection *must* be considered in all cases of manslaughter; and
- the degree of provocation is a critical factor in deciding the sentence.

The guidelines for this are:

Degree of provocation	Sentence range	Starting point
Low	10 years to life	12 years' custody
Substantial	4–9 years	8 years' custody
High	if custody is absolutely necessary, up to 4 years	3 years' custody

Figure 14.4 Sentencing guidelines on manslaughter through provocation

14.4 Powers of the courts

As already indicated, the courts have several different types of sentences available to them. There are four main categories: custodial sentences, community sentences, fines and discharges. The courts also have the power to make additional orders such as compensation orders, and, in motoring offences have other powers such as disqualification from driving.

14.4.1 Custodial sentences

A custodial sentence is the most serious punishment that a court can impose. Custodial sentences range from 'weekend' prison to life imprisonment. They include:

- mandatory and discretionary life sentences
- fixed term sentences
- custody plus (short-term sentence)
- intermittent custody
- suspended sentences.

Custodial sentences are meant to be used only for serious offences. Section 152 of the Criminal Justice Act 2003 says that the court must not pass a custodial sentence unless it is of the opinion that the offence (or combination of offences):

'was so serious that neither a fine alone nor a community sentence can be justified.'

The age of the offender is also important as young offenders should only be given a custodial sentence as a last resort. Where a young offender is given a custodial sentence they are always held in separate units from adults.

The court must state its reason for imposing a custodial sentence, and in the case of the Magistrates' Court, that reason must be written on the warrant of commitment and entered in the court register.

In the guidelines on suggested 'entry points' published by the Magistrates' Association, a custodial sentence is advised for offences such as assaulting a police officer in the execution of his duty, and burglary of a residential property.

Mandatory life sentences

The only sentence a judge can impose for murder is a life sentence. However, the judge is allowed to state the minimum number of years' imprisonment that the offender must serve before being eligible for release on licence. This minimum term is now governed by s 269 and Sched 21 to the Criminal Justice Act 2003. This gives judges clear starting points for the minimum period to be ordered. The starting points range from a full life term down to 12 years. A whole life term should be set where the offence falls into one of the following categories:

- the murder of two or more persons, where each murder involves a substantial degree of premeditation or planning or the abduction of the victim or sexual or sadistic conduct
- the murder of a child if involving the abduction of the child or sexual or sadistic motivation
- a murder done for the purpose of advancing a political, religious or ideological cause, or
- a murder by an offender previously convicted of murder.

Cases which have a starting point of 30 years include where the murder is of a police or prison officer in the course of his duty, or a murder using a firearm or explosive or the sexual or sadistic murder of an adult or a murder that is racially or religiously aggravated. For any offence of murder which is not specifically given a starting point of a whole life term or 30 years, a starting point of 15 years is given. Where the offender was under the age of 18 at the time of the offence this period is 12 years. Once the judge has decide on the starting point, any aggravating or mitigating factors must then be considered.

Aggravating factors which can increase the minimum term ordered by the judge include the fact that the victim was particularly vulnerable because of age or disability, or any mental or physical suffering inflicted on the victim before death. Mitigating factors include the fact that the offender had an intention to cause grievous bodily harm rather than an intention to kill, a lack of premeditation or the fact that the offender acted to some extent in self-defence (though not sufficient to give him

a defence). Where there are mitigating factors the judge can set a minimum term of less than any of the starting points.

A sentence of life imprisonment has normally to be imposed where an offender over the age of 18 is convicted of a second serious sexual or violent offence. The judge can set an appropriate minimum time to be served in prison. Where there are 'exceptional circumstances' the judge does not have to impose a life sentence.

Discretionary life sentences

For other serious offences such as manslaughter, rape and robbery the maximum sentence is life imprisonment, but the judge does not have to impose it. The judge has a discretion in sentencing and can give any lesser sentence where appropriate. This can even be a fine or a discharge.

Fixed-term sentences

For other crimes, the length of the sentence will depend on several factors, including the maximum sentence available for the particular

Inside of a prison

crime, the seriousness of the crime and the defendant's previous record. Imprisonment for a set number of months or years is called a 'fixed-term' sentence.

Prisoners do not serve the whole of the sentence passed by the court. Anyone sent to prison is automatically released after they have served half of the sentence. Only offenders aged 21 and over can be given a sentence of imprisonment.

Home Detention Curfew

The Crime and Disorder Act 1998 allows early release from prison on condition that a curfew condition is included. The period of curfew is increased with the length of sentence. There is no automatic right to be released on curfew; each prisoner is assessed to see if he or she is suitable. If a Home Detention Curfew order is not made, then the prisoner must serve half the sentence before release on licence.

The reason for introducing such Home Detention Curfews is to encourage recently released prisoners to structure their lives more effectively as well as prevent re-offending. Also by releasing prisoners early in this way the prison population is reduced.

Extended sentences

Section 85 of the Powers of Criminal Courts (Sentencing) Act 2000 gives the sentencing court power to pass an extended sentence for a sexual or violent offence. This means that the offender is given a custodial sentence plus a further period (the 'extension period') during which the offender is at liberty on licence. The extension period cannot exceed 10 years for a sexual offence or five years for a violent offence.

The idea behind this sentence is to have greater control over sexual offenders when they leave prison. Such offenders are also required to register with the police so that it is known where they are living.

Intermittent custody

The Criminal Justice Act 2003 brought in intermittent custody. This was where the defendant spent weekends or other periods in prison but was free (and able to live at home) for the rest of the week. This penalty was introduced by the Criminal Justice Act 2003 and pilots began in January 2004. In 2006, however, the Government announced that intermittent custody would be abolished. It had not been used in many cases. In addition, it was 'blocking' prison places, as the offenders only used the cells at weekends. With an increase in the prison population, those places were needed for ordinary prisoners.

Minimum sentences

There is a minimum sentence of seven years for anyone aged 18 or over who is convicted on three separate occasions of dealing in Class A drugs. There is also a minimum sentence of three years for those convicted of burglary of a residential building for a third time. In both these cases judges can impose a lesser sentence if there are exceptional circumstances.

Suspended prison sentences

An adult offender may be given a suspended prison sentence of up to two years (six months maximum in the Magistrates' Court). This means that the sentence does not take effect immediately. The court will fix a time during which the sentence is suspended; this can be for any period up to two years. If, during this time, the offender does not commit any further offences, the prison sentence will not be served. However, if the offender does commit another offence within the period of suspension, then the prison sentence is 'activated' and the offender will serve that sentence together with any sentence for the new offence.

Activity

Read the following extract from an article in the *New Law Journal* and answer the questions below.

Taking responsibility

Fifty-eight per cent of all prisoners and three in four young offenders are re-convicted within two years of release, *write Finola Farrant and Joe Levenson*. Why is this and what can be done?

Prisoners have many of the characteristics of social exclusion:

- 26 per cent have spent time in care as a child;

- 47 per cent of women in prison have no educational qualifications;

- 66 per cent of men in prison do not have a job at the time of their conviction; and

- eight per cent of female prisoners have previously been admitted to a psychiatric hospital…

The Prison Reform Trust recently published *Barred Citizens: Volunteering and Active Citizenship by Prisoners*, which examined and identified the benefits of volunteering and active citizenship by prisoners. Volunteering can offer a means of improving the employment prospects of prisoners by providing work experience, improving skills and confidence and enabling prisoners to gain a work reference…

Prisoners currently face great difficulties finding employment after release because of low educational attainment, health problems, a lack of suitable housing and obsolete skills. Ex-prisoners also frequently face discrimination from employers…

Volunteering, especially when it involves undertaking community placements, allows prisoners to build or maintain links with the outside world.

Taken from an article in *New Law Journal*,
6 August 2002

Questions

1. What percentage of prisoners re-offend within two years of release?

2. What problems do many of those who are convicted have prior to their conviction?

3. What problems are faced by prisoners when they finish their sentence?

4. What solution does the article suggest for some of these problems?

5. Suggest other ways in which offenders could be prepared to reintegrate into society.

The article refers to the work of the Prison Reform Trust. Look up this organisation on the Internet at *www.prisonrefomtrust.org.uk*.

A suspended sentence should only be given where the offence is so serious that an immediate custodial sentence would have been appropriate, but there are exceptional circumstances in the case that justify suspending the sentence.

A suspended sentence of imprisonment is one where the offender will only serve the custodial period if he breaches the terms of the suspension. The prison sentence can only be between 28 and 51 weeks. The period of suspension can be between six months and two years. The idea is that the threat of prison during this period of suspension will deter the offender from committing further offences. If the offender complies with the requirements of the suspended sentence he will not serve the term of imprisonment.

The suspended sentence can be combined with any of the requirements used in a community order (see section 14.4.3). If the offender fails to meet the requirements the suspended sentence may be 'activated'. This means that the offender will be made to serve the term of imprisonment. Prior to the Criminal Justice Act 2003, a suspended sentence could only be combined with a fine or a compensation order, leaving the offender unsupervised. As a result a suspended sentence was seen as a 'soft option' and rarely used by the courts.

Sentences for young offenders

There has been a lot of debate as to whether young offenders, particularly those under the age of 15, should be given custodial sentences. Government policy on this point has changed frequently during the past few years. It is argued that many young offenders need help rather than punishment and that this is best provided by sentencing orders which keep the offender in the community. Custodial units for young offenders have often been called 'universities of crime'. However, there are at the moment several different types of custodial sentence which can be given, depending on the type of offence, the age of the offender and whether he or she has offended before.

Young Offenders' Institutions

Offenders aged 18 to 20 can be sent to a Young Offenders' Institution as a custodial sentence. The minimum sentence is 21 days and the maximum is the maximum allowed for the particular offence. If the offender becomes 21 years old while serving the sentence, he will be transferred to an adult prison.

Detention and training orders

The Crime and Disorder Act 1998 created a new custodial sentence, called a detention and training order, for young offenders. The sentence must be for a specified period with a minimum of four months and a maximum of 24 months. In between these, the order can be for six months, eight months, 10 months, 12 months or 18 months. No other length of time can be given.

A detention and training order can be passed on offenders from the age of 12 to the age of 21, but for those under the age of 15 this order can only be made if they are persistent offenders.

There is also power for the Home Secretary to extend the use of detention and training orders to offenders aged 10 and 11. If this is introduced it can only apply where the court is of the opinion that only a custodial sentence is adequate to protect the public from further offending.

Detention for serious crimes

For very serious offences, the courts have additional power to order that the offender be detained for longer periods. For 10- to 13-year-olds this power is only available where the crime committed carries a maximum sentence of at least 14 years' imprisonment for

Comment

Critics of the use of custodial sentences for young offenders point out that such penalties do not appear to have any reformative effective. Home Office research in 1994 revealed that for male prisoners, 82 per cent of those aged 17–20 re-offended within two years of being released, while the figure for those aged 15–16 was even higher at 92 per cent. However, there are also statistics to show that persistent offenders are likely to re-offend regardless of whether they are given a custodial sentence or a community-based one.

Since 1997 one of the aims of the Labour Government has been to try to prevent young offenders becoming persistent offenders. They have introduced a range of new non-custodial measures for dealing with young offenders. These include referrals to Youth Offending Teams and action plan orders which can create an intensive programme aimed at rehabilitation.

---

adults, or is an offence of indecent assault on a woman under s 14 of the Sexual Offences Act 1956. For 14- to 17-year-olds, it is also available for causing death by dangerous driving, or for causing death by careless driving while under the influence of drink or drugs. The length of detention imposed on the young offender cannot be more than the maximum sentence available for an adult.

Originally, 10- to 13-year-olds were not included in these provisions, but the law was amended in 1994 to include them, after a court had been unable to give a custodial sentence to a 13-year-old boy who had been found guilty of raping a 12-year-old girl.

Detention at Her Majesty's Pleasure

Any offender aged 10–17 who is convicted of murder must be ordered to be detained during Her Majesty's Pleasure. This is an indeterminate sentence which allows the offender to be released when suitable. The judge in the case can recommend a minimum number of years that should be served before release is considered, and the Lord Chief Justice will then set the tariff.

If an offender reaches 21 while still serving a sentence he or she will be transferred to an adult prison.

14.4.2 Community sentences

Prior to the Criminal Justice Act 2003, the courts had individual community sentences which they could impose on an offender. They could combine some of these sentences, in particular unpaid work with a supervision order. Also, they could add requirements about treatment and residence to a supervision order, but they could not use a whole range of orders.

The Criminal Justice Act 2003 created one community order under which the court can combine any requirements they think are necessary. These requirements include all the previous existing community sentences which became available as 'requirements' and can be attached to the sentence. There are also new 'requirements' available. The sentencers can 'mix and match' requirements allowing them to fit the restrictions and rehabilitation to the offender's needs. The sentence is available for offenders aged 16 and over. The full list of requirements available to the courts is set out in s 177 of the Criminal Justice Act 2003. This states:

'177(1) *Where a person aged 16 or over is convicted of an offence, the court by or before which he is convicted may make an order imposing on him any one or more of the following requirements:*

(a) as unpaid work requirement

(b) an activity requirement

(c) a programme requirement

(d) a prohibited activity requirement

(e) a curfew requirement

(f) an exclusion requirement

(g) a residence requirement

(h) a mental health treatment requirement

(i) a drug rehabilitation requirement

(j) an alcohol treatment requirement

(k) a supervision requirement, and

(l) in the case where the offender is aged under 25, an attendance centre requirement.'

Each of these is defined within the Criminal Justice Act 2003. Most are self-explanatory from their name, such as drug rehabilitation and alcohol treatment. Much crime is linked to drug and alcohol abuse and the idea behind these two requirements is to tackle the causes of crime, and hopefully prevent further offences. Mental health treatment is also aimed at the cause of the offender's behaviour. The main other requirements are explained briefly below.

Unpaid work requirement

This requires the offender to work for between 40 and 300 hours on a suitable project organised by the probation service. The exact number of hours will be fixed by the court, and those hours are then usually worked in eight-hour sessions, often at weekends. The type of work involved will vary, depending on what schemes the local probation service have running. The offender may be required to paint school buildings, help build a play centre or work on conservation projects. When Eric Cantona, the French footballer, was found guilty of assaulting a football fan, the court ordered that he help at coaching sessions for young footballers.

One criticism is that the number of hours is not enough – other countries which run similar schemes can impose much longer hours. However, re-offending rates are lower than for other community sentences. Also the number of hours was increased from 240 to 300 by the Criminal Justice Act 2003.

Prohibited activity requirement

This requirement allows a wide variety of activities to be prohibited. The idea is to try to prevent the defendant from committing another crime of the type he has just been convicted of. Often the defendant is forbidden to go into a certain area where he has caused trouble. In some cases the defendant has been banned from wearing a 'hoodie'. In 2006, a defendant who was found guilty of criminal damage was banned from carrying paint, dye, ink or marker pens.

Curfew requirement

Under these, an offender can be ordered to remain at a fixed address for between 2 and 12

This is the government's latest idea for a community sentence.

hours in any 24-hour period. This order can last for up to six months and may be enforced by electronic tagging (where suitable). Courts can only make such an order if there is an arrangement for monitoring curfews in their area. Such monitoring can be done by spot-checks, with security firms sending someone to make sure that the offender is at home or offenders may be electronically tagged. There are also pilot schemes on using satellite technology to track those who are tagged.

The cost of tagging is quite expensive, being estimated at £675 per offender per month. However, this does compare favourably with the cost of keeping an offender in prison as the estimated cost of this is £1,555 per month per offender.

Statistics show that in the first two years of using electronic tagging, a very high percentage (80+) of offenders completed the tagging period successfully.

Exclusion requirement

Offenders are ordered not to go to certain places. The order can specify different places for different periods or days. This is intended to keep offenders away from areas where they are most likely to commit crime. For example, a persistent shoplifter could be banned from certain shopping areas. The order can be for up to two years for offenders 16 and over, and a maximum of three months for those under 16.

Supervision requirement

For this requirement the offender is placed under the supervision of a probation officer for a period of up to three years. During the period of supervision the offender must attend appointments with the supervising officer or with any other person decided by the supervising officer.

The Criminal Justice Act 2003 states that a supervision requirement may be imposed for the purpose of 'promoting the offender's rehabilitation'.

14.4.3 Fines

This is the most common way of disposing of a case in the Magistrates' Court where the maximum fine is £5,000 for an individual offender. The magistrate can impose a fine of up to £20,000 on businesses who have committed offences under various regulatory legislation, such as health and safety at work. In the Crown Court only a small percentage of offenders are dealt with by way of a fine.

Unpaid fines

One of the problems is the number of unpaid fines. This has two negative effects: it makes the punishment ineffective; and it leads to defendants being imprisoned for non-payment. In order to overcome these, the Courts Act 2003 introduced the concept of discharge of fines by unpaid work. Pilots on this were run between September 2004 and March 2005 in various areas of the country. The fine which is owed is remitted at a rate of £6 per hour of unpaid work.

14.4.4 Discharges

These may be either a conditional discharge or an absolute discharge. A conditional discharge means that the court discharges an offender on the condition that no further offence is committed during a set period of up to three years. It is intended to be used where it is thought that punishment is not necessary. If an offender re-offends within the time limit, the court can then impose another sentence in place of the conditional discharge, as well as imposing a penalty for the new offence. Conditional discharges are widely used by Magistrates' Courts for first-time minor offenders.

An absolute discharge means that,

effectively, no penalty is imposed. Such a penalty is likely to be used where an offender is technically guilty but morally blameless. An example could be where the tax disc on a vehicle has fallen to the floor – it is technically not being displayed and an offence has been committed. So, in the unlikely situation of someone being prosecuted for this, the magistrates, who would have to impose some penalty, would most probably decide that an absolute discharge was appropriate.

Activity

Look at the bar chart on the opening page of this chapter which shows the types of sentence used in the Magistrates' and the Crown Courts and answer the following questions.

1. What type of sentence are offenders most likely to be given at the Crown Court?

2. What two types of sentence are offenders most likely to be given at the Magistrates' Courts?

3. Why do you think the sentences used most frequently are different for the two courts?

4. Which two types of sentence show the biggest difference in percentages given at the Crown Court and at the Magistrates' Courts?

5. Why do you think the percentages for these two types of sentence are different in the Magistrates' Court and the Crown Court?

14.4.5 Disqualification from driving

Where a defendant is charged with a driving offence, the courts may also have the power to disqualify that person from driving for a certain period of time. The length of the disqualification will depend on the seriousness of the driving offence. Usually the courts will impose a fine as well as disqualification. For a first-time drink-driving offence the courts have to disqualify the defendant for a minimum of 12 months, unless there are very exceptional reasons not to disqualify. If an offender has a previous drink-drive conviction, then the minimum is usually three years' disqualification.

The courts can use this power to disqualify in any other crime where the offender has used a vehicle to commit an offence. For example a defendant who drives a car in order to do a burglary could be disqualified from driving, but this power is not often used.

14.4.6 Other powers available to the courts

The courts have other powers which are aimed at compensating victims and/or making sure that the defendant does not benefit from his or her crimes.

Compensation orders and restitution orders

Courts can make an order that the defendant pay a sum of money to his victim in compensation. They are encouraged to use this order by the fact that they must give reasons if they do not make a compensation order in any case in which they have the power to do so. In the Magistrates' Court the maximum amount of compensation is £5,000.

If the defendant still has the property he obtained from the victim, then the courts can make an order that the property is returned. This is called a restitution order.

- to stay away from certain places
- to comply with arrangements for his education
- to make reparation.

Fines

The maximum amount of a fine varies with the age of the offender: 10- to 13-year-olds can only be fined a maximum of £250, while for 14- to 17-year-olds the maximum is £1,000. Those aged 18 and over are subject to the normal maximum of the Magistrates' Court of £5,000.

Reparation Orders

A Reparation Order may be imposed on offenders under the age of 18. This order cannot be made in combination with a custodial sentence, Community Service Order, a combination order, a Supervision Order or an Action Plan Order.

An order will require the offender to make reparation as specified in the order:

- to a person or persons who were victims of the offence or were otherwise affected by it, or
- to the community at large.

The order is for a maximum of 24 hours' work and the reparation order must be completed under supervision within three months of its imposition. An order for direct reparation to a victim can only be made with that person's consent.

Discharges

These may be used for an offender of any age, and are commonly used for first-time young offenders who have committed minor crimes.

However, the courts cannot conditionally discharge an offender in the following circumstances:

- Where a child or young offender who is

convicted of an offence has been warned within the previous two years; unless there are exceptional circumstances which must be explained in open court
- Where the offender is in breach of an anti-social behaviour order
- Where the offender is in breach of a sex offender order.

Reprimands and warnings

These are not sentences passed by a court, but methods by which the police can deal with offenders without bringing the case to court. For either a reprimand or warning to be given there must be evidence that a child or young person has committed an offence and admits it. In addition, the police must be satisfied that it would not be in the public interest for the offender to be prosecuted. A reprimand or warning can only be given if the offender has never been convicted of any offence.

There is a limit to the number of times and the occasions on which an offender can be 'cautioned'. The first step is the reprimand. This can only be given if the child or young person has not been previously reprimanded or warned. Even then it should not be used where the constable considers the offence to be so serious as to require a warning.

An offender may be warned only if he has not been warned before or if an earlier warning was more than two years before. When warned the child or young offender must be referred to a Youth Offending Team. This team assesses the case and, unless it considers it inappropriate to do so, arranges for the offender to participate in a rehabilitation scheme.

14.5.2 Parental responsibility

If the parents agree, they can be bound over to keep their child under control for a set period of up to one year. If the child commits an offence during this period the parents will forfeit a sum of money up to a maximum of £1,000. If a parent unreasonably refuses to be bound over, the court has the power to fine that parent instead. Parents can also be bound over to ensure that a young offender complies with a community sentence.

Where an offender under 16 years old is fined or ordered to pay compensation, the court must require the offender's parents to pay, and the financial situation of the parent is taken into account in deciding the amount of the order.

Parenting orders

This is intended to offer training and support to parents to help change their children's offending behaviour. In this way it is more practical than the existing provisions which merely make a parent responsible for their child's offending behaviour. Under such an order a parent can be required to attend counselling or guidance sessions for up to three months on a maximum basis of once a week.

In addition, the parent may be required to comply with conditions imposed by the courts; for example, escort the child to school or ensure that a responsible adult is present in the home in the evening to supervise the child. A court may make a parenting order where:

- The court makes a child safety order
- The court makes an anti-social behaviour order (or sex offender order) in respect of a child
- A child or young person is convicted of an offence
- A parent is convicted of an offence relating to truancy under the Education Act 1996.

An order should only be made if it is desirable in the interests of preventing the conduct which gave rise to the order. Where a person under the age of 16 is convicted of an offence,

the court should make a parenting order unless it is satisfied that it is not desirable in the interests of preventing the conduct which gave rise to the order. In this case the court must state in open court that it is not satisfied and explain why not.

14.5.3 Youth Offending Teams

The Crime and Disorder Act made it the duty of each local authority to establish one or more Youth Offending Teams (YOTs) in their area. The main idea in establishing these teams is to build on co-operation between agencies involved, especially social services and the probation service. These teams are to co-ordinate the provision of youth justice services in the area.

A YOT must include a probation officer, a local authority social worker, a police officer, a representative of the local health authority and a person nominated by the chief education officer. Any other appropriate person may also be invited to join the team.

The role of YOTs is highlighted by the fact that, under s 66 of the Crime and Disorder Act 1998, any offender who is warned must be referred to the local YOT. Youth courts may also refer offenders to the YOT.

14.6 Mentally ill offenders

The law recognises that, so far as possible, mentally ill offenders should not be punished but should receive treatment. Where an offence has been committed by an offender who is mentally ill, the courts have a wider range of powers available to them. In addition to the ordinary sentences which can be given, there are special provisions aimed at treating such offenders in a suitable way.

The main additional powers available to the courts are to: give the offender a community

Activity

Suggest a suitable sentence for the following offenders and explain what the aim of the sentence would be.

Questions

1. Kevin, aged 22, has been found guilty by the magistrates of two charges of criminal damage. The amount of damage involved is estimated at £600. He is single, unemployed and has no previous convictions.

2. Melanie, aged 15, appeared before the local youth court and admitted shoplifting on five occasions. She also admitted two offences of taking and driving a car without the owner's consent. She has appeared before the youth court on two previous occasions for similar offences.

3. Andrew, aged 26, has been found guilty at the Crown Court of an assault causing grievous bodily harm. He committed this offence while on bail charged with another offence of violence.

sentence, with a requirement that he or she attends for treatment; make a hospital order or to make a restriction order under s 41 of the Mental Health Act 1983.

A community order requiring the offender to have treatment will be made where the court is satisfied that the mental condition is treatable, and that there is no need to make a hospital order. A hospital order will be made if the condition makes it appropriate that the offender should stay in hospital for treatment.

However, there are some cases in which the protection of the public is a key element. Under s 41 of the Mental Health Act 1983 offenders with severe mental problems, who are considered to be a danger to the community, can be sent to a secure hospital such as Broadmoor. Magistrates' Courts cannot make such an order; it can only be made by a Crown Court. The order can be that the offender be detained for a set period or, where necessary, for an indefinite period. If an offender is

ordered to be detained for an indefinite period, the hospital can only discharge him with the permission of the Home Secretary or the Mental Health Review Tribunal.

14.7 Anti-Social Behaviour Orders

These are civil orders not criminal penalties. They are usually referred to by the abbreviation of ASBOs. They can be imposed when a person has behaved in an anti-social manner. The type of behaviour included under the term 'anti-social' is very wide. For example, they may have harassed or intimidated people or been frequently drunk or high on drugs and caused a nuisance in public or to neighbours: they may even have done several acts of minor criminal damage.

Under an ASBO the person can be ordered

not to go to certain areas or take part in certain types of behaviour. Breaking an ASBO is a criminal matter and the offender can then be sentenced for the breach.

The intention of ASBOs is both to protect the community and to try to prevent the person's behaviour from deteriorating further into truly criminal activity.

Activity

Look up the website **www.together.gov.uk** to find examples of when anti-social behaviour orders have been made.

14.8 Penal policies and their effects

Sentencing policies have an effect on the number of offenders who are sent to prison. The United Kingdom sends a higher percentage of its population to prison than any other European Union country. The changes in sentencing policy over the last few years are reflected in the changing size of prison population as the Government has first attempted to reduce the number of defendants sent to prison for relatively minor offences, and then (to some extent) reversed their policies in an effort as being seen as the party of 'law and order'.

However, under the Criminal Justice Act 2003, the Government has introduced tougher community penalties to try to avoid using custodial sentences.

14.8.1 Prison population

There has been concern that the number of people in prison (known as the prison

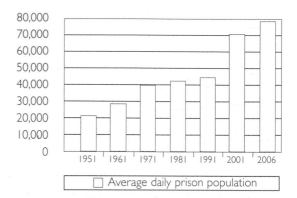

Figure 14.6 *Average daily prison population for England and Wales 1951–2006*

population) has risen rapidly in recent years. In fact the increase has been going on for the past 50 years, as is shown by Figure 14.6.

In addition, the Government has forecast that the prison population is likely to rise to 93,000 by 2009.

It can be argued that the population of England and Wales has increased during this period and so some increase should be expected. However, the population increase has not been that great and the number of prisoners per 100,000 of the general population confirms that there has indeed been a great increase in the number of people sent to prison. In 1951 there were only 50 per 100,000 of the population in prison by 2001 this had risen to 136. By 2004 the United Kingdom had the highest rate of prison population per 100,000 in the whole of Europe.

14.8.2 Women and sentencing

Numerically there are far fewer women in prison than men. In 2006 there were 4,800 women in prison. It is also true that, for indictable offences, women are more likely to be given a discharge or a community sentence than men, and are less likely to be fined or

Chapter 15
The legal profession

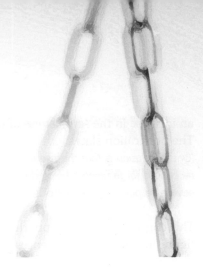

In England and Wales there are two types of lawyers (barristers and solicitors) jointly referred to as the legal profession. Most countries do not have this clear-cut division among lawyers: a person will qualify simply as a lawyer, although, after qualifying, it will be possible for them to specialise as an advocate, or in a particular area of law. This type of system is seen in this country in the medical profession, where all those wishing to become doctors take the same general qualifications. After they have qualified, some doctors will go on to specialise in different fields, perhaps as surgeons, and will take further qualifications in their chosen field.

In England, not only are the professions separate, but there is no common training for lawyers, although there have been increasing calls for this. As far back as 1971 the Ormrod Committee was in favour of a common education for all prospective lawyers. In 1994 the Lord Chancellor's advisory committee on legal education, under Lord Steyn, recommended that, instead of having separate training for barristers and solicitors, 'the two branches of the profession should have joint training. All those qualifying would then work for six months or a year at a solicitors', with those who wished to become barristers going on to do extra training at the Bar. Yet despite these recommendations, the training of the two professions remains separate.

15.1 Solicitors

There are over 100,000 solicitors practising in England and Wales and they are controlled by their own professional body, the Law Society.

15.1.1 Training

To become a solicitor it is usual to have a law degree, although those with a degree in a subject other than law can do an extra year's training in core legal subjects, and take the Common Professional Examination. The next stage is the one-year Legal Practice Course. This is much more practically based than the previous Law Society Finals course and includes training in skills such as client-interviewing, negotiation, advocacy, drafting documents and legal research. There is also an emphasis on business management, for example, keeping accounts.

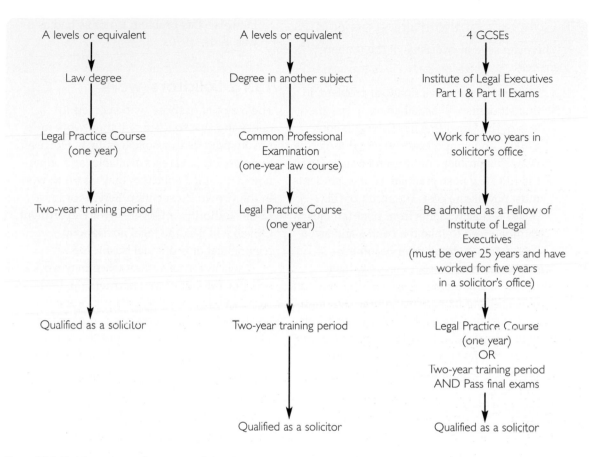

Figure 15.1 *Training routes to become a solicitor*

Training contract

Even when this course has been passed, the student is still not a qualified solicitor. He or she must next obtain a training contract under which they work in a solicitors' firm for two years, getting practical experience. This training period can also be undertaken in certain other legal organisations such as the Crown Prosecution Service, or the legal department of a local authority. During this two-year training contract the trainee will be paid, though not at the same rate as a fully qualified solicitor, and will do his own work, supervised by a solicitor. He will also have to complete a 20 day Professional Skills Course which builds on the skills learnt on the LPC. At the end of the time, the trainee will be admitted as a solicitor by the Law Society and his name will be added to the roll (or list) of solicitors. Even after qualifying, solicitors have to attend continuing education courses to keep their knowledge up to date.

Non-graduate route

There is also a route under which non-graduates can qualify as solicitors by first becoming legal executives. This route is only open to mature candidates and takes longer than the graduate route. The three routes to becoming a solicitor are shown in Figure 15.1.

Criticisms of the training process

There are several criticisms of the training process.

1. The first of these is a financial problem, in that students will usually have to pay the fees of the Legal Practice Course (about £7,000) and support themselves during this year. This problem has arisen because, as the LPC is a post-graduate course, students must pay all the cost. The result of this policy is that students from poor families cannot afford to take the course and are therefore prevented from becoming solicitors, even though they may have obtained a good law degree. Other students may take out bank loans, so that although they qualify, they start the training period with a large debt. In order to overcome this problem a few universities have started offering four year degree courses, combining a law qualification and a practical course, so students pay only the university fees. This financial problem is also one faced by prospective barristers. The problem has increased since universities started charging £3,000 a year from 2006.

2. A point common to barristers, is that non-law graduates do only one year of formal law for the Common Professional Course. The Ormrod Committee which reported on legal education in 1971 thought that the main entry route should be via a law degree, but in practice 25 per cent of solicitors will not have taken a law degree. One critic posed the question of whether the public would be satisfied with doctors who have only studied medicine for one year, concentrating on only six subjects. Yet this is precisely what is occurring in the legal profession.

3. A third problem is one of over-supply, so that students who have passed the LPC are unable to obtain a training contract.

However this problem is not as bad as it was in the 1990s.

15.1.2 Solicitors' work

The majority of those who succeed in qualifying as a solicitor will then work in private practice in a solicitors' firm. However, there are other careers available, and some newly-qualified solicitors may go on to work in the Crown Prosecution Service or for a Local Authority or Government Department. Others will become legal advisers in commercial or industrial businesses.

A solicitor in private practice may work as a sole practitioner or in a partnership. There are some 9,000 firms of solicitors, ranging from the small 'high street' practice to the big city firms. The number of partners is not limited, and some of the biggest firms will have over a hundred partners as well as employing assistant solicitors.

The type of work done by a solicitor will largely depend on the type of firm he or she is working in. A small high street firm will probably be a general practice advising clients on a whole range of topics such as consumer problems, housing and business matters and family problems. A solicitor working in such a practice is likely to spend some of his time interviewing clients in his office and negotiating on their behalf, and a large amount of time dealing with paperwork. This will include:

- writing letters on behalf of clients
- drafting contracts, leases or other legal documents
- drawing up wills
- dealing with conveyancing (the legal side of buying and selling flats, houses, office buildings and land).

The solicitor may also, if he wishes, act for some of his clients in court. Standing up in court and putting the client's case, and questioning witnesses is known as advocacy. Some solicitors will specialise in this and spend much of their time in court.

Specialising

Although some solicitors may be general practitioners handling a variety of work it is not unusual, even in small firms, for a solicitor to specialise in one particular field. The firm itself may only handle certain types of cases (perhaps only civil actions) and not do any criminal cases, or a firm may specialise in matrimonial cases. Even within the firm the solicitors are likely to have their own field of expertise. In large firms there will be an even greater degree of specialisation with departments dealing with one aspect of the law. The large city firms usually concentrate on business and commercial law. Amounts earned by solicitors are as varied as the types of firm, with the top earners in big firms on £500,000 or more, while at the bottom end of the scale some sole practitioners will earn less than £30,000.

Conveyancing

Prior to 1985 solicitors had a monopoly on conveyancing: this meant that only solicitors could deal with the legal side of transferring houses and other buildings and land. This was changed by the Administration of Justice Act 1985 which allowed people other than solicitors to become licensed conveyancers. As a result of the increased competition in this area, solicitors had to reduce their fees, but even so they lost a large proportion of the work. This led to a demand for wider rights of advocacy.

Rights of advocacy

All solicitors have always been able to act as advocates in the Magistrates' Courts and the County Courts, but their rights of audience in the higher courts used to be very limited. Normally a solicitor could only act as advocate in the Crown Court on a committal for sentence, or on an appeal from the Magistrates' Court, and then only if he or another solicitor in the firm had been the advocate in the original case in the Magistrates' Court.

Key Facts		
	Original rights	To present cases in County Court and Magistrates' Court also at Crown Court on committal for sentence or appeal from Magistrates' Court
	Practice Direction 1986	Following *Abse* v *Smith* allowed to make statement in High Court in cases in which terms had been agreed
	Courts and Legal Services Act 1990	Solicitors allowed to apply for certificate of advocacy to conduct cases in the higher courts. Must have experience of advocacy, take course and pass examinations
	Access to Justice Act 1999	Solicitors to have full rights of audience

Figure 15.2 Key fact chart on solicitors' rights of audience

solicitors, and also barristers and licensed conveyancers, where the professions' own regulatory bodies did not provide a satisfactory answer. Under the Access to Justice Act 1999 the Ombudsman has power to order that the solicitor concerned should pay compensation or that the Law Society itself should compensate the client.

15.2 Barristers

There are about 12,000 barristers in independent practice in England and Wales. Collectively barristers are referred to as 'the Bar' and they are controlled by their own professional body – the General Council of the Bar. All barristers must also be a member of one of the four Inns of Court: Lincoln's Inn, Inner Temple, Middle Temple and Gray's Inn, all of which are situated near the Royal Courts of Justice in London.

15.2.1 Training

Entry to the Bar is normally degree-based, though there is a non-degree route for mature entrants, under which a small number of students qualify. As with solicitors, graduate students without a law degree can take the one year course for the Common Professional Examination in the core subjects, in order to go on to qualify as a barrister. All student barristers have to pass the Bar Vocational Course which emphasises the practical skills of drafting pleadings for use in court, negotiation and advocacy.

Until 1997 only the Inns of Court School of Law (Bar School) could run this course, but since September 1997 six other bodies have been validated to offer the course. These are: the BPP Law School and the College of Law in London, and Law Schools in Nottingham, Northumbria, Bristol and Cardiff. This allows

more students to obtain a place on the Bar Vocational Course, but brings the same problems that solicitors are facing, with more people qualifying than there are work placements available for.

All student barristers must join one of the four Inns of Court and used to have to dine there 12 times before being called to the Bar. Since October 1997 students may attend in a different way, for example a weekend residential course. This will help students on the courses outside London as travelling costs will be lower. The idea behind the rule requiring all trainee barristers to dine was that they met senior barristers and judges and absorbed the traditions of the profession. In practice, few barristers dine at their Inns and students are unlikely to meet anyone except other students.

Once a student has passed the Bar Vocational Course, he or she is then 'called to the Bar'. This means that they are officially qualified as a barrister. However, there is still a practical stage to their training which must be completed. This is called pupillage.

Pupillage

After the student has passed the Bar Vocational Course there is 'on the job' training where the trainee barrister becomes a pupil to a qualified barrister. This effectively involves 'work shadowing' that barrister, and can be with the same barrister for 12 months or with two different pupil masters for six months each. There is also a requirement that they take part in a programme of continuing education organised by the Bar Council. After the first six months of pupillage, barristers are eligible to appear in court and may conduct their own cases. During pupillage trainee barristers are paid a small salary, usually about half the amount paid to trainee solicitors.

The various training routes are shown in Figure 15.3.

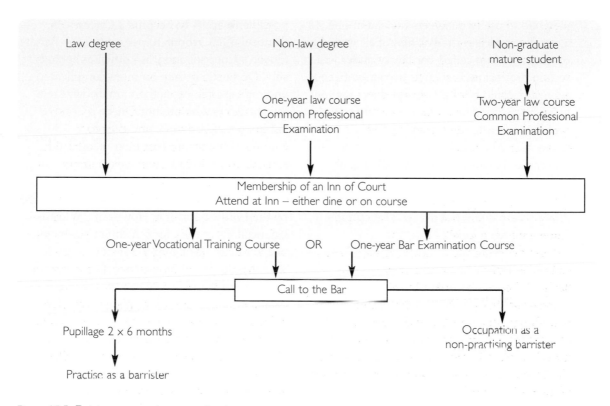

Figure 15.3 *Training routes to become a barrister*

15.2.2 Barristers' work

Barristers practising at the Bar are self-employed, but usually work from a set of chambers where they can share administrative expenses with other barristers. Most sets of chambers are fairly small comprising of about 15–20 barristers. They will employ a clerk as a practice administrator – booking in cases and negotiating fees – and they will have other support staff. One of the problems facing newly qualified barristers is the difficulty of finding a tenancy in chambers. Many will do a third six-month pupillage and then 'squat' as an unofficial tenant before obtaining a place. The rule on having to practise from chambers has been relaxed, so that it is technically possible for barristers to practise from home. However, despite the fact that a tenancy in chambers is not essential, it is still viewed as

the way to allow a barrister to build a successful practice.

The majority of barristers will concentrate on advocacy, although there are some who specialise in areas such as tax and company law, and who rarely appear in court. Barristers have rights of audience in all courts in England and Wales. Even those who specialise in advocacy will do a certain amount of paperwork, writing opinions on cases, giving advice and drafting documents for use in court.

Direct access

Originally it was necessary for anybody who wished to instruct a barrister to go to a solicitor first. The solicitor would then brief the barrister. This was thought to create unnecessary expense for clients, as it meant they had to use two lawyers instead of one. As a result of criticism the Bar first of all started to operate a system called Bar Direct under which certain professionals such as accountants and surveyors could brief a barrister direct without using a solicitor. This was extended to other professionals and organisations. Then in September 2004 the Bar granted direct access to anyone (business or individual). It is no longer necessary to go to a solicitor in order to instruct a barrister for civil cases. However, direct access is still not allowed for criminal cases or family work.

Cab rank rule

Normally barristers operate what is known as the cab rank rule under which they cannot turn down a case if it is on the area of law they deal with and they are free to take the case. However, where clients approach a barrister direct, the cab rank rule does not apply. Barristers can turn down a case which would require investigation or support services which they cannot provide.

Employed barristers

The employed Bar, which includes those barristers working for the Crown Prosecution Service, can appear in the Magistrates' Court, but used not to be able to conduct cases in the Crown Court, High Court or appellate courts. As these barristers will have done exactly the same training as the independent Bar, this was seen as being unnecessarily restrictive. The Access to Justice Act 1999 allowed barristers working for the CPS or other employers to keep their rights of audience. The Act also allowed barristers who work in solicitors' firms to keep the right to present cases in court.

Queen's Counsel

After at least 10 years as a barrister or as a solicitor with an advocacy qualification, it is possible to apply to become a Queen's Counsel (QC). About 10 per cent of the Bar are Queen's Counsel and it is known as 'taking silk'. QCs usually take on more complicated and high-profile cases than junior barristers (all barristers who are not Queen's Counsel are known as 'juniors'), and they can command higher fees for their recognised expertise. Often a QC will have a junior barrister to assist with the case.

Until 2004 Queen's Council were appointed by the Lord Chancellor. However, the Lord Chancellor's criteria for selecting QCs have been criticised as being too secretive. There was also the fact that less than 10 per cent of QCs are women and only a very few are from ethnic minorities. In turn, this has an effect on the composition of the judiciary since senior judges are usually chosen from the ranks of Queen's Counsel. The position of women and ethnic minorities in the legal profession is considered in more detail in section 15.5.

Also, in 2003, the Office of Fair Trading (OFT) stated that it thought the position of QC was not of benefit to the public. It said:

- QCs do not necessarily offer a better service
- the QC title is too generic and does not tell purchasers about the area of specialisation
- the system focuses on advocacy skills whereas users require a range of skills such as legal advice and case management
- there is no monitoring of quality or incentive to keep standards high once the title has been conferred.

This led to the Lord Chancellor announcing in May 2003 that the processing of applications for appointment in 2003 would be suspended while the whole system was reviewed. It was followed in July 2003 by the issue of a consultation paper *The Future of Queen's Counsel*.

The Bar wanted the position of QC to be

kept and the Bar Council replied to the consultation paper claiming that the QC system serves the public interest because it:

- is a conspicuous brand that enhances the standing of UK legal services abroad
- is a publicly recognised mark of quality of advocacy
- provides a resource for public inquires;
- promotes competition by supplementing market information
- is a tool for promoting diversity as an increasing number of minority ethnic barristers approach silk seniority.

On this last point, ethnic minority barristers pointed out that the numbers eligible to apply for silk were just about to increase.

Finally, in 2004 the Lord Chancellor, the Bar Council and the Law Society agreed a new system for appointment.

New appointment system

Selection of who should become a QC is now made by an independent selection panel. Lawyers apply to become QCs. They have to pay a fee of £2,500. Applicants provide references (these can include references from clients) and are interviewed by members of the panel. The panel then recommends those who should be appointed to the Lord Chancellor.

The first appointments of QCs under the new system were made in 2006. 443 applied and 175 were appointed. Of these, 33 were women (48.5 per cent of female applicants), 10 ethnic minority (41.7 per cent of such applicants) and four solicitors (33.3 per cent of solicitor applicants).

The most notable fact is the number of women who were successful – but this may only reflect the fact that there are more women in the profession.

15.2.3 Complaints against barristers

Where a barrister receives a brief from a solicitor he or she does not enter into a contract with his client and so cannot sue if their fees are not paid. Similarly, the client cannot sue for breach of contract. However, they can be sued for negligence. In *Saif Ali* v *Sydney Mitchell and Co* (1980) it was held that a barrister could be sued for negligence in respect of written advice and opinions. In that case a barrister had given the wrong advice about who to sue, with the result that the claimant was too late to start proceedings against the right person.

In *Hall (a firm)* v *Simons* (2000) the House of Lords held that lawyers could also be liable for negligence in the conduct of advocacy in court. This decision overruled the earlier case of *Rondel* v *Worsley* (1969) in which barristers were held not to be liable because their first duty was to the courts and they must be 'free to do their duty fearlessly and independently'.

The Law Lords in *Hall (a firm)* v *Simons* felt that in light of modern conditions it was no longer in the public interest that advocates should have immunity from being sued for negligence. They pointed out that doctors could be sued and they had a duty to an ethical code of practice and might have difficult decisions to make when treating patients. There was no reason why advocates should not be liable in the same way.

They also pointed out that allowing advocates to be sued for negligence would not be likely to lead to the whole case being re-argued. If an action against an advocate was merely an excuse to get the whole issue litigated again, the matter would almost certainly be struck out as an abuse of process.

	Solicitors	Barristers
Professional body	Law Society	Bar Council
Basic qualifications another	Law degree OR degree in another subject PLUS Common Professional Exam	Law degree OR degree in subject PLUS Common Professional Exam
Vocational training	Legal Practice Course	Bar Vocational Course
Practical training	Training contract	Pupillage
Number in profession	100,000	12,000 (including 800 QCs)
Method of working	Firm of partners OR as sole practitioner	Self-employed, practising in chambers
Rights of audience	Normally only County Court and Magistrates' Court After Access to Justice Act 1999 will be able to have full advocacy rights	All courts
Relationship with client	Contractual	Normally through solicitor BUT accountants and surveyors can brief barristers directly
Liability	Liable in contract and tort to clients May also be liable to others affected by negligence (*White v Jones*)	No contractual liability BUT liable for negligence (*Hall v Simons*)

Figure 15.4 Key fact chart comparing solicitors and barristers

Bar Standards Board

Complaints against barristers are handled by the Bar Standards Board. If there was poor service, the Board can order the barrister to pay compensation of up to £5,000 to the client. The complaints process is overseen by an independent Lay Complaints Commissioner.

Senate of the Inns of Court

Barristers can be disciplined by the Senate of the Inns of Court if they fail to maintain the standards set out in their Code of Conduct. In extreme cases the Senate can disbar a barrister from practising.

Legal Services Ombudsman

As set out earlier in section 15.1.3, there has been a Legal Services Ombudsman since 1991, whose work involves investigating complaints about all the legal professions. There are comparatively few complaints against barristers and the Ombudsman has found that the Bar Council usually handles about 90 per cent of complaints satisfactorily.

15.3 Legal Services Bill 2006

15.3.1 Background

In 2001 a report by the Office of Fair Trading recommended that unjustified restrictions on competition in the legal profession should be removed.

In 2004 the Clementi Report into the legal profession was published (*Review of the Regulatory Framework for the Legal Services in England and Wales – Final Report*). The main recommendations were that:

- there should be a new complaints body which is independent of the professions
- there should be a legal services board as regulator over all the legal professional bodies
- Legal Disciplinary Practices (LPDs) should be permitted where there are barristers, solicitors and non-lawyers working together in the same practice
- non-lawyers would be allowed to own and manage LPDs, but there would be

safeguards to make sure that they were 'fit to own' such a practice.

15.3.2 The Legal Services Bill

The Government introduced this Bill into Parliament in the Autumn of 2006. It starts by setting out regulatory objectives for legal services. These are:

(a) supporting the constitutional principle of the rule of law

(b) improving access to justice

(c) protecting and promoting the interests of consumers

(d) promoting competition in the provision of services

(e) encouraging a strong, diverse and effective legal profession

(f) increasing public understanding of the citizen's legal rights and duties

(g) promoting and maintaining adherence to the professional principles.

Legal Services Board

The Bill provides for the creation of the Legal Services Board. The role of the Board is to have independent oversight regulation of the legal profession. It will consist of a Chairman and seven to 10 members appointed by the Secretary of State. The first Chairman must be a non-lawyer and the majority of members must also be non-lawyers.

The Home Affairs Committee reported on the Bill when it was in draft form. The committee was concerned that the Secretary of State was involved in the appointment of the chairman and members of the Board. It felt that this prevented the Board from being independent of the Government. The Government, however, has kept this provision in the final Bill.

Complaints about legal services

The Bill has provision for establishing the Office for Legal Complaints to handle all complaints in respect of the legal profession. The Office will have a Chairman and between six and eight members. The Chairman must be a non-lawyer and the majority of members must also be non-lawyers.

The location of this Office is to be in the West Midlands and staff will be drawn largely from the Law Society's Consumer Complaints Service. This is the organisation that has been frequently criticised for its inefficient handling of complaints.

The Bar is concerned that its complaints handling will become less efficient under the new system. Also, the Home Affairs Committee reporting on the draft Bill recommended that approved regulators such as the Bar Standards Board should have flexibility to handle service and conduct of complaints, but the Government rejected this recommendation.

Alternative Business Structures (ABS)

Under the present system there are restrictions on the types of business structures in the legal profession. The main restrictions are:

- barristers and solicitors cannot operate from the same business
- lawyers are not allowed to enter into partnership with non-lawyers
- on non-lawyers being involved in the ownership or management of legal businesses
- legal practices cannot operate as a companies.

So, generally, barristers and solicitors cannot work together, nor can lawyers and non-lawyers work together in legal businesses. The Legal Services Bill will change this by allowing:

- legal businesses to include lawyers and non-lawyers
- legal businesses to include barristers and solicitors
- non-lawyers to own legal businesses
- legal businesses to operate as companies.

The Home Affairs Committee Report on the draft Bill pointed out that the provisions in the Bill go well beyond the recommendations of Sir David Clementi. It thought that there is potential for conflict of interest in ABS firms, both between lawyers and shareholders and between lawyers and non-lawyers. The Committee was also worried about:

- the speed of approach
- the level of uncertainty about the impact of the reforms, particularly on access to justice in rural areas and legal aid provisions.

The Committee has urged the Government to take a step-by-step approach in introducing alternative business structures. However, the Government says that no prescribed timetable is necessary and sees no reason to delay implementation.

Activity

Find out whether the Legal Services Bill 2006 is now an Act. Try looking on the Internet at *www.opsi.gov.uk*. If it is not there, look at *www.parliament.uk* to see if the Bill is still going through Parliament.

15.4 Fusion

A major debate used to be whether the two professions should be merged into one profession. The advantages of fusion were thought to be:

- reduced costs as only one lawyer would be needed instead of a solicitor and a barrister
- less duplication of work because only one person would be doing the work, instead of a solicitor preparing the case and then passing it on to a barrister
- more continuity as the same person could deal with the case from start to finish

The disadvantages of fusion were seen as:

- a decrease in the specialist skills of advocacy
- loss of the independent bar and the lack of availability of advice from independent specialists at the bar

- less objectivity in consideration of a case; at the moment the barrister provides a second opinion
- loss of a cab-rank principle under which barristers have to accept any case offered to them (except when they are already booked on another case for the same day). This principle allows anyone to get representation, even if their case is unpopular or unlikely to win.

The argument for fusion is no longer so important since the changes made by the Courts and Legal Services Act 1990 and the Access to Justice Act 1999 mean that barristers

Activity

Read the following extract and answer the questions below.

Reforms to tackle racism and sexism at the Bar

[A report by a Working Party under Lord Justice Thorpe into the recruitment, training and regulation of barristers] found that the Benchers, senior barristers over 15 years call and who are responsible for running the Inns, were 'overwhelmingly' male and white. In 1999 out of the 1,028 Benchers among the four Inns only 66 were female, and only 8 were of ethnic minority origin. The Working Party, unsurprisingly, found 'as a fact' that ethnic minorities and women were under-represented on the benches of the Inns. In addition, there was no evidence that the Inns had reviewed their selection procedure for the Bench since the

introduction of an Equal Opportunity Code in 1997 or had considered how to address the problem of under-representation.

The report also found evidence of 'systematic bias in favour of whites and against students and against students belonging to "other" ethnic groups' in the award of scholarships and bursaries by the Inns'...

The host of detailed recommendations which are now being implemented to redress the situations include: applications for Inns' membership, scholarships, grants, pupillage, pastoral care and training, discipline and grievances, Benchers, other governing bodies of the Inns, staff and the operation of equal opportunities policies.

Taken from an article in *New Law Journal,* 8 March 2002

Questions

1. Name the four Inns of Court.

2. What role do Benchers perform in an Inn?

3. In 1999 how many Benchers were women?

4. In 1999 how many Benchers were from an ethnic minority background?

5. What other area of bias does the extract mention?

6. The last paragraph mentions 'pupillage'. What is pupillage?

7. Why is it important that there should be no bias in considering applications for membership of Inn or grants or scholarships?

and solicitors can take a case from start to finish. Under the Access to Justice Act barristers have the right to do litigation (i.e. the preliminary work in starting a case) which has in the past always been done by solicitors. At the same time solicitors have wider rights of advocacy and may represent clients in all courts.

When the Legal Services Bill becomes law there will even less need for the professions to be fused. Barristers and solicitors will be able to work together in the same legal business.

15.5 Women and ethnic minorities in the legal profession

The legal profession has an image of being white male-dominated. Both women and ethnic minorities are under-represented in the higher levels of the legal professions.

Women

Women are forming an increasing number of the entrants to the professions. They now make up over half of new solicitors and half of new entrants to the Bar. As a result of the increasing numbers of women studying law there are now greater numbers of women in both professions: 30 per cent of members of the Bar and 42 per cent of solicitors are female. Despite this there are very few women at the higher levels in either profession. For example, at the bar only about 12 per cent of QCs are women. Women solicitors tend to be in junior positions as assistant solicitors or junior partners, even though a third of practising solicitors are women.

One of the reasons put forward to explain this is that the increase in entrants is a fairly recent phenomenon. Twenty years ago there were comparatively few women going into the legal professions, and so it is not so surprising that there are correspondingly fewer women in senior positions.

In the solicitors' profession about 23 per cent of partners are women. This figure is increasing, but a survey in 2001 found that many women solicitors did not want to become partners.

Women also tend to earn less than their male counterparts, even when they do achieve higher status, especially in the solicitors' ranks.

Women solicitors do not earn the same level of salary as male solicitors. Even the starting salaries of women are lower. The gap becomes bigger the higher up the profession, with men earning on average £15,000 more per year than women.

Examination Questions

1. (a) Describe the different training and rights of audience of barristers **and** solicitors.
   (b) Explain how the changes to training and rights of audience in the last fifteen years have improved services for clients.

   OCR 2569, January 2003

2. (a) To what extent have recent developments effectively fused the legal professions of barrister and solicitor? *[10 marks]*
   (b) Explain the significance of the Clementi Style Reforms on the future of the legal practice in England and Wales. *[15 marks]*

   LW2 WJEC, June 2006

Chapter 16

The judiciary

When speaking of judges as a group, they are referred to as the judiciary. There are many different levels of judges, but the basic function is the same at all levels: judges are there to adjudicate on disputes in a fair, unbiased way, applying the legal rules of this country. There is no clear-cut division between civil and criminal judges, as many judges at the various levels are required to sit for both types of case. This in itself causes problems as, before their appointment, most judges will have specialised in one area of law. The head of the judiciary is the Lord Chief Justice.

When considering judges the first point is that there is a marked difference between what are called superior judges and inferior judges. This affects the method of appointment, the training, the work and the terms on which they hold office, so it is as well to start by understanding which judges are involved at each level.

16.1 Types of judges

16.1.1 Superior judges

Superior judges are those in the High Court and above. Starting from the top and working down these are:

- The Lords of Appeal in Ordinary (the Law Lords) in the House of Lords
- The Lords Justices of Appeal in the Court of Appeal
- High Court judges (known as puisne judges) who sit in the three divisions of the High Court and, note that in addition, judges from the Queen's Bench Division also sit in the Crown Court

The head of the House of Lords is the Lord Chancellor. Specific judicial posts heading the different divisions of the Court of Appeal and the High Court are as follows:

- **The Lord Chief Justice** is the head of the judiciary. He is the President of the Criminal Division of the Court of Appeal
- **The Master of the Rolls**, President of the Civil Division of the Court of Appeal
- **The President of the Queen's Bench Division**
- **The President of the Family Division of the High Court**, the senior judge in that division. In 1999 the first woman President was appointed
- **The Chancellor of the High Court**, who is head of the Chancery Division.

16.1.2 Inferior judges

The inferior judges are:

- Circuit Judges who sit in both the Crown Court and the County Court
- Recorders who are part-time judges sitting usually in the Crown Court, though some may be assigned to the County Court
- District Judges who hear small claims and other matters in the County Court
- District Judges (Magistrates' Court) who sit in Magistrates' Courts in London and other major towns and cities
- Chairmen of tribunals.

16.2 Qualifications

The relevant qualifications for the different judicial posts are set out in the Courts and Legal Services Act 1990. This Act broke the previous

The Lord Chief Justice, Lord Phillips of Worth Matravers

monopoly that the Bar held on all superior judgeships, by basing qualifications on the relevant advocacy qualifications, and providing for promotion from one level to the next.

To become a judge at any level it is necessary to have qualified as a barrister or solicitor. It is no longer essential to have practised, as the Courts and Legal Services Act provided for academic lawyers to be appointed. In 1994, the Lord Chancellor lifted the ban which prevented lawyers in the civil service and Crown Prosecution Service from becoming judges. These changes have all helped to widen the pool of potential candidates for judgeships, and may eventually help to make the composition of the bench a wider cross-section of society.

The qualifications for each level of judge are set out below.

16.2.1 Law Lords

These are appointed from those who hold high judicial office, for example, as a judge in the Court of Appeal, or from those who have been qualified to appear in the Supreme Court for at least 15 years. As the House of Lords is the final appellate court for Scotland and Northern Ireland as well, judges can also be appointed from those who have practised as an advocate in Scotland for at least 15 years or as a member of the Bar in Northern Ireland for at least 15 years or held high judicial office in their own legal system.

In recent times all the appointments have been from those holding high judicial office, either in the English Court of Appeal of in the equivalent courts or Scotland and Northern Ireland.

16.2.2 Lords Justices of Appeal

These must have a 10-year High Court qualification or be an existing High Court judge. In recent times all Lords Justices of Appeal have been appointed from existing High Court judges.

16.2.3 High Court judges

In order to be eligible to be appointed as a High Court judge it is necessary either to have had the right to practice in the High Court for at least 10 years or to have been a Circuit judge for at least two years. Prior to the Courts and Legal Services Act 1990 only those who had practised as a barrister for at least 10 years were eligible.

These qualification routes give solicitors the chance to become High Court judges, either by promotion from a Circuit judgeship as happened in 1993 to the first solicitor to be appointed, or by holding a certificate of advocacy for the required time. Note that a second solicitor was appointed to the High Court bench in 2000 and promoted to the Court of Appeal in 2007.

It is also possible for academic lawyers (who have not practised as barristers or solicitors) to be appointed. One of the first academics to be appointed to the High Court was Brenda Hale, who is now the first woman judge in the House of Lords.

16.2.4 Circuit Judges

There are different routes to becoming a Circuit Judge. The candidate can either have had rights of audience for at least 10 years in either the Crown Court or the County Court or have been a Recorder. The route via being a Recorder has existed since 1971 and allows solicitors who do not have the required certificate of advocacy a route into the judiciary. About 10 per cent of Circuit Judges are solicitors.

The Courts and Legal Services Act 1990 also allows for promotion after being a District Judge, stipendiary magistrate or chairman of

an employment tribunal for at least three years. These provisions have widened the pool of potential judges and are gradually leading to a better cross-section among the judges at this level.

The usual route to becoming a Circuit Judge is to be appointed as a Recorder first and then be promoted to a Circuit Judge.

16.2.5 Recorders

This is a part-time post. The applicant must have practised as a barrister or solicitor for at least 10 years, though in practice it is rare to be appointed with less than 15 years' experience. Usually an applicant is appointed as a Recorder in training first and then appointed as a Recorder.

16.2.6 District Judges

These need a seven-year general qualification. This means they can be appointed from either barristers or solicitors, but in practice the vast majority of District Judges in the County Court are solicitors. District Judges in the Magistrates' Courts need the same qualifications. About two-thirds of these are former solicitors.

16.3 Selection

16.3.1 History

Until 2005, the Lord Chancellor was the key figure in the selection of superior judges. The Lord Chancellor's Department would keep information on all possible candidates. These files would contain confidential information and opinions from existing judges on the suitability of each person. The contents of these files were secret.

When there was a vacancy for a judicial

position in the House of Lords, the Court of Appeal or the High Court, the Lord Chancellor would consider the information in these files and decide which person he thought was the best for the post. That person would then be invited to become a judge.

Not surprisingly, this system of selection was seen as secretive. It was also felt that it favoured white males, as there were few women in the higher ranks of the judiciary.

Matters improved for High Court judgeships as, from 1998, vacancies were advertised and any qualified person could apply. However, even then, the Lord Chancellor continued to invite people to become judges, rather than appoint solely from those who applied.

The major role of the Lord Chancellor in appointment was very controversial as the Lord Chancellor is a political appointment. (See section 16.9 for further information on the Lord Chancellor.) It was thought that the appointment of judges should be independent from any political influence. So the method of appointment was changed by the Constitutional Reform Act 2005.

The following sections will explain how appointments are now made.

16.3.2 The Law Lords

There are 12 Lords of Appeal in Ordinary who sit in the Appellate Committee of the House of Lords (this is the correct title for the House of Lords in its judicial capacity).

Law Lords are made life peers and are entitled to sit in the House of Lords in its legislative capacity and take part in debates. The appointments are made by the Queen after being nominated by the Prime Minister; in fact, the normal procedure is understood to be that the Lord Chancellor draws up a short list in order of preference and the Prime Minister selects from this list. In nearly all

cases the first choice candidate of the Lord Chancellor will be the one who is appointed, but it is known that Mrs Thatcher on at least one occasion vetoed the first choice and nominated the second choice.

This system of selection will remain until the new Supreme Court replaces the House of Lords.

The first women judge to sit as a Law 'Lord' was appointed in January 2004. She is Lady Hale and she had previously been a judge in the Court of Appeal.

16.3.3 Judges of the new Supreme Court

When the Supreme Court is established, probably in 2009, judges for this court will be selected according to the method set out in Part 3 of the Constitutional Reform Act 2005. This states that when there is a vacancy, the Lord Chancellor must convene a Supreme Court selection commission.

This commission must include the President and the Deputy President of the Supreme Court and one member of the Judicial Appointments Commission. As the Supreme Court is also the final court of appeal for Scotland and Northern Ireland, the commission must also include a member of the Judicial Appointments Board for Scotland and the Northern Ireland Judicial Appointments Commission.

The commission will decide the selection process to be used. It will then use that process to select a candidate and report that selection to the Lord Chancellor.

Under s 29 of the Constitutional Reform Act 2005, the Lord Chancellor can reject that candidate or ask the commission to reconsider. This can only be done if the Lord Chancellor is of the opinion that the person selected is not suitable for the office or that there is evidence

used to form part of the panel. This means there may be one Lord Justice of Appeal sitting with two High Court judges.

In law reports Court of Appeal judges are referred to as Lord Justice or Lady Justice, but when their judgments are being quoted they are usually referred to by their surname followed by LJ, for example, Arden LJ.

16.5.3 High Court judges

Each judge in the High Court will be assigned to one of the Divisions. There are 72 judges in the Queen's Bench Division, 17 in the Chancery Division and 18 in the Family Division.

There are also Deputy High Court judges who sit to help with the workload.

The main function of High Court judges is to try cases. These are cases at first instance, because it is the first time the case has been heard by a court. They will hear evidence from witnesses, decide what the law is and make the decision as to which side has won the case. If the claim is for damages (an amount of money) the judge decides how much should be awarded to the winning claimant. The type of work dealt with by each Division is described more fully in Chapter 9. When hearing first instance cases, judges sit on their own. In some rare cases there may be a jury.

High Court judges also hear some appeals. These are mainly from civil cases tried in the County Court. The judges in the Queen's Bench Division also hear criminal appeals from the Magistrates' Courts by a special case stated method. These are appeals on law only. When sitting to hear appeals, there will be a panel of two or three judges.

Judges from the Queen's Bench Division also sit to hear criminal trials in the Crown Court. When they do this they sit with a jury. The jury decide the facts and the judge decides

the law. Where a defendant pleads guilty or is found guilty by a jury, the judge then has to decide on the sentence.

In law reports, High Court judges are referred to as Mr Justice or Mrs Justice, but when their judgments are being quoted they are usually referred to by their surname followed by J, for example, Dobbs J.

Activity

Look up law reports on the Internet. Try *www.bailii.org*.

TRY TO FIND

1. A law report in which there was a female judge.

2. A report of the Court of Appeal in which at least one of the judges is only of High Court level.

3. A report from the High Court in which the judge sitting is only a Deputy High Court judge.

16.5.4 Inferior judges

Circuit Judges sit in the County Court to hear civil cases and also in the Crown Court to try criminal cases. In civil cases they sit on their own (it is very rare to have a jury in a civil case in the county court). They decide the law and the facts. They make the decision on who has won the case.

In criminal cases they sit with a jury. The jury decide the facts and the judge decides the law. Where a defendant pleads guilty or is found guilty by a jury, the judge then has to decide on the sentence.

Recorders are part-time judges who are

Court	Judge	Qualification	Role
House of Lords	Lords of Appeal in Ordinary Also known as Law Lords	15-year supreme court qualification *or* hold high judicial office	Hear appeals on points of law Civil and criminal cases
Court of Appeal	Lord Justices of Appeal	10-year supreme court qualification *or* be an existing High Court judge	Hear appeals Criminal cases against conviction and/or sentence Civil cases on the finding and /or the amount awarded
High Court	High Court judges Also known as puisne judges	10-year supreme court qualification *or* Be a Circuit judge for 2 years	Sit in one of the three Divisions Hear first instance cases and decide liability and remedy Some appeal work
Crown Court	High Court judges	See above	Try cases with a jury
	Circuit judges	10-year Crown Court or County Court qualification or be a recorder or district judge for 3 years	Decide the law
	Recorders	10-year Crown Court or County Court qualification	Pass sentence on guilty defendants
County Court	Circuit judges	See above	Civil cases decide liability and remedy
County Court	District judges	7-year general qualification	District judges hear small claims
Magistrates' Courts	District judges (Magistrates' Courts)	7-year general qualification	Criminal cases – decide law and verdict Pass sentence on guilty defendants Some family work

Figure 16.1 *Key facts chart of qualifications, selection and appointment of judges*

appointed for a period of five years. They are used mainly in the Crown Court to try criminal cases, but some sit in the County Court to help with civil cases.

District Judges sit in the County Court to deal with small claims cases (under £5,000) and can also hear other cases for larger amounts.

District Judges (Magistrates' Courts) sit to try criminal cases in the Magistrates' Courts. They sit on their own and decide facts and law. When a defendant pleads guilty or is found guilty,

they also have to decide on the sentence.

They may also sit to hear family cases, but this will usually be with two lay magistrates.

16.6 Composition of the Bench

One of the main criticisms of the Bench is that it is dominated by elderly, white, upper-class males. There are very few women judges, and even fewer judges from ethnic minorities. With the introduction of a younger retirement age, the average age of judges will be slightly reduced, but it is unusual for any judge to be appointed under the age of 40, with superior judges usually being well above this age.

16.6.1 Women in the judiciary

The number of women in judicial posts is very small, although there has been an improvement in recent years. During the 1990s there was an increase in the number of women appointed to the High Court. The first woman judge in the Queen's Bench Division was appointed in 1992, and the first in the Chancery Division in 1993.

The first woman in the Court of Appeal was appointed in 1988. This was Lady Butler-Sloss. The legal system was so unused to women in the higher levels of the judiciary that when she was appointed she had to be addressed in court as My Lord, and in law reports her title was written as Lord Butler-Sloss!

In 1994 the then Master of the Rolls (the head of the Civil Division of the Court of Appeal) announced that in future she should be addressed as My Lady. However, it was not until the Courts Act 2003 that the official title of women judges in the Court of Appeal became Lady Justice of Appeal.

It was not until 1999 that a second woman was appointed to the Court of Appeal, and a third in 2000. In February 2001 the first all-female Court of Appeal panel sat. The first, and so far only, woman judge in the House of Lords was appointed in 2004.

By the beginning of 2007 the total number of women judges in the High Court was still only ten out of just over 100 judges, with only three women out of 37 judges in the Court of Appeal.

Lower down the judicial ladder, there are slightly more women being appointed than in

the past. At the beginning of 2007, 11 per cent of Circuit Judges and 14 per cent of Recorders were female. The highest percentages of women were for District Judges (23 per cent).

16.6.2 Ethnic minorities

In 2004 the first ethnic minority judge was appointed to the High Court. Even at the lower levels, ethnic minorities are still poorly represented. At the beginning of 2007 only 1.5 per cent of Circuit Judges and 4.5 per cent of Recorders were from an ethnic minority. These percentages have not changed much over the past five years. However, there have been improvements at the lowest levels, with over 8 per cent of Deputy District Judges (Magistrates' Courts) being from an ethnic minority.

It will be interesting to see if the new appointments system leads to greater diversity.

16.6.3 Educational and social background

At the higher levels judges tend to come from the upper levels of society, with many having been educated at public school and nearly all attending Oxford or Cambridge University. A survey by the magazine, *Labour Research*, found that of the 85 judges appointed from 1997 to mid-1999, 73 per cent had been to public school and 79 per cent to Oxbridge. Judges (especially superior judges) will have spent at least 20 years working as barristers and mixing with a small group of like-minded people. As a result, judges are seen as out of touch with society. Occasionally the media report actions or comments which appear to support this view, for example, where a judge said of an eight-year-old rape victim that she 'was no angel'. Since 1995 training in human awareness has been given to prevent such

Activity

Read the following newspaper article and answer the questions below.

Do you fancy being a High Court judge? Forget the whisper over a drink at your Inn of Court or the traditional "tap on the shoulder". Dust off your CV and send in an application. And then prepare yourself for an "interview" with a selection panel. This is the new world of appointing judges…

The selection process will be undertaken by the Judicial Appointments Commission, the independent body set up under the Constitutional Reform Act in 2005 to take over responsibility for selecting judges from the Lord Chancellor's officials.

There has been advertising for High Court judges before – but they were selected on paper. This time, the candidates will undergo a face-to-face discussion – and that, with references and their own application form, will combine to inform the selection.

Baroness Usha Prashar, who is chairman of the 15 lay and judicial commissioners and 105 staff, will now be responsible for 500 to 700 appointments a year, including the High Court…

The aim she says is for a much more transparent process that will encourage a greater diversity of candidates. "Up to now the process was perceived to be very secretive and not very open. There was a view that it was those who you knew who counted and that probably deterred a lot of people who felt they would not get a fair deal. This will be objective and transparent and hopefully that will encourage more people to apply."

Taken from an article by Francis Gibb, *The Times*, 31 October 2006

Questions

1. Who was responsible for appointing judges under the old system?

2. Who is responsible for appointing judges now?

3. Describe the problems with the old system of appointing judges.

4. Describe how the new system operates.

5. Explain whether you think that the new system will encourage a wider range of applicants for judgeships.

Research

Look up the judicial website *www.judiciary.gov.uk.*

1. Look up the names of the judges in the House of Lords. Choose any two and look at their biographies. Find out the following matters:

   (a) Which school did they go to?

   (b) At which university did they get their degree?

   (c) When did they first become a judge?

   (d) When did they become a judge in the House of Lords?

2. Find out how many woman judges there are in the Court of Appeal.

3. Find out how many ethnic minority judges there are in the High Court.

offensive remarks. Lord Taylor, a former Lord Chief Justice, who was one of the few senior judges who had attended a state school, pointed out that judges live in the real world and do ordinary things like shopping in supermarkets.

16.7 Training

The training of judges is carried out by the Judicial Studies Board, which was set up in 1979. Most of the training is, however, focused at the lower end of the judicial scale, being aimed at recorders. Once a lawyer has been appointed as a recorder in training, they go on a one-week course run by the Judicial Studies Board, and then shadow an experienced judge for a week. After this they will sit to hear cases, though there will be one-day courses available from time to time, especially on the effect of new legislation.

Critics point out that the training is very short, and that even if all the people involved are experienced lawyers this does not mean that they have any experience of doing such tasks as summing up to the jury or sentencing.

There is also the fact that some recorders will not have practised in the criminal courts as lawyers, so their expertise is limited and a one-week course a very short training period.

There is no compulsory training given to new High Court judges, although they are invited to attend the courses run by the Judicial Studies Board. The attitude of the judiciary to training has changed considerably over the last 20 years. Training used to be seen as insulting to lawyers who had spent all their working lives in the courts building up expertise in their field. It was also seen as a threat to judicial independence. However, the need for training is now fully accepted.

Human awareness training

In 1993 the Judicial Studies Board recommended that training should include racial awareness courses. This was accepted by the Lord Chancellor and all Circuit judges and recorders now have to attend a course designed to make them aware of what might be unintentionally discriminatory or offensive, such as asking a non-Christian for their Christian name. The Board has also introduced training in human awareness, covering gender awareness, and disability issues. The training explores the perceptions of unrepresented parties, witnesses, jurors, victims and their families, and tries to make judges more aware of other people's viewpoints.

Legal research

Another problem that exists is the lack of research facilities for judges at all levels – this is especially true of the appellate courts, where the cases are likely to involve complex legal points. The judges in the Court of Appeal have only four days a month for legal reading, and, unlike many foreign courts, there are no lawyers attached to the court to research the law. In the European Court of Justice there are Advocates General who are independent lawyers working for the court, whose task is to research legal points and present their findings.

16.7.1 Should there be a 'career' judiciary?

In many continental countries becoming a judge is a career choice made by students once they have their basic legal qualifications. They will usually not practise as a lawyer first, but instead are trained as judges. Once they have qualified as a judge they will sit in junior posts and then hope to be promoted up the judicial ladder. This has two distinct advantages over the system in use in this country:

- The average age of judges is much lower, especially in the bottom ranks. In this country an assistant recorder will normally be in their late thirties or early forties when appointed, and the average age for appointment to the High Court Bench tends to be late forties/early fifties
- Judges have had far more training in the specific skills they need as judges.

The disadvantage of the continental system is that judges may be seen as too closely linked to the government as they are civil servants. In this country judges are generally considered as independent from the government. This point of judicial independence is explored more fully in section 16.10.

Elected judges

In the USA judges at state and local level are elected to their posts. This may cause pressure groups to canvass voters actively for or against judges, according to the views the judges hold. Judges in the federal courts are appointed by the President but the appointment has to be confirmed by the Senate. Before voting on a new appointee the Senate can question him or her about their background and past life and this is usually televised. This makes the appointment system very public, but can lead to political overtones in the appointment system, with one political party voting for a candidate and the opposing party voting against that candidate.

16.8 Retirement and dismissal

It is important that judges should be impartial in their decisions and, in particular, that the Government cannot force a judge to resign if that judge makes a decision with which the Government of the day disagrees. In this country judges are reasonably secure from political interference. The only exception to this rule is the Lord Chancellor. His is a political appointment and the Prime Minister can dismiss the Lord Chancellor at any time, just as the Prime Minister has the right to dismiss any other Cabinet member. The Lord Chancellor will also change with a change of Government.

forward by groups such as the local political parties, trade unions and chambers of commerce. To try and encourage as wide a range of potential candidates as possible committees have advertised for individuals to put themselves forward with advertisements being placed in local papers, or newspapers aimed at particular ethnic groups, and even on buses! For example, in Leeds, radio adverts have been used and people encouraged to come to open evenings at their local Magistrates' Court in order to get as wide a spectrum of potential candidates as possible.

The intention is to create a panel that is representative of all aspects of society. In 1966 the then Lord Chancellor, Lord Gardiner, issued a directive to advisory committees telling them to bear in mind people's political allegiances in order to get a balance. At the time this caused a stir, but the reason behind it was to try to get better balanced panels of magistrates. That directive said:

'The Lord Chancellor cannot disregard political affiliations in making appointments, not because the politics of an individual are a qualification or a disqualification for appointment, but because it is important that justices should be drawn from all sections of the community and should represent all shades of opinion.

This object would not be attained if appointments were made in too large a degree from supporters of any one political party. It is the aim of the Lord Chancellor to preserve a proper balance by the appointment of suitable parties from the main political parties, and, if they can be found, from persons who are independent of any political party.

For these reasons the Lord Chancellor wishes advisory committees to have regard for the political affiliations of the persons whom they recommend for appointment.'

This is still the case today – Lord Irvine, the then Lord Chancellor, wanted to find an alternative way of getting a good social balance on magistrates' panels. However, he announced in 1999 that he had reluctantly concluded that, for the moment, political balance remained the most practicable method.

A balance of occupations is also aimed at. The Lord Chancellor has set down 11 broad categories of occupations, and advisory committees are recommended that they should not have more than 15 per cent of the bench coming from any one category.

17.4.2 Interview process

There is usually a two-stage interview process. At the first interview the panel tries to find out more about the candidate's personal attributes, in particular looking to see if they have the six key qualities required. The interview panel will also explore the candidate's attitudes on various criminal justice issues such as youth crime or drink driving. The second interview is aimed at testing candidates' potential judicial aptitude and this is done by a discussion of at least two case studies which are typical of those heard regularly in magistrates' courts. The discussion might, for example, focus on the type of sentence which should be imposed on specific case facts.

The advisory committees will interview candidates and then submit names of those they think are suitable to the Lord Chancellor. He will then appoint new magistrates from this list. Once appointed, magistrates may continue to sit until the age of 70.

17.5 Composition of the Bench today

The traditional image of lay justices is that they are 'middle-class, middle-aged and middle-minded'. This image is to a certain extent true.

Most magistrates are in the 45–65 age bracket. Magistrates under the age of 40 are still rare. The majority are supporters of the Conservative party; this is so even in areas where there is a high Labour vote. A report, *The Judiciary in the Magistrates' Courts* (2002), which had been commissioned jointly by the Home Office and the Lord Chancellor's Department found that lay magistrates:

- were drawn overwhelmingly from professional and managerial ranks; and
- 40 per cent of them were retired from full-time employment.

However, in other respects the bench is well balanced: 49 per cent of magistrates are women as against 10 per cent of professional judges. Also, ethnic minority are reasonably well represented in the magistracy. The National Strategy for the Recruitment of Lay Magistrates (2003) gave the statistics for ethnic minority lay magistrates as being 6 per cent of the total number of lay magistrates as against 7.9 per cent of the population as a whole. This compares very favourably to the professional judiciary where less than 1 per cent are from ethnic minority backgrounds.

The relatively high level of ethnic minority magistrates is largely a result of campaigns to attract a wider range of candidates. A major campaign was launched by the Lord Chancellor's Department in March 1999. Under this, adverts encouraging people to apply were placed in some 36 different newspapers and magazines. Adverts were placed in national newspapers and also in TV guides and women's magazines. In an effort to encourage those from ethnic minorities to apply, adverts also appeared in such publications as the *Caribbean Times*, the *Asian Times* and *Muslim News*. This led to an increase in the number of ethnic minority appointments.

The Lord Chancellor has encouraged disabled people to apply to become magistrates. In 1998 the first blind lay magistrates were appointed.

17.6 Magistrates' duties

They have a very wide workload which is mainly connected to criminal cases, although they also deal with some civil matters, especially family cases. They try 97 per cent of all criminal cases and deal with preliminary hearings in the remaining 3 per cent of criminal cases. This will involve Early Administrative Hearings, remand hearings, bail applications and committal proceedings. They also deal with civil matters which include the enforcing of debts owed to the utilities (gas, electric and water), non-payment of the council tax and non payment of television licenses. In addition they hear appeals from the refusal of a local authority to grant licences for the sale of alcohol and licences for betting and gaming establishments.

Youth Court

Specially nominated and trained justices form the Youth Court panel to hear criminal charges against young offenders aged 10–17 years old. These magistrates must be under 65 and a panel must usually include at least one man and one woman. There is also a special panel for the Family Court to hear family cases including orders for protection against violence, affiliation cases, adoption orders and proceedings under the Children Act 1989.

Appeals

Lay magistrates also sit at the Crown Court to hear appeals from the Magistrates' Court. In these cases the lay justices form a panel with a qualified judge.

Activity

Read the following article and answer the questions below.

Calling all those who would be magistrates

The public perceives a JP as a middle-aged, middle-class person who 'knows the right people'. Up to a point, this is true; it may well be the 'right people' who suggest you apply to be a JP. But after that, you're on your own. Your application and references will be thoroughly vetted, and you will undergo a searching interview. However, if you are appointed, you will probably be nearer 40 than 30 – possibly older.

Why don't we see younger JPs? 'Lack of maturity/experience' is usually given as the reason for not appointing many applicants in the 25 to 30 age group, but this begs the question of why comparatively few JPs are in their thirties or forties.

Since most defendants are under 40, why aren't there more JPs of a similar age? It is unlikely that the selection procedure is at fault – age is not a qualification *per se*. A more probable reason is that people from this age group submit fewer applications, which may well be through lack of awareness. For example, did you know that you do not have to be nominated by someone else – you can nominate yourself? Why don't we see more 'recruitment' advertising that emphasises this point? Perhaps the Lord Chancellor's Department thinks it would not be able to cope.

More probably, it is outside factors that inhibit younger applicants. JPs have to sit at least 26 times a year, plus 'training days'. How many people can take this kind of time off work? Will their employer pay them? Will they be passed over for promotion because they are 'hardly ever there'? Employers do not take kindly to someone who wants to take off more than two days a month. Civic responsibility does not contribute to company profits. Nevertheless, employers should take the wider view and encourage service as a JP. Spin-off from this policy would be employees who have received training in analysing situations in a structured manner – a rarity in many firms.

If we grant that there is a preponderance of 40 to 60-year-olds on the bench, it is not surprising that many an 18-year-old driver considers the bench that fined him £100 for speeding were a bunch of old fogeys and that he has not had a hearing by his peers.

If you think that *he* has a point, how do you think a young *black* person feels? Only about 6 per cent of newly appointed magistrates come from ethnic minorities, creating an enormous imbalance from the point of view of race.

In practice, the standard complement of three JPs in court ensures that an extremist view held by one member cannot decide the verdict. And, if such views *were* expressed by a JP, he or she could well be asked to resign. The lay magistracy is certainly not a breeding ground for any kind of racial bias.

But, as the old adage that is repeated *ad nauseam* has it, 'Justice must be seen to be done'. And many a convicted defendant from an ethnic minority may feel that he or she did not have a fair hearing purely and simply because all the JPs were white. It won't be true but that doesn't stop him or her from thinking it.

There is no easy answer as to why ethnic minorities are under-represented. It may be that many are in blue-collar jobs, and therefore cannot take the time off work. Perhaps they feel they will be out of place in an institution that is dominated by white people? Or do they fear rejection by their own people?

Nobody is suggesting that positive discrimination be practised in order to boost the number of JPs from ethnic minorities. But with constant criticism of the fact that there is a disproportionate number of such people in prison, surely it would be a positive step to encourage applications actively from ethnic minorities?

Taken from an article by Derek Edmunds in *The Times*, 21 February 1995

Questions

1. What reasons does the article put forward for the lack of young JPs?
2. Why is it suggested that there should be more young JPs?
3. Why does the article suggest that more magistrates from ethnic minorities should be appointed?
4. Do you think that it is necessary for the lay bench to be a wide cross-section of society? Give reasons for your answer.

17.7 Training of lay magistrates

The training of lay magistrates is supervised by the Magistrates' Committee of the Judicial Studies Board. This Committee has drawn up a syllabus of the topics which lay magistrates should cover in their training. However, because of the large numbers of lay magistrates, the actual training is carried out in local areas, sometimes through the clerk of the court, sometimes through weekend courses organised by universities with magistrates from the region attending.

Since 1998 magistrates' training has been monitored more closely. There were criticisms prior to then that, although magistrates were required to attend a certain number of hours training, there was no assessment of how much they had understood. In 1998 the Magistrates New Training Initiative was introduced (MNTI 1). In 2004 this was refined by the Magistrates National Training Initiative (MNTI 2).

The framework of training is divided into four areas of competence, the first three of which are relevant to all lay magistrates. The fourth competence is for chairmen of the bench. The four areas of competence are:

1. Managing yourself – this focuses on some of the basic aspects of self-management in relation to preparing for court, conduct in court and ongoing learning.
2. Working as a member of a team – this focuses on the team aspect of decision-making in the Magistrates' Court.
3. Making judicial decisions – this focuses on impartial and structured decision-making.
4. Managing judicial decision-making – this is for the chairman's role and focuses on working with the legal adviser, managing the court and ensuring effective, impartial decision-making.

For delivering training there are Bench Training and Developmental Committees (BTDCs) and s 19(3) of the Courts Act 2003 sets out a statutory obligation on the Lord Chancellor to provide training and training materials.

17.7.1 Training of new magistrates

There is a syllabus for new magistrates which is divided into three parts. These are:

1. **Initial introductory training**:
   this covers such matters as understanding the organisation of the Bench and the administration of the court and the roles and responsibilities of those involved in the Magistrates' Court.
2. **Core training**:
   this provides the new magistrate with the opportunity to acquire and develop the key skills, knowledge and understanding required of a competent magistrate.
3. **Activities**:
   these will involve observations of court sittings and visits to establishments such as a prison or a probation office.

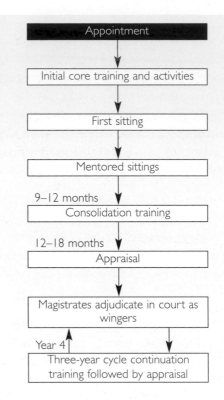

Figure 17.1 New magistrates' training and appraisal pathway (taken from MNTI2 Handbook issued by the Judicial Studies Board)

The training programme for new magistrates should normally follow the pattern set out in Figure 17.1.

17.7.2 Mentors

Each new magistrate keeps a Personal Development Log of their progress and has a mentor (an experienced magistrate) to assist them. The initial introductory training is covered before the new magistrate starts sitting in court. They will also take part in a structured court room observation of cases on at least three occasions. These should be arranged so that they see different aspects of the work and should include preliminary decisions such as bail, a short summary trial and sentencing.

17.7.3 Training sessions

These are organised and carried out at local level within the 42 court areas. Much of the training is delivered by Justices' Clerks. The Judicial Studies Board intends that most training should still be delivered locally. However, they take into account the need to collaborate regionally and nationally where appropriate. In particular, the training of Youth and Family Panel Chairmen will be delivered nationally for Areas which do not have enough such Chairmen requiring training to run an effective course locally.

17.7.4 Appraisal

During the first two years of the new magistrate sitting in court, between eight and eleven of the sessions will be mentored. In the same period the magistrate is also expected to attend about seven training sessions. After two years, or whenever it is felt that the magistrate is ready, there will be an appraisal of the magistrate to check if they have acquired the competencies.

Any magistrate who cannot show that they have achieved the competencies will be given extra training. If they still cannot achieve the competencies, then the matter is referred to the local Advisory Committee, who may recommend to the Lord Chancellor that the magistrate is removed from sitting.

This new scheme involves practical training 'on the job'. It also answers the criticisms of the old system where there was no check made on whether the magistrate had actually benefited from the training session they attended.

Those magistrates who chair the bench are also appraised for this role, so that the quality of the chairing in court is improving.

17.8 Retirement and removal

The retirement age is 70, but when magistrates become 70 they do not officially retire – instead their names are placed on the Supplemental List. This means that they can no longer sit in the Magistrates' Court. However, they can continue to carry out some administrative functions mainly connected with signing documents. Lay magistrates who move from the commission area to which they were appointed cannot continue as magistrates in that area. If they wish to continue as magistrates their names will be placed on the Supplemental List until there is a vacancy in their new area. Lay magistrates may, of course, resign from office at any time and many will resign before reaching 70.

17.8.1 Removal

Section 11 of the Courts Act 2003 gives the Lord Chancellor the power to remove a lay justice for the following reasons:

- on the ground of incapacity or misbehaviour
- on the ground of a persistent failure to meet such standards of competence as are prescribed by a direction given by the Lord Chancellor; or
- if the Lord Chancellor is satisfied that the lay justice is declining or neglecting to take a proper part in the exercise of his functions as a justice of the peace.

Up to now removal for misbehaviour usually occurs when a magistrate is convicted of a criminal offence. There are about 10 such removals each year. However, on occasions in the past there have been removals for such matters as taking part in a CND march or

<table>
<tr><td rowspan="6" style="writing-mode: vertical-lr;">Key Facts</td></tr>
<tr><td>Qualifications</td><td>Live or work near
Need common sense, integrity
Disqualified for serious criminal record, bankruptcy or work that is incompatible</td></tr>
<tr><td>Appointment</td><td>By Lord Chancellor on the recommendation of local advisory committees</td></tr>
<tr><td>Training</td><td>Four basic competencies:
Personal Development Log of progress
Mentors and mentored sessions
Attend about seven training sessions
Appraisal</td></tr>
<tr><td>Composition of bench</td><td>29,000 lay magistrates, 50.3 per cent men, 49.7 per cent women
Over-representation of Conservative supporters
Under-representation of young working class</td></tr>
<tr><td>Work</td><td>Summary trials
Ancillary matters e.g. issuing warrants, bail applications
Youth court
Family court</td></tr>
</table>

Figure 17.2 Key fact chart on lay magistrates

transvestite behaviour. There was considerable criticism of the Lord Chancellor's use of his power of removal in such circumstances and it unlikely that such behaviour today would lead to removal from the bench.

17.9 The magistrates' clerk

Every bench is assisted by a clerk. These are now also referred to as legal advisers. The senior clerk in each court has to be qualified as a barrister or solicitor for at least five years. The clerk's duty is to guide the magistrates on questions of law, practice and procedure. This is set out in s 28(3) of the Justices of the Peace Act 1979 which says:

'It is hereby declared that the functions of a justices' clerk include the giving to the justices . . . of advice about law, practice or procedure on questions arising in connection with the discharge of their functions.'

The clerk is not meant to assist in the decision-making and should not normally retire with the magistrates when they go to make their decision. In *R* v *Eccles Justices, ex parte Farrelly* (1992) the Queen's Bench Divisional Court quashed convictions because the clerk had apparently participated in the decision-making process.

Clerks deal with routine administrative matters and in May 1993 were given increased powers so that they can now issue warrants for arrest, extend police bail, adjourn criminal proceedings. The Crime and Disorder Act 1998 also gives clerks the powers to deal with Early Administrative Hearings.

17.10 Advantages of lay magistrates

17.10.1 Cross-section of society

Lay magistrates provide a wider cross-section on the bench than would be possible with the use of professional judges. This is particularly true of women with 49 per cent of magistrates being women compared with 10 per cent of professional judges. Also, ethnic minorities are reasonably well represented in the magistracy.

In 1999 the Lord Chancellor announced this campaign to attract a wider range of magistrates, but he pointed out that the magistracy was already very diverse:

'Magistrates come from a wide range of backgrounds and occupations. We have magistrates who are dinner ladies and scientists, bus drivers and teachers, plumbers and housewives. They have different faiths and come from different ethnic backgrounds, some have disabilities. All are serving their communities, ensuring that local justice is dispensed by local people. The magistracy should reflect the diversity of the community it serves.'

Lay magistrates are more representative than District Judges in the Magistrates' Courts. In 2000 a report, *The Judiciary in the Magistrates' Courts*, pointed out that in comparison to lay magistrates, District Judges were:

- younger; but
- mostly white and male.

17.10.2 Local knowledge

Lay magistrates used to have to live within 15 miles of the area covered by the commission, in order that they would have local knowledge of particular problems in the area. Under the Courts Act 2003 there is no longer a formal requirement that they should live in or near the area in which they sit as a magistrate, although it is intended that normally magistrates will continue to sit in the local justice area in which they reside. However, if there is a good reason to do otherwise, for example, where it is easier for the magistrate to sit in the area where he or she works, then this is allowed.

Even though lay magistrates live or work in the relevant justice area, it is sometimes argued that they do not have any real knowledge of the problems in the poorer areas. This is because most magistrates come from the professional and managerial classes and will live in the better areas. However, their main value is that they will have more awareness of local events, local patterns of crime and local opinions than a professional judge from another area.

Another problem is that during the last 10 years, some 125 Magistrates' Courts have been closed. This causes problems of access and attendance as in some areas people have long journeys to their 'local' court. It also means that the advantage of lay magistrates having local knowledge is being lost.

17.10.3 Cost

The use of unpaid lay magistrates is cheap. The report *The Judiciary in the Magistrates' Courts* (2000) found that at that time the cost of using lay magistrates was £52.10 per hour. As against this the cost of using district judges in the magistrates' courts was £61.78 an hour. When this is multiplied by the number of hours' work carried out by lay magistrates in the course of the year, it is obvious that the cost of replacing them with professional judges would be several millions of pounds. In addition, there would also be the problem of recruiting sufficient qualified lawyers.

The cost of a trial in the Magistrates' Court

Members of the forces

Full-time serving members of the forces may be excused from jury service if their commanding officer certifies that their absence from duty (because of jury service) would be prejudicial to the efficiency of the service.

18.3.6 Discretionary excusals

Anyone who has problems which make it very difficult for them to do their jury service, may ask to be excused or for their period of service to be put back to a later date. The court has a discretion to grant such an excusal but will only do so if there is a sufficiently good reason. Such reasons include being too ill to attend court or suffering from a disability that makes it impossible for the person to sit as a juror, or being a mother with a small baby. Other reasons could include business appointments that cannot be undertaken by anyone else, examinations or holidays that have been booked.

In these situations the court is most likely to defer jury service to a more convenient date, rather than excuse the person completely. This is stated in the current guidance for summoning officers which is aimed at preventing the high number of discretionary excusals. The guidance states that:

'The normal expectation is that _everyone_ summoned for jury service will serve at the time for which they are summoned. It is recognised that there will be occasions where it is not reasonable for a person summoned to serve at the time for which they are summoned. In such circumstances the summoning officer should use his/her discretion to defer the individual to a time more appropriate. Only in extreme circumstances, should a person be excused from jury service.'

If a person is not excused from jury service they must attend on the date set or they may be fined up to £1,000 for non-attendance.

This fact, that everyone is now expected to do jury service, is controversial. This is because, as well as the old category of 'excusable as of right', there was also a category of people who were ineligible for jury service. This included judges and others who had been involved in the administration of justice within the previous 10 years. This category was also abolished by the Criminal Justice Act 2003. This means that judges, lawyers, police, etc. are eligible to serve on juries. Many people feel that this could lead to bias or to a legally well-qualified juror influencing the rest of the jury.

Judges on jury service

In June 2004 (just two months after the rules on jury service changed) a judge from the Court of Appeal, Lord Justice Dyson, was summoned to attend as a juror. This prompted the Lord Chief Justice, Lord Woolf, to issue observations to judges who are called for jury service. These point out that:

- a judge serves on a jury as part of his duty as a private citizen
- excusal from jury service will only be granted in extreme circumstances
- deferral of jury service to a later date should be sought where a judge has judicial commitments which make it particularly inconvenient for him to do jury service at the time he was called to do so
- at court if a judge knows the presiding judge or other person in the case, he should raise this with the jury bailiff or a member of the court staff if he considers it could interfere with his responsibilities as a juror
- it is a matter of discretion for an individual judge sitting as a juror as to whether he discloses the fact of his judicial office to the other members of the jury

- judges must follow the directions given to the jury by the trial judge on the law and should avoid the temptation to correct guidance which they believe to be inaccurate as this is outside their role as a juror.

The point about letting the court know when someone involved in the case is personally known to the juror is also relevant to practising lawyers who are called for jury service. It was noticeable that when a Queen's Counsel was summoned for jury service at the Central Criminal Court (the Old Bailey) in the summer of 2004, he was prevented from sitting in each case that he was called for, on the grounds that he knew one or more people involved in each trial.

Activity

Discuss whether you think the following people should sit on a jury:

1. A woman who was fined for shoplifting a month ago.

2. A man who was fined and disqualified from driving for taking cars without the consent of the owner.

3. A doctor who works in general practice.

4. A doctor who works in an accident and emergency unit of a busy city hospital.

5. A Circuit Judge who frequently tries cases in the Crown Court.

18.4 Selecting a jury

At each Crown Court there is an official who is responsible for summonsing enough jurors to try the cases that will be heard in each two week period. This official will arrange for names to be selected at random from the electoral registers, for the area which the court covers. This is done through a computer selection at a central office. It is necessary to summons more than 12 jurors as most courts have more than one court-room and it will not be known how many of those summonsed are disqualified – or will be excused. In fact, at the bigger courts up to 150 summons may be sent out each fortnight.

Those summonsed must notify the court if there is any reason why they should not or cannot attend. All others are expected to attend for two weeks' jury service, though, of course, if the case they are trying goes on for more than two weeks they will have to stay until the trial is completed. Where it is known that a trial may be exceptionally long, such as a complicated fraud trial, potential jurors are asked if they will be able to serve for such a long period.

18.4.1 Vetting

Once the list of potential jurors is known, both the prosecution and the defence have the right to see that list. In some cases it may be decided that this pool of potential jurors should be 'vetted', i.e. checked for suitability. There are two types of vetting.

Routine police checks

Routine police checks are made on prospective jurors to eliminate those disqualified. In *R v Crown Court at Sheffield, ex parte Brownlow* (1980) the defendant was a police officer and the defence sought permission to vet the jury panel for convictions. The judge gave

Court	Crown Court
Qualifications	18–70 age Registered to vote Resident in UK for at least five years since age 13
Disqualified	Sentenced to five years' or more imprisonment – disqualified for life Served a prison sentence OR suspended sentence OR a community order – disqualified for 10 years On bail – disqualified while on bail
Excusals	Members of the armed forces Discretionary – ill, business commitments, or other 'good reason'
Selection	A central office selects names from the lists of electors Summons sent to these people Must attend unless disqualified or excused
Vetting	May be checked for criminal record – *R v Mason* (1980) In cases of national security may be subject to a wider check on background subject to Attorney-General's guidelines
Challenges	Individual juror may be challenged for cause, e.g. knows defendant Whole panel may be challenged for biased selection – but no right to a multi-racial jury (*R v Ford* (1989)) Prosecution may 'stand by' any juror
Function	Decide verdict – Guilty or Not guilty Sole arbiters of fact but judge directs them on law
Verdict	Must try for a unanimous verdict BUT if cannot reach a unanimous verdict then a majority verdict can be accepted of 10:2 or 11:1

Figure 18.2 Key fact chart on the use of juries in criminal cases

permission but the Court of Appeal, while holding that it had no power to interfere, said that vetting was 'unconstitutional' and a 'serious invasion of privacy' and not sanctioned by the Juries Act 1974. However, in *R v Mason* (1980) where it was revealed that the Chief Constable for Northamptonshire had been allowing widespread use of unauthorised vetting of criminal records, the Court of Appeal approved of this type of vetting. Lawton LJ pointed out that, since it is a criminal offence to serve on a jury whilst disqualified, the police were only doing their normal duty of preventing crime by checking for criminal records. Furthermore, the court said that, if in the course of looking at criminal records convictions were revealed which did not disqualify, there was no reason why these should not be passed on to prosecuting counsel, so that this information could be used in deciding to stand by individual jurors (see section 18.4.3 for information on the right of stand by).

Juror's background

A wider check is made on a juror's background and political affiliations. This practice was brought to light by the 'ABC' trial in 1978 where two journalists and a soldier were charged with collecting secret information. It was discovered that the jury had been vetted for their loyalty. The trial was stopped and a new trial ordered before a fresh jury. Following these cases, the Attorney-General published guidelines in 1980 on when political vetting of jurors should take place. These guidelines were revised in 1988 in a Practice Note (Jury: Stand By: Jury Checks) (1988) and state that:

(a) vetting should only be used in exceptional cases involving:
   • national security where part of the evidence is likely to be given *in camera*
   • terrorist cases.
(b) vetting can only be carried out with the Attorney-General's express permission.

18.4.2 Selection at court

The jurors are usually divided into groups of 15 and allocated to a court. At the start of a trial the court clerk will select 12 out of these 15 at random. If there are not enough jurors to hear all the cases scheduled for that day at the court, there is a special power to select anyone who is qualified to be a juror from people passing by in the streets or from local offices or businesses. This is called 'praying a talesman'. It is very unusual to use this power but it was used at Middlesex Crown Court in January 1992 when about half the jury panel failed to turn up after the New Year's holiday and there were not sufficient jurors to try the cases.

18.4.3 Challenging

Once the court clerk has selected the panel of 12 jurors, these jurors come into the jury box to be sworn in as jurors. At this point, before the jury is sworn in, both the prosecution and defence have certain rights to challenge one or more of the jurors. There are two challenges which can be made and, in addition, the prosecution has a special right of 'stand by'. These are:

• to the array
• for cause
• prosecution right to stand by jurors.

To the array

This right to challenge is given by s 5 of the Juries Act 1974 and it is a challenge to the whole jury on the basis that it has been chosen in an unrepresentative or biased way. This challenge was used successfully against the 'Romford' jury at the Old Bailey in 1993 when, out of a panel of 12 jurors, nine came from Romford, with two of them living within 20 doors of each other in the same street. In *R v Fraser* (1987) this method of challenging a jury was also used, as the defendant was of an ethnic minority background but all the jurors were white. The judge in that case agreed to empanel another jury. However, in *R v Ford* (1989) it was held that if the jury was chosen in a random manner then it could not be challenged simply because it was not multi-racial.

For cause

This involves challenging the right of an individual juror to sit on the jury. To be successful the challenge must point out a valid reason why that juror should not serve on the jury. An obvious reason is that the juror is disqualified, but a challenge for cause can also be made if the juror knows or is related to a witness or defendant. If such people are not removed from the jury there is a risk that any subsequent conviction could be quashed. This occurred in *R* v *Wilson* and *R* v *Sprason* (1995) where the wife of a prison officer was summoned for jury service. She had asked to be excused attendance on that ground, but this request had not been granted. She served on the jury which convicted the two defendants of robbery. Both defendants had been on remand at Exeter prison where her husband worked. The Court of Appeal said that justice must not only be done, it must be seen to be done and the presence of Mrs Roberts on the jury prevented that, so that the convictions had to be quashed.

Prosecution right to stand by jurors

This is a right that only the prosecution can exercise. It allows the juror who has been stood by to be put to the end of the list of potential jurors, so that they will not be used on the jury unless there are not enough other jurors. The prosecution does not have to give a reason for 'standing by', but the Attorney-General's guidelines issued in 1988 make it clear that this power should be used sparingly.

Peremptory challenge

Before 1989 the defence used to have the right to challenge jurors without giving any reason. Initially the right allowed seven jurors to be removed in this way, but this number was reduced to three before the right was abolished altogether because of abuse of the system. The problem arose mainly in trials where there were several defendants each with a right of peremptory challenge. This meant that an unbalanced jury could result. For example, it was used in the Cyprus Secrets case in 1986 to get a young jury, in the Greenham Common case in 1985 to get an all-female jury and in 1982 in the Bristol riots case to provide an all-black jury.

18.4.4 Criticisms of the selection of juries

Use of electoral register

The method of selecting jurors from the list of registered voters is open to criticism as it does not always give a representative sample of the population. It excludes some groups such as the homeless who cannot register to vote. Also not every one who is eligible registers to vote. This is especially true of the young and ethnic minorities. While the poll tax was operating in the early 1990s the number of people registered to vote went down by well over a million. All these facts cast doubt on the representative nature of the electoral register.

Multi-racial juries

One of the problems is whether it is desirable for the jury to be racially mixed, where the defendant or victim is from an ethnic minority. Research in 1979 by Baldwin and McConville found that ethnic minorities were severely under-represented on juries. They looked at a sample of 3,912 jurors and found there were only 28 jurors from ethnic minorities, while census figures indicated that the figure should have been 10 times higher. However, more recent research by Zander and Henderson in 1993 found that non-white jurors made up 5 per cent of jury panels. This was only just below the proportion in the population, as a whole, of 5.9 per cent. Despite this, there is no guarantee that there will be any ethnic minority jurors on a particular case and, as decided in *R* v *Ford* (1989), there is no power for the judge to empanel a multi-racial jury.

Surprisingly, up until 1870 there was statutory power, where a non-English person was on trial, for a jury to be specially selected so that it contained equal numbers of English people and foreigners.

Disqualified jurors

Although some checks are carried out, many disqualified people fail to disclose this fact and sit on juries. One survey of Inner London juries estimated that one in every 24 jurors was disqualified. In one instance at Snaresbrook Crown Court a man with 15 previous convictions sat as a juror in three cases and was the jury foreman in two of them. He later admitted that as far as he was concerned all defendants were not guilty unless they 'had been molesting kids'.

Excusals

If there are too many discretionary excusals it may lead to an unrepresentative jury. In 1979 Baldwin and McConville found that young mothers were often excused so that women were under-represented on juries. However, the research in 1993 by Zander and Henderson found that women were proportionately represented, so this problem may no longer exist. Home Office research in 1999 found that over one in every three jurors was excused from serving. The main reasons for excusal were medical conditions, looking after children or elderly relatives and business commitments. This wide spread use of the discretionary excusal can again prevent juries from being a true cross-section of the local population. The new guidance on discretionery excusals should lead to more representative juries.

Prosecution's right of 'stand by'

The prosecution's right of stand by was kept even when the defence's peremptory challenge was withdrawn. This might be seen as giving the prosecution an advantage in 'rigging' the jury, particularly when combined with vetting. However, even when a jury has been vetted, it does not always give the prosecution an advantage. This was seen in *Ponting's Case*, where the defendant was charged with an offence against the Official Secrets Acts and the jury was vetted. Despite the vetting the jury returned a not guilty verdict (see section 18.6.2 for further comment on this case).

18.5 The jury's role in criminal cases

The jury is used only at the Crown Court for cases where the defendant pleads not guilty. This means that a jury is used in about 20,000 cases each year.

18.5.1 Split function

The trial is presided over by a judge and the functions split between the judge and jury. The judge decides points of law and the jury decides the facts. At the end of the prosecution case, the judge has the power to direct the jury to acquit the defendant if he decides that, in law, the prosecution's evidence has not made out a case against the defendant. This is called a directed acquittal and occurs in about 10 per cent of cases.

Where the trial continues, the judge will sum up the case at the end, to the jury and direct them on any law involved. The jury retire to a private room and make the decision on the guilt or innocence of the accused in secret. Initially the jury must try to come to a unanimous verdict, i.e. one on which they are all agreed. The judge must accept the jury verdict, even if he or she does not agree with it. This long established principle goes back to *Bushell's Case* (1670). The jury do not give any reasons for their decision.

18.5.2 Majority verdicts

If, after at least two hours (longer where there are several defendants), the jury have not reached a verdict, the judge can call them back into the courtroom and direct them that he can now accept a majority verdict. Majority verdicts have been allowed since 1967. Where there is a full jury of 12, the verdict can be 10–2 or 11–1 either for guilty or for not guilty. If the jury has fallen below 12 for any reason (such as the death or illness of a juror during the trial) then only one can disagree with the verdict. That is, if there are 11 jurors, the verdict can be 10–1; if there are 10 jurors it can be 9–1. If there are only nine jurors the verdict must be unanimous. A jury cannot go below nine.

Majority verdicts were introduced because of the fear of jury 'nobbling', that is jurors being bribed or intimidated by associates of the defendant into voting for a not guilty verdict. When a jury had to be unanimous, only one member need be bribed to cause a 'stalemate' in which the jury were unable to reach a decision. It was also thought that the acquittal rates in jury trials were too high and majority decisions would result in more convictions.

Where the jury convict a defendant on a majority verdict, the foreman of the jury must announce the numbers both agreeing and disagreeing with the verdict in open court. This provision is contained in s 17(3) of the Juries Act 1974 and is aimed at making sure the jury have come to a legal majority, and not one, for

example of eight to four, which is not allowed. However, in *R* v *Pigg* (1983), the Court of Appeal held that, provided the foreman announced the number who had agreed with the verdict, and that number was within the number allowed for a majority verdict, then the conviction was legal. It did not matter that the foreman had not also been asked how many disagreed with the verdict. About 20 per cent of convictions by juries each year are by majority verdict.

18.5.3 Secrecy

The jury discussion takes place in secret and there can be no inquiry into how the jury reached its verdict. This is because section eight of the Contempt of Court Act 1981 makes disclosure of anything that happened in the jury room a contempt of court which is a criminal offence. It is a contempt 'to obtain, disclose or solicit any particulars of statements made, opinions expressed, arguments advanced or votes cast by members of a jury in the course of their deliberations in any legal proceedings'. The section was brought in because newspapers were paying jurors large sums of money for 'their story'. This is obviously not desirable, but the total ban on finding out what happens in the jury room means that it is difficult to discover whether jurors have understood the evidence in complex cases.

In January 2005 a consultation paper, *Jury Research and Impropriety*, was issued by the Government. This proposed allowing 'sensitively conducted' research into jury discussions. The Summary of Responses to this document was published in November 2005. This showed:

- the majority of respondents were in favour of allowing some form of research into the approach of juries to cases they tried

- BUT about 75 per cent of respondents were against allowing an independent party access to the deliberating room
- most respondents also rejected the idea of using CCTV to research jury deliberations.

The Government's conclusion is that further research into the jury decision-making process would be valuable. However, this can be done without losing the secrecy of jury discussions. For example, a shadow jury could be used. This is an 'unofficial' jury which watches the case and then discusses it with CCTV cameras in the room.

18.6 Advantages of jury trial

18.6.1 Public confidence

On the face of it, asking 12 strangers who have no legal knowledge and without any training to decide what may be complex and technical points is an absurd one. Yet the jury is considered as one of the fundamentals of a democratic society. The right to be tried by one's peers is a bastion of liberty against the state and has been supported by eminent

Activity

Read the following article and use it as a basis for a discussion on 'jury equity'.

Jet case verdict is hard to understand, says Minister

Talks with the Home Office and the Attorney-General are being sought by the Treasury Minister Michael Jack into the acquittal of a group of women who caused £1.5 million of damage to a British Aerospace Hawk destined for Indonesia.

Mr Jack, MP for Fylde, said yesterday: 'I, and I am sure many others, find this jury's decision difficult to understand. It would appear there is little question about who did this damage. For whatever reason that damage was done, it was just plain wrong. The ramifications of the case are, however, very important in terms of future security, jobs and the question of being able to do damage and getting off with it.'

On Tuesday, the jury at Liverpool Crown Court cleared Lotta Kronlid, 28, Andrea Needham, 30, and Joan Wilson, 33, of causing criminal damage to the jet at a BAe factory at Warton, near Preston, in January. They and a fourth defendant, Angela Zelter, 45, were cleared of conspiring to damage the jet.

The women admitted breaking into a hangar and using hammers to damage the £10 million aircraft. However, they denied the charges claiming that their actions were justified. The jury accepted their claim that they had a lawful excuse to damage the aircraft because they were using reasonable force to prevent a greater crime. They said that disarming the jet, one of a consignment of 24 bought by Indonesia, would prevent it being used against the civilian population in East Timor.

Taken from an article by Kate Alderson in
The Times, 2 August 1996

damages that will be awarded. The awards vary greatly as each jury has its own ideas and does not follow past cases. The amount is, therefore, totally unpredictable which makes it difficult for lawyers to advise on settlements. Judges look back to past awards when deciding awards of damages in personal injury cases, and then apply an inflation factor so that there is consistency between similar cases. Juries in defamation cases cause particular problems with very large awards; one judge called it 'Mickey Mouse' money. In 1989 Lord Aldington was awarded £1.5 million; this is the highest award to date. If the amounts in personal injury cases are compared to this, it can be seen that this size of award would only be given to a very severely injured person who had been permanently disabled.

Until 1990 the Court of Appeal had no power to correct awards which were thought to be far too high. They could only strike out the award and order a re-trial. This was both time-consuming and expensive and rarely happened. As a result of cases in which there were over-generous awards, Parliament enacted s 8 of the Courts and Legal Services Act 1990 which gives the Court of Appeal special powers in such cases. This allows the Court of Appeal to order a new trial or substitute such sum as appears proper to the court, if they feel the damages were excessive or inadequate. This power was first used in a case brought by the MP Teresa Gorman where the Court of Appeal reduced the damages awarded to her by the jury from £150,000 to £50,000. It was also used in *Rantzen v Mirror Group Newspapers* (1993) when the award to Esther Rantzen, the founder of 'Childline' (a charity set up to help abused children) over allegations that she had deliberately kept quiet about the activities of a suspected child abuser, was reduced from £250,000 to £110,000.

18.8.2 Unreasoned decision

The jury does not have to give a reason either for its decision or for the amount it awards. A judge always gives a judgment, this makes it easier to see if there are good grounds for an appeal.

18.8.3 Bias

The problems of bias in civil cases is different to that encountered in criminal cases. In some defamation cases the claimants and/or the defendants may be public figures so that jurors will know and possibly hold views about them. Alternatively there is the fact that the defendant in a defamation case is often a newspaper and jurors may be biased against the press or may feel that 'they can afford to pay'.

18.8.4 Cost

Civil cases are expensive and the use of a jury adds to this as the case is likely to last longer. At the end of the case the losing party will have to pay all the costs of the case which may amount to hundreds of thousands of pounds. As a result of this, the Lord Chancellor has introduced some reforms so that defamation actions will be less costly. Firstly, with the increase in County Court jurisdiction, parties can now agree that their case should be transferred to the County Court. Here a jury of eight may be used and the trial is likely to be less expensive than one in the High Court. Secondly, the parties may also agree to the case being tried by a judge alone without a jury. The Defamation Act 1996 allows the claimant to seek a limited sum (up to £10,000) in a quick procedure dealt with by a judge. This allows those who want to clear their name and get immediate compensation at a lower cost to do so.

18.9 Alternatives to jury trial

Despite all the problems of using juries in criminal cases, there is still a strong feeling that they are the best method available. However, if juries are not thought suitable to try serious criminal cases, what alternative form of trial could be used?

18.9.1 Trial by a single judge

This is the method of trial in the majority of civil cases which is generally regarded as producing a fairer and more predictable result. Trial by a single judge is also used for some criminal trials in Northern Ireland. These are called the Diplock courts and were brought in on the recommendation of Lord Diplock to replace jury trial because of the special problems of threats and jury nobbling that existed between the different sectarian parties.

However, there appears to be less public confidence in the use of judges to decide all serious criminal cases. The arguments against this form of trial are that judges become case-hardened and prosecution-minded. They are also from a very elite group and would have little understanding of the background and problems of defendants. Individual prejudices are more likely than in a jury where the different personalities should go some way to eliminating bias. But, on the other hand, judges are trained to evaluate cases and they are now being given training in racial awareness. This may make them better arbiters of fact than an untrained jury.

18.9.2 A panel of judges

In some continental countries cases are heard by a panel of three or five judges sitting together. This allows for a balance of views, instead of the verdict of a single person. However, it still leaves the problems of judges becoming case-hardened and prosecution-minded and coming from an elite background. The other difficulty is that there are not sufficient judges and our system of legal training and appointment would need a radical overhaul to implement this proposal. It would also be expensive.

18.9.3 A judge plus lay assessors

Under this system the judge and two lay people would make the decision together. This method is used in the Scandinavian countries. It provides the legal expertise of the judge, together with lay participation in the legal system by ordinary members of the public. The lay people could either be drawn from the general public, using the same method as is used for selecting juries at present or a special panel of assessors could be drawn up as in tribunal cases. This latter suggestion would be particularly suitable for fraud cases.

18.9.4 A mini-jury

Finally, if the jury is to remain, then it might be possible to have a smaller number of jurors. In many continental countries when a jury is used there are nine members. For example in Spain, which reintroduced the use of juries in certain criminal cases in 1996, there is a jury of nine. Alternatively a jury of six could be used for less serious criminal cases that at the moment can have a full jury trial, as occurs in some American states.

Examination Questions

Read the following extract carefully before answering the questions based on it.

'A senior judge has been summoned to sit as a juror in a criminal trial. Lord Justice Dyson, of the Court of Appeal, is the first High Court judge and possibly the first member of the judiciary, to be called to jury service… The move is part of a Government initiative to draw jurors from as broad a cross-section of society as possible. Most people have a one in six chance of sitting on a jury, and about 480,000 people are summoned for jury service each year, although more that half of these are later excused service … Judge George Bathurst-Norman discharged a QC from a jury at the Old Bailey trial recently after learning that he recognised the prosecuting counsel. The judge expressed concern that the QC would understand legal matters other jurors would not.'

(a) What is the role of the jury?   *[5 marks]*

(b) What are the dangers, if any, in increasing the cross-section off society eligible to act as jurors?   *[5 marks]*

(c) To what extent are jurors representative of society?   *[15 marks]*

LWI WJEC, January 2005

Chapter 19

Legal aid and advice

When faced with a legal problem, the average person will usually need expert help from a lawyer, or from someone else with expertise in the particular type of legal difficulty. Most often the need is just for advice, but some people may need help in starting court proceedings and/or presenting their case in court. For the ordinary person seeking legal assistance there are three main difficulties:

1. **Lack of knowledge.** Many people do not know where their nearest solicitor is located or, if they do know this, they do not know which solicitor specialises in the law involved in their particular case.

2. **People often have a fear of dealing with lawyers**; they feel intimidated.

3. **The final difficulty is one of cost.** Solicitors charge from about £100 an hour for routine advice from a small local firm, to over £300 an hour for work done by a top city firm of solicitors in a specialist field.

19.1 Access to justice

Where a person cannot get the help they need, it is said they are being denied access to justice. Access to justice involves both an open system of justice and also being able to fund the costs of a case. There have been various schemes aimed at making the law more accessible to everyone – for example, the national network of Citizens' Advice Bureaux was started in 1938 and now operates in most towns. More recently the Law Society has relaxed the rules so that solicitors are allowed to advertise and inform the public of the areas of law they specialise in.

However, the problem of cost still remains a major hurdle. A judge, Mr Justice Darling, once said 'The law courts of England are open to all men like the doors of the Ritz hotel'. In other words, the courts are there for anyone to use but cost may prevent many people from seeking justice. The cost of civil cases in the High Court will run into thousands of pounds. Even in the cheaper County Court the cost will possibly be more than the amount of money recovered in damages. There is the additional risk in all civil cases that the loser has to pay the winner's costs. In criminal cases a person's liberty may be at risk and it is essential that they should be able to defend themselves properly.

19.2 History of legal aid and advice schemes

A system of Government-funded legal aid and advice began after the report by the Rushcliffe Committee in 1945. This was the era of the development of the Welfare State and access to legal services was viewed as being as important as access to medical services.

The Government accepted the proposals in principle and this led to the Legal Aid and Advice Act 1949. The initial scheme only covered civil cases. It was not until 1964 that the scheme was extended to criminal cases. Other parts of the scheme were gradually set up. The main areas of advice came from the Green Form scheme of advice which was set up in 1972. Then, following the Police and Criminal Evidence Act 1984, duty solicitor schemes in police stations and Magistrates' Courts were established. The entire system was consolidated in the Legal Aid Act 1988, when the handling of civil legal aid was taken from the Law Society and given to a specially created Legal Aid Board.

Eligibility

When the scheme started in 1949, about 80 per cent of the population were eligible. This was in line with the idea of the Rushcliffe Committee that the scheme should be available not only to the poor but also to those of moderate means. Because the financial limits for qualifying did not keep pace with inflation, the number qualifying gradually went down to about 48 per cent by 1978. In 1979 the limits were revised upward and once more nearly 80 per cent of the population qualified. This did not last long and in 1993 there were severe cuts to the limits so that only 40 per cent qualified and many of these had to pay large contributions towards their funding.

19.3 The Access to Justice Act 1999

The cost of funding cases under the legal aid scheme was very expensive. There were also criticisms that advice was not available to those who really needed it. In their White Paper, *Modernising Justice*, which preceded the Access to Justice Act, the Government stated that it needed to tackle the following problems:

* inadequate access to good quality information and advice
* the inability to control legal aid
* the need to target legal aid on real legal needs, within a budget the taxpayer can afford.

The advice sector was described as 'fragmented and unplanned' with the result that providers of legal services could not work together to achieve the maximum value and effect.

Under the Access to Justice Act the old legal aid scheme was replaced by two new schemes. These are the Community Legal Service for civil matters and the Criminal Defence Service for criminal cases. The Community Legal Service came into effect on 1 April 2000. The Criminal Defence Service started in April 2001. To oversee the public funding of legal services there is a Legal Services Commission.

19.3.1 The Legal Services Commission

Section 1 of the Access to Justice Act 1999 set up the Legal Services Commission. The members of the Commission are appointed by the Lord Chancellor. When appointing members he should try to make sure that, between them, they have a wide range of expertise and experience. This expertise should cover the advice sector and other legal

Figure 19.1 *Public funding system under the Legal Services Commission*

services, the work of the courts, consumer affairs, social conditions and management.

The Legal Services Commission took over funding of civil cases from the Legal Aid Board. It is responsible for managing the Community Legal Service Fund and it is able to make contracts with providers of all types of legal service. The Commission is also responsible for developing local, regional and national plans to match the delivery of legal services to needs and priorities which have been identified. It also has a role in respect of criminal legal aid and the Criminal Defence Service.

Figure 19.1 shows the organisation of the public funding system under the Legal Services Commission.

The Community Legal Service employs 1,500 permanent staff at 12 offices across England, one office in Wales and a head office in London.

19.3.2 The Community Legal Service

The Access to Justice Act 1999 establishes a Community Legal Service which provides the following services for matters involving civil law:

- General information about the law and legal system and the availability of legal services
- Legal advice

- Help in preventing or settling or otherwise resolving disputes about legal rights and duties
- Help in enforcing decisions by which such disputes are resolved
- Help in relation to legal proceedings not relating to disputes.

This scheme includes advice, assistance and representation by lawyers and, as well, the services of non-lawyers. It also covers services such as mediation. The money to pay for this service is met by the Community Legal Service Fund.

19.3.3 The Community Legal Service Fund

This fund is maintained by the Legal Services Commission from money paid to the Commission by the Lord Chancellor. The Lord Chancellor is responsible for determining how much is appropriate each year though, obviously, he has to work within the Government's total budget. This means that there is a set limit for the fund and it is a main difference from the old legal aid system which was demand led. In other words, under the old system, Government funding was provided for any case which qualified; while under the present system there is a limit or cap on the amount of money available and it is possible that some people will be refused funding because the money has run out.

Within the set budget for the Community Legal Service Fund, there are two sub-budgets – civil and family. The Legal Services Commission has limited flexibility to switch money between the two. Money is allocated to regional offices of the Commission according to the amount identified as necessary for that area. However, this can result in one area not having enough to fund all the cases it needs to, while in another area there is enough funding. To help this problem very expensive cases are funded on a case-by-case basis through individually negotiated contracts from a central fund.

The effect of capping

In July 2004 the Constitutional Affairs Select Committee published a report into legal funding for civil cases and pointed out that:

'Provision for civil legal aid has been squeezed by the twin pressures of the Government's reluctance to devote more money to legal aid and the growth in criminal legal aid, as well as the cost of asylum cases ... The Government should ring fence the civil and criminal legal aid budgets so that funding for civil work is protected and is considered quite separately from criminal defence funding.'

19.3.4 Excluded matters

Certain types of civil legal matters **cannot** be funded by the Community Legal Service Fund. These are:

- Allegations of negligently caused injury, death or damage to property, apart from allegations of clinical negligence
- Conveyancing
- Boundary disputes
- The making of wills
- Matters of trust law
- Defamation or malicious falsehood
- Matters of company or partnership law, or
- Other matters arising out of the carrying on of a business.

Most of these were excluded from receiving legal aid under the previous system, but some of the categories used to be able to get help. In particular, people who suffer injury or damage through someone else's negligence used to be able to get legal aid, but are now excluded from Government funding. This type of case can be funded by conditional fees (see section 19.4).

Court cases

Funding is available for cases in the County Court, High Court and appeal courts. However, cases for amounts of under £5,000 cannot get funding. There is also another 'gap' in the system as funding is not available for most tribunal hearings. The exceptions are cases before the Mental Health Tribunal, which are funded because they involve the liberty of the individual, as the Mental Health Tribunal decides whether detention of people under the Mental Heath Acts is justified. It is also hoped that there will be funding for cases before immigration tribunals.

Even where funding is allowed, individuals must show that they meet the other criteria before funding will be given. These criteria are discussed in section 19.2.7.

19.3.5 Different types of help

As already seen, the Government provides funds for paying for advice and representation in civil cases. There are various limitations on what areas of law and the types of cases that can be funded. In addition, the person making the application must show that they are within strict financial limits for them to qualify for public funding help.

The system covers different levels of help and representation. For civil cases the levels are:

- Legal Help – this covers advice but does not include issuing or conducting court proceedings

- Help at Court – this allows help (ie advice) and advocacy at a court or tribunal, although without formally acting as legal representative in the proceedings
- Legal Representation – this covers all aspects of a case including starting or defending court proceedings and any advocacy needed in the case
- Support Funding – this allows partial funding of cases which are otherwise being pursued privately, eg a very high cost case under a conditional fee agreement.

In addition there are two other levels of service available in family cases. The main one is Approved Family Help which provides advice, negotiation, the issuing of proceedings and, where relevant, any conveyancing work. The other service is Family Mediation which covers the cost of using mediation to resolve a family dispute.

New advice services

During 2003–04 the Community Legal Service invested in innovative projects intended to break down geographical, time and other barriers to make advice more accessible. These included:

- *www.justask.org.co* (now known as *www.cls.direct.org.uk*) offering around the clock legal information online
- advice surgeries in health and community centres in isolated parts of the country
- a video-conference link putting people in touch with trained solicitors
- access to duty solicitors in County Courts for people who face eviction from their home
- telephones in county and combined courts connecting people to legal advisers
- one-stop-shops enabling abused women to receive advice and counselling under one roof
- a new national telephone helpline to offer debt, welfare benefits and education-related advice from Summer 2004.

CLS Direct

The telephone service, CLS Direct, has increasingly been used. In the year ending 31 March 2006, there were over 509,000 telephones calls to the service. Many of the calls were from those in disadvantaged sections of society, as 70 per cent of callers who were tested would have been eligible for legal aid.

Community Legal Advice Centres

In March 2006 the Government introduced the concept of a Community Legal Advice Centre (CLAC), a one-stop service providing advice on debt, welfare benefits, community care, housing and employment. The first two such centres were set up in Leicester and Gateshead. The Legal Services Commission intends that there will eventually be about 75 CLACs.

19.3.6 Priority for funding

Section 6 of the Access to Justice Act 1999 states that priorities shall be set in accordance with any directions given by the Lord Chancellor. In February 2000 the Lord Chancellor directed the Legal Services commission to give priority to child protection cases and cases where a person is at risk of loss of life or liberty. The available resources should be managed so that all cases in these categories that meet the merits criteria can be funded.

After that the Commission should give high priority to:

- other cases concerning the welfare of children
- domestic violence cases
- cases alleging serious wrong-doing or breaches of human rights by public bodies, and
- 'social welfare' cases, including housing proceedings, and advice about employment rights, social security entitlements and debt.

This direction only covers advice about most 'social welfare' matters. Funding is not available for representation in employment tribunals or social security tribunals.

19.3.7 Funding criteria

Under s 7 of the Access to Justice Act 1999, regulations are issued on financial eligibility for funding. This is known as means testing and there are two matters taken into consideration. These are the person's disposable income and their disposable capital:

Disposable income

Disposable income is calculated by starting with the gross income and taking away

- tax and national insurance
- housing costs
- childcare costs or maintenance paid for children
- an allowance for each dependant
- a standard allowance for employment (where the person is employed).

People receiving Income Support or Income Based Job Seeker's Allowance automatically

Monthly disposable income	Monthly contribution
Band A	¼ of income in excess of the band
Band B	+ ⅓ of income in excess of the band
Band C	+ ½ of income in excess of the band

qualify, assuming their disposable capital is below the set level.

There is a minimum amount of disposable income below which the applicant does not have to pay any contribution towards their funding. For income levels above this minimum level, a monthly contribution has to be paid. The more in excess of the minimum the greater the amount of the contribution. Monthly disposable income is graded into bands. Those bands are:

There is a maximum amount above which the person will not qualify for help. This idea of minimum and maximum levels is shown in Figure 19.2.

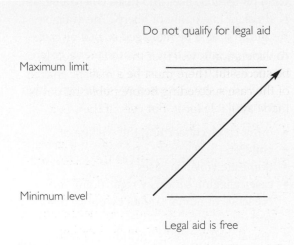

Do not qualify for legal aid

Maximum limit

Increasing contribution for those between the two limits

Minimum level

Legal aid is free

Figure 19.2 *Minimum and maximum limits for legal aid*

Disposable capital

Disposable capital is the assets of the person, such as money in a bank or savings account, stocks and shares or expensive jewellery. For Legal Help, Help at Court and representation in immigration matters the maximum limit for disposable capital is £3,000. Funding is not available if the person has assets worth more than this.

For the other publicly funded services there is a minimum limit for disposable capital of £3,000 and a maximum of £8,000. If the assets are below £3,000, then no contribution is payable. If the person has over £3,000 but under £8,000 they will have to pay the extra above £3,000 as a contribution towards their funding. If they have more than £8,000 they must use their own money to fund any legal case, although once they have spent the money in excess of £8,000 they can become eligible for funding.

Where a person owns a home the value of that home is taken into account in deciding the disposable capital. This is done by deducting the amount of mortgage, but only up to £100,000, from the current value of the property. If the amount left after this exceeds £100,000 then all the excess is counted as disposable capital.

Example:

House current market value	£220,000
Mortgage £140,000 – can only deduct £100,000	£100,000
leaves	£120,000
Deduct allowance of £100,000 from the value	= £20,000

So this remaining amount of £20,000 is counted as disposable capital. Clearly this is over the maximum limit allowed for disposable capital and, therefore, the person would not qualify to receive funding.

Criteria for funding

There is a code about provision of funded services. This code sets out criteria on which it is decided whether to fund services. The factors which are considered are:

- the likely cost of funding and the benefit which may be obtained
- the availability of sums in the Community Legal Fund
- the importance of the matters for the individual
- the availability of other services
- the prospects of success
- the conduct of the individual
- the public interest and
- such other factors as the Lord Chancellor may require the Commission to consider.

So even if a person is financially poor enough to qualify for help, other factors will also be considered. For example, if another type of service such as mediation is thought to be a better way of dealing with the case, then the case will not qualify. Also if it is thought that the applicant could fund the case in another way such as by a conditional fee agreement, funding is not available.

Merits of the case

Another factor which is taken into consideration is whether the case is likely to be successful. There must be a realistic chance of the case succeeding before public money is made available for it. But even if there is a realistic chance of success this is not a guarantee that funding will be given. The test is now wider. Do the merits of the case, in the context of the Government's priorities and available resources, justify public spending? It cannot be assumed that any case necessarily has an automatic right to public funding because of its intrinsic merits.